DOWSING

DOWSING

THE ULTIMATE GUIDE FOR THE 21ST CENTURY

Elizabeth Brown

HAY HOUSE

Australia • Canada • Hong Kong • India
South Africa • United Kingdom • United States

First published and distributed in the United Kingdom by:
Hay House UK Ltd, 292B Kensal Rd, London W10 5BE. Tel.: (44) 20 8962 1230;
Fax: (44) 20 8962 1239. www.hayhouse.co.uk

Published and distributed in the United States of America by:
Hay House, Inc., PO Box 5100, Carlsbad, CA 92018-5100. Tel.: (1) 760 431 7695 or
(800) 654 5126; Fax: (1) 760 431 6948 or (800) 650 5115. www.hayhouse.com

Published and distributed in Australia by:
Hay House Australia Ltd, 18/36 Ralph St, Alexandria NSW 2015. Tel.: (61) 2 9669 4299;
Fax: (61) 2 9669 4144. www.hayhouse.com.au

Published and distributed in the Republic of South Africa by:
Hay House SA (Pty), Ltd, PO Box 990, Witkoppen 2068. Tel./Fax: (27) 11 467 8904.
www.hayhouse.co.za

Published and distributed in India by:
Hay House Publishers India, Muskaan Complex, Plot No.3, B-2, Vasant Kunj, New Delhi –
110 070. Tel.: (91) 11 4176 1620; Fax: (91) 11 4176 1630. www.hayhouse.co.in

Distributed in Canada by:
Raincoast, 9050 Shaughnessy St, Vancouver, BC V6P 6E5. Tel.: (1) 604 323 7100;
Fax: (1) 604 323 2600

The author of this book does not dispense medical advice or prescribe the use of any
technique as a form of treatment for physical or medical problems without the advice
of a physician, either directly or indirectly. The intent of the author is only to offer
information of a general nature to help you in your quest for emotional and spiritual
wellbeing. In the event you use any of the information in this book for yourself, which is
your constitutional right, the author and the publisher assume no responsibility for your
actions.

A catalogue record for this book is available from the British Library.

ISBN 978-1-84850-220-8

Printed in the UK by CPI William Clowes Ltd, Beccles, NR34 7TL.

All of the papers used in this product are recyclable,
and made from wood grown in managed, sustainable forests and
manufactured at mills certified to ISO 14001 and/or EMAS.

Dedicated with love and infinite gratitude to:

Beryl and Nic, my first teachers, who gave me a voice.
Piers, for the courage and confidence to make it heard.
My great-grandfather, Benjamin Evans,
who taught me everything he knew.
And Tom Worrell, who, one auspicious night at the foot of the Blue
Ridge Mountains of Virginia, taught me to dowse…

CONTENTS

ACKNOWLEDGEMENTS

With deepest gratitude to:

Dr Salah Al-Rashed and my students in Kuwait, whose warmth and enthusiasm for dowsing were the catalyst for this book.

Everyone at Hay House, for all your amazing support, energy and expertise. It is both a privilege and an honour to be part of the Hay House family.

My father, who taught me, as a child, that there is no excuse for not knowing something – always ask a question.

All my teachers everywhere, in every realm, for your constant and loving guidance, irrepressible humour and joy.

Eri Griffin, for your beautiful illustrations.

Tim Lawson, for your technical expertise … I am in awe!

Phil Argyle – this book would have been poorer without your astonishing talents.

And Dr Harry Oldfield – thank you for your open mind and your open heart.

All those who so generously and graciously gave of their time, experience and expertise:

Dr Jude Currivan, George Applegate, Dr Konstantin Korotkov, Dr Mark Atkinson, Dr David Hamilton, Maire Denhoffer, Dr Keith Souter, David Ashworth, Clive Thompson, Dan Kahn, Monsignor Peter Fleetwood, Professor Chris French and Peter Taylor. And the late dear, wise, irrepressible Hamish Miller.

Peter Ford, my literary mentor, for your guidance and awesome skills in the delivery of the written word.

Annie Reed Henderson and Lee Farrington for your insightful observations and wonderful humour.

And to all those without whom the writing of this book would simply not have been possible:

All my clients and students, each and every one of you, thank you for your trust, your willingness to come on a journey with me and for teaching me so much.

Team Twelve, for whom my love and trust know no bounds, for your guidance and patience. I hope you like your book.

My editor and agent, Kathy Sorley – thank you for sharing this journey with me. Your skills of the written word, instant grasp of any situation and insightful intuition still astonish me. I am truly blessed to have had your endless guidance and support.

And my husband, Piers, without whom this book would not – literally – have been possible. You gave me the space, the unfailing encouragement and support. You willingly and graciously assumed the role of chief cook and bottle-washer and carried it out with aplomb for longer than was fair or just. It is your infinite patience, steadfast belief and love that have enabled this book to be written. My gratitude is beyond words.

PROLOGUE

Annie was sleeping peacefully in the bedroom of her pretty terraced cottage. It was 3:15 a.m. Around her the streets of a fashionable London suburb also soundlessly slumbered.

The roar of a vehicle speeding down her quiet side street suddenly shattered the silence. Braking abruptly, it drew to a halt immediately outside her home. Jolted upright by the noise, she deftly moved to the window, now very much awake.

Concealed by the voile panels, she watched a man leap out of an unmarked white van and begin pacing up and down directly in front of her gate. Her stomach involuntarily tightened. *Oh no*, she thought with trepidation, *we're about to be burgled*. She reached for her phone, her eyes remaining glued to the ominous figure.

She watched, all senses on alert, as he continued to pace. Peering at his form, now made eerie by the lamplight, she remained frozen, trying to anticipate his next move.

With a start she realized he had something in his hands – obviously the tools of his trade. She watched as he handled them with the ease of someone who knew what he was doing. Riveted, she followed his shadow as he wandered back and forth, back and forth, brandishing a pair of pointed metal objects.

Then, upon reaching her neighbour's gate, he stopped abruptly in his tracks.

What *on Earth* was he doing?

Then it hit her…

Her trepidation melted into amusement.

And the dowsing rods in his hands began to spin rapidly.

At this signal, a door opened in the white van and a second man leaped out. Brandishing an aerosol can of paint, he sprayed the outline of a blue square on the pavement directly underneath the spinning rods.

Job done, the two men jumped back on board, and the anonymous white van sped off into the night…

Annie returned to the comfort of her bed with a wry smile on her face. The only thing on her mind as she drifted off to sleep was, whoever would believe her story?

INTRODUCTION

It may be said with great confidence that dowsing has contributed and continues to contribute to geology, geophysics, ecology, medicine, and the economy of those countries where dowsers conduct their operations.
Professor Alexander Dubrov, Russian Academy of Science

If dowsers are operating by mere chance, it's pretty amazing how they can be so successful.
Amit Goswami, PhD, theoretical quantum physicist and Professor Emeritus, University of Oregon

Let's get one thing straight from the start.

Dowsing works.

If it didn't, it wouldn't have pluckily survived hundreds, if not thousands, of years of being ridiculed by the general public, dismissed with barely disguised contempt by mainstream science and denounced as the work of the devil by religious groups. Over the centuries dowsers have suffered the gamut from the indignity of scorn to the injustice of imprisonment.

And yet ... dowsing is flourishing today as never before.

This is the most exciting time for this ancient art, which now finds itself on the cutting edge of science. Dowsers have known for centuries of the validity and integrity of their skills. But the science to explain, endorse and legitimize the practice has lagged behind. That is, until recently; new discoveries in physics are now placing dowsing firmly on the threshold of proof.

Not that there has been any need to endorse dowsing, as the proof is in the results. Dowsers are today employed worldwide: on the payroll of countless utility companies; by police forces to locate crime scenes and missing persons, living or dead; to work hand-in-hand with the police and other authorities in engineering maintenance and road safety; by oil companies to sink wells; by mining companies to locate diamonds and precious metals; by farmers and the owners of factories and golf-courses to find water for irrigation. There is also a thriving community of doctors and homoeopaths employing its benefits in diagnosis and treatment. And volunteer water dowsers are selflessly changing the lives of whole villages on the African continent by locating water quite simply for their survival.

Even more dramatically, dowsing was used by the US Marine Corps in Vietnam to detect underground mines and booby traps, and by American intelligence agencies to locate missing planes and contraband drugs. In a recent conversation, internationally renowned Russian research scientist Dr Konstantin Korotkov told me that his team regularly used dowsing first, before confirming their findings with technology, 'because it is quicker'!

You won't necessarily hear of these dowsers. Why? Because their employers choose to keep silent, fearing ridicule and embarrassment. But they continue to employ the dowsers nevertheless. How do I know? Because I am a professional dowser. And over the years I have talked to my fellow dowsers, men and women, about how they employ their skills, their passion for dowsing and their challenges and successes.

Having dowsed for more than 20 years now, I can say that this is the book I would like to have read when I first started out. There is much here that I was never taught but wish I had been. Perhaps something you read will resonate with you and encourage you to become a dowser, give you a leg-up to be a better dowser or inspire you to be the best dowser you can possibly be. Or maybe you are simply curious about how this ancient art can have so many modern applications in contemporary life.

Please know that I am not a scientist, nor do I have any aspirations in that direction. Inevitably, as there is no pre-established language to portray the realms of consciousness and subtle energies, I have had to use some terminology that would be deemed to be scientific. I have tried to balance this by also using the language of music. In all cases, the words are used in the spirit of trying to convey the message in the simplest, least pretentious, most accessible way. But, to borrow from Sir Isaac Newton, it is the fact that I 'stand on the shoulders of giants' that has made the writing of this book possible. At every opportunity I have sought to give these men and women, scientists and non-scientists, full and just recognition for their remarkable, pioneering and very often brave endeavours.

Though not a scientist, I am, however, a dowser. I was first taught to dowse by an extraordinary and inspiring man who teaches Native Americans their lost intuitive arts and whose missions include restoring the balance of our planet and the implementation of environmentally sustainable water technologies. And for most of my life, since the age of 14, I have been trained in, and exposed to, many and varied aspects of subtle energies. In that time, I have amassed a broad and intensive spectrum of dowsing experience. Along with the privilege of working with private and corporate clients in over 20 countries, from Australia to Iceland, Argentina to Kuwait, I have established a track record of professional integrity and am the grateful recipient of a formidable but humbling list of testimonials.

Now I am writing this book to introduce dowsing to you as one of the most natural means of enhancing and enriching your life and the lives of others. At a time in the Western world when we are, on a daily basis, bombarded and overwhelmed by *choices*, dowsing is an invaluable tool to help us discern truth from non-truth, to enable us to see past the 'advice' and 'recommendations' of those who operate from hidden agendas and hold vested interests that are not in our own best good. Dowsing also offers an alternative to the sensationalistic and confusing sound-bite headlines from an over-enthusiastic and persuasive media, giving us a means of taking responsibility for our own health and well-being and what is and is not to our *individual* benefit.

This book is also written to bring dowsing up to date, to leave behind the unhelpful, provocative terminology such as 'water-witching' and 'doodle-bugging', to remove it from the realms of the mysterious, the spooky and the occult, and finally, after centuries of being abused, misunderstood and misinterpreted, to restore its purity as a means of connecting, through its phenomenal mechanics, with the infinite field of the universe.

In short, with considerable first-hand experience of its unquestionable benefits, I am both honoured and committed to giving dowsing its deserved place in the 21st century, at this crucial coming together of science and human consciousness.

PART I
WHAT, WHEN AND WHO

CHAPTER ONE

WHAT IS DOWSING?

Dowsing is a conscious attunement to the field of consciousness that non-locally connects each and every one of us with the cosmos as a whole.

Jude Currivan, PhD, cosmologist, author, dowser

Dowsing has undergone a paradigm shift from the useful but relatively mundane science of finding water sources, lumps of metal and old drains, to the realms of a spiritual search into the mysteries of human consciousness and its relationship with the earth.

Hamish Miller, dowser, author, *The Definitive Wee Book on Dowsing*

To look at the origins, mechanics and practical applications of dowsing, we first have to determine how wide we will allow our definition of dowsing to be. Many traditionalists in the dowsing community believe that the only pure form of dowsing is water divining and, at a stretch, divining for oil, gas and minerals, thus it is defined as 'a means of searching or finding out'. For the purposes of this book, and in acknowledgement of new discoveries in the fundamental nature of the universe, I suggest that dowsing be redefined in the following manner: 'a way of finding out by accessing information, with directed intent, using a means outside the five recognized senses and culminating in a physical response within the human body'. As we will see, this may be with, or without, the use of a dowsing tool.

The most common image of dowsing is of a man (usually old, with grey hair and a beard!) holding a forked hazel branch looking – or divining – for underground water. He asks questions of the stick related to finding water: the location of the nearest source, the depth it can be found at, the volume of the flow and the extent of its potability. The stick – or dowsing or 'divining' rod – moves in response to his questions and indicates the location of underground water. This is known as *water divining*.

The second most commonly recognized image of dowsing is a person observing reactions from a hand-held pendulum (a weight suspended on a short thread). When a question is asked, the pendulum swings in response, predominantly with a circular motion, indicating either *yes* or *no* answers. This methodology is a means of *information dowsing*.

Kinesiological testing, known also as muscle testing, would also fit within our definition of dowsing. There are many methods of kinesiology, using various muscles within the body. Perhaps the most commonly known method is the use of the deltoid muscle in the arm as a reactor muscle. Two people are needed. When the arm of the subject is extended and, at a given signal, light pressure applied by a tester, the muscle will test 'strong' or 'weak' in response to any given statement or stimuli. Conversely, some practitioners of kinesiology *do not need their subject to be present*. They employ their own body as a kinesiological indicator by using various muscle reactions of their own hand in response to questions or stimuli. The dictionary definition of kinesics is 'the study of body movements that convey information in the absence of speech'.

All these are means of accessing or finding out information not immediately obvious to us with the naked eye. We are using the human body as a reactor or a connector to a field of information, which subsequently culminates in an observable physical manifestation of minute muscular responses.

So dowsing can be described as a means of *searching* – for water, oil, gas, minerals, underground cables, pipes or caverns, archaeological artefacts or anything missing or lost; *identifying* leaks, stress fractures, environmental pollutants, electromagnetic fields, nutritional deficiencies, black spots, the sex of pigeons, crime scenes, Earth energies and subtle energies; or *accessing information* about the environment, nature, health and well-being and, well, just about anything you can possibly want to know!

And, as dowsing has a remarkably wide range of applications, the craft is divided into categories. There are two main classifications:

The first is **field dowsing** *– where you are in the presence or vicinity of that for which you are searching, for example on a site determining the location of water or the presence of electromagnetic fields. The dowsing tool will react at, or point to, the spot where the physical target can be found.*

The second classification is **remote dowsing***, which has two different modes:* **map dowsing** *and* **information dowsing***. Map dowsing entails using a map (or plan or diagram) as a means of focus to discern information pertaining to that map, for example exploring for water, oil or minerals or determining the location of electromagnetic fields. Information dowsing is when no map is necessary and the subject or object may either be thousands of miles away or perhaps in the form of a concept, idea or a theory that has no obvious physical presence, and by dowsing in this fashion we are doing exactly what the term suggests: accessing information. How this is possible and how this is accomplished we will explore in detail later on.*

Despite the more traditional preference for the term 'divining', 'dowsing' and 'divining' are currently interchangeable, with 'dowsing' being viewed as a more contemporary term. One dictionary definition of 'divination' as 'the act or practice of divining: seeking to know the future or hidden things by magical means' is limiting and does nothing to help the dowsing cause. The associations surrounding the word 'magical' once again confine dowsing to the realms of the unscientific, the entertainment business or the downright dodgy.

To the modern mind, in this age of advanced technology, any image of dowsing exercises incredulity and draws criticisms of 'unproven and unscientific'. But running side by side with technological advances of a magnitude barely imaginable a century ago are extraordinary scientific discoveries in the fields of consciousness, intent and the interconnection of everything in the universe. Dismissing dowsing outright as 'unscientific' does not serve us well. Instead, I believe the field of dowsing practices is in perfect accord with new discoveries in the field of quantum exploration.

It was not always so!

Chapter Two

THE CHANGING PERCEPTION OF DOWSING

We have come from advanced societies whose special technologies suited the great mental capacities of the inhabitants, and we are heading back in that direction. We have come from societies where the inhabitants reliably sensed deeper dimensions of the universe than we presently do, so that they readily manipulated space, time and matter...
Professor William A. Tiller, PhD, Stanford University

There should be no enmity among seekers after truth.
Auctoritates Aristotelis

It is important that we examine dowsing in the context of its history. Besides substantiating its longevity and illustrating its many practical applications, this will help us to better understand the common perception of dowsing to date and its somewhat shaky reputation within institutional science, religious groups and the unacquainted public.

Dowsing has existed in various forms around the planet for as long as humankind has been aware of a field of information or believed that an organized intelligence is at work, existing outside the individual conscious mind. Although it is assumed by many to have originally come about as a primordial survival tool, a means of finding water, I believe this to be only part of the story. To the highly evolved ancient civilizations (those that predate by thousands of years those of Ancient Greece, Egypt and Mesopotamia), living in a state of intuitive consciousness was a way of life. After the demise of these civilizations, subsequent cultures tried to find a way back to what their advanced ancestors had done naturally. It is likely then that the use of a dowsing instrument to physically demonstrate their link to the consciousness field, the field of all knowledge, ran concurrently with its use as a practical tool of discovery.

There are many claims of pictorial evidence of early dowsing or divining with a forked stick, for example cave drawings and pictographs from 8000 BC. Unfortunately, these are at best over-enthusiastic and at worst totally unsubstantiated. Experts in the field confirm that interpreting prehistoric rock art is notoriously inexact, and many fall into the trap of seeing what they want to see. However, Sheila Ostrander and Lynn Schroeder, authors of the informative *Psychic Discoveries Behind the Iron Curtain*, write, 'Bas reliefs from early Egypt portray water diviners equipped with dowsing rods and even headgear with antennae. Kings of ancient China, like King Yu (2200 BC), are pictured carrying dowsing rods.'

A reliable reference is noted in the meticulously researched and detailed dowsing history *The Divining Hand*. Author Christopher Bird states, 'As far back as the fifth century BC, the father of history, Herodotus, wrote of the use of willow divining rods among the Scyths, a nomadic Iranian people who roved the prairies of what is now southern Russia.'

The history of dowsing up to the 1500s is chequered and more difficult to verify – not least because for centuries dowsing and similar activities fell under the heading of the occult and had to be practised covertly in order to avoid charges of witchcraft or even the death sentence. The Catholic Church fought to retain any form of 'divination' (in the broadest sense of the term) as its exclusive domain: a papal bull in the 14th century, issued by Pope John XXII, forbade the 'use of a ring to obtain answers in the manner of the devil' – 'a ring' was a type of pendulum apparently used as an alternative to a dowsing rod.

However, in the past 500 years dowsing has gone through periods of relative respectability. Some of the best-substantiated reports and pictorial evidence come in the form of a work by German physician and mining expert Georg Bauer, who wrote under the pseudonym Georgius Agricola. Called *De Re Metallica* (The Nature of Minerals) and published in 1556, this landmark book in the evolving story of dowsing is illustrated with German woodcuts clearly showing the participation of dowsers in the mining of minerals. From that point onwards, dowsing is well documented, with mining and water-finding references, along with the successful location of items as diverse as archaeological sites, underground tunnels and criminals. Endorsement was not forthcoming from either the Catholic or Protestant Church, however, after Martin Luther relegated dowsing to the realms of witchcraft and denounced it as the 'work of the devil'.

Conversely, the cause *for* dowsing was helped enormously by the support of Queen Elizabeth I later in the 16th century. She was keen to introduce mineral dowsing to England to keep pace with the commercial success gained by Germany. She invited German mining experts and dowsers to England to – very successfully – locate mineral mines in the north of England, Cornwall and Wales. But this was the time of the English Renaissance, before the emergence of the so-called Age of Reason. An era when the world was very different, when knowledge of the metaphysical was the norm and magic was not a derogatory term in the field of science. A time before Newtonian physics, when there was little differentiation between science and the arts. A world where alchemy and chemistry were indistinguishable, astronomy and astrology were one practice and Galileo Galilei, Johannes Kepler and Tycho Brahe cast horoscopes as an integral part of their work.

And an age when many of the clergy of the Christian Church were active dowsers.

What?

Yes, despite the best efforts of the Church, records from the 17th and 18th centuries are littered with the involvement of priests, abbots and a bishop or two in dowsing. Their imagination was fired by the dowsing phenomenon sweeping Europe, a phenomenon not scientifically proven but rendered irresistible by the weight of empirical evidence. With the education, the means and the influence, the priests either instructed in dowsing experiments or fully participated themselves.

Early adherents included Father Bernard Caesius, who surmised that the rod, rather than mysteriously moving by itself, was physically moved by the dowser; Father Athanasius Kirchner, who spent half a lifetime conducting experiments to render dowsing more scientifically acceptable; the Abbé de Vallemont, who wrote a treatise on the dowsing rod suggesting, very sensibly, that its movement resulted from a combined reaction of the dowser and what they were dowsing; and the Bishop of Grenoble, who supervised experiments on water dowsing and whose name has been given to the infamous (in dowsing circles!) *Bishop's Rule*, a method of identifying the depth below ground of a watercourse.

This prelatical trend continued into 20th-century France and included the Abbé Mermet, who, after a lifetime of research on dowsing, published a book entitled *How I Proceed in the Discovery of Near or Distant Water, Metals, Hidden Objects and Illnesses*, and the Abbé Alexis Bouly, originally an extremely successful water dowser who, having established a reputation for locating water for commercial use in France and across Europe, went on to make his mark working for the military. Not only was he able to locate unexploded World War I shells buried underground but also to determine whether they were of German, Austrian or French manufacture *prior* to the unearthing.

Bouly founded the Society of Friends of Radiesthesia (his new word for dowsing) and committed himself to a lifetime of research in the health field in general and microbes in particular.

In recognition of his remarkable achievements he was awarded the highest decoration in France, the Chevalier de la Legion d'Honneur. Even more remarkable was his acceptance speech: 'This cross of the Legion of Honour is awarded in my person to all practitioners of dowsing. For my own part, the award represents the crowning of a life I have tried to dedicate to the service of God and the good of humanity.'

Bouly inspired the extraordinary Father Jean-Louis Bourdoux, who, having spent years as a missionary in the Brazilian jungles, was prompted to use dowsing to identify the medicinal and healing properties of indigenous plants. Following many years of study, the result was *Practical Notions of Radiesthesia for Missionaries*.

These three pioneering clerics were the inspiration for the life's work of a fourth groundbreaking Catholic priest, the accomplished Father Jean Jurion. His extraordinary achievements can be summed up as follows: 30 years dedicated to health dowsing, a study of homoeopathy, the amassing of the medical records of 30,000 patients, a 2,000-page treatise detailing everything he had ever learned about homoeopathy and dowsing for health, and an astonishing track record for accuracy and efficiency. He also dispensed with the pretension and superstition that surrounded dowsing – which direction one needed to face, what to wear, the type of material a dowsing tool should be made from – concluding that he could dowse under *any* conditions without limitation. This artless approach was badly needed – and long overdue. More important was the realization that 'his most spectacular achievements were related to cases that he thought practically impossible to solve because doctors had given up on them' – what we recognize today in dowsing terms as *a need*.

Despite this, or perhaps because of it, Father Jean Jurion was dragged in and out of court by the French medical authorities, who, as the Church before them, were possessive of what they saw as their exclusive domain. Even under these circumstances of extreme provocation, he continued to display dignity and patient-focused dedication. Before his death in 1977, he made the thought-provoking observation that 'In countries such as the

Netherlands, Germany and Great Britain, *no law forbids doctors from working together with unorthodox healers* [my italics].'

With contributions from various scholars, an array of clerics, master miners, doctors and professors, countless experiments were conducted over several hundred years. In conclusion, the dowsing phenomenon was variously attributed to emanations, invisible corpuscles, mysterious exhalations, magnetic fields, electrical influences, radiation(s), waves, vapours and, of course, from the incredulous authorities and public, pure fraud, sleight of hand or some sort of pact with the devil.

This 'work of the devil' nail in the dowsing coffin was reinforced for centuries, and astonishingly has continued up until the present day. Visionary, author and spiritual teacher David Ashworth recalls a time in the 1990s when he and a colleague were asked to dowse a church in Sheffield. The invitation had actually come from the dean, who had witnessed what he described as an 'amazing light' that had appeared in the crypt, and wanted to find out more. Whilst dowsing around the columns in the crypt, David and his colleague came across a young woman who was eating her lunchtime sandwiches. Suddenly realizing what they were doing, she cried out in alarm, accusing them of being evil and engaging in the work of the devil. Then, without allowing them so much as an explanation, she ran off in disgust.

The contradictory participation of the Catholic Church in the evolving story of dowsing is interesting. When I first approached the Catholic Communications Network (CCN) in 2008 for clarification on the Church's current position, I was told, 'The issue here is whether dowsing is classified as an occult practice. Since dowsing is a form of divination (using a divining rod), it could also be associated with the supernatural.' The relevant extract from the Catholic Church's teaching document (*The Catechism*) was also forwarded to me:

> *All forms of divination are to be rejected: recourse to Satan or demons, conjuring up the dead or other practices falsely supposed to 'unveil' the future. Consulting*

horoscopes, astrology, palm reading, interpretation of omens and lots, the phenomena of clairvoyance, and recourse to mediums all conceal a desire for power over time, history, and, in the last analysis, other human beings, as well as a wish to conciliate hidden powers. They contradict the honour, respect, and loving fear that we owe to God alone.

Goodness!

Once again dowsing is relegated to the levels of demons and the devil. But when I gently questioned this, suggesting that water dowsing had no connection with the occult, instead being the human body's physical reaction to both electromagnetic and quantum fields, and stating that I would find it difficult to believe that the Church would have any problem with water dowsers going out to Africa and saving the lives of whole communities by locating water and helping with the digging of wells, the response was revealing: 'We need someone who understands the scientific side of dowsing. Dowsing in the form detailed [in my email] looks OK.'

So it is not dowsing as such that is the problem, only what dowsing is *believed to be.* The CCN media co-ordinator had unintentionally hit on the crux of the matter that has dogged the reputation of dowsing for hundreds of years: it is unfairly handicapped by ignorance, supposition and superstition, the assumption of what it might be rather than the understanding of what it actually is. All this results from the simple fact that there has never been any official or accepted agreement of what dowsing is and how it works. This book will clarify both.

Probably not surprisingly, the Catholic Church was unable to find anyone versed in 'the scientific side of dowsing'. They did put me in touch, however, with a delightfully accommodating Consultor for the Pontifical Council for Culture and the Pontifical Council for Inter-religious Dialogue. An ex-Vatican official, Monsignor Peter Fleetwood stated that he did not recognize the oft-repeated dowsing myth that the Pope 'has given his blessing to dowsing as long as it is used for the benefit of mankind'. He explained:

> Many people ascribe to the Pope statements made by Vatican 'officials' as if every statement made by every person working at every level in the offices of the Holy See has the same authority. People are generally positively disposed, but if there is no resident expert 'in house' they have enormous difficulty answering questions that are not at the centre of their normal agenda.

So to date it appears that, despite the participation throughout history of exceptionally talented clerical dowsers, and today's more open-minded priests (and bishops, I am reliably informed), the official view of the Vatican still stands as 'all forms of divination are to be rejected'.

Any ability to access information or truth – the very essence of dowsing – can prove threatening to those who seek power and control and who prefer to keep the populace in ignorance. And disappointingly, there are those today who have closed minds and feel similarly threatened due to myriad alternative agendas.

Some of the best news about dowsing today comes from Russia. There it has become a legitimate field of study and dowsers are referred to as *biolocation operators*, as 'it is more scientific'. In a lecture given to the British Society of Dowsers' International Congress in 1993, Professor Alexander Dubrov outlined the then-current state of dowsing in Russia – and it made quite an impact.

The practice of dowsing had actively started to develop after 1960, he explained, culminating in the first all-Union seminar of dowsing in Moscow in 1968 and, in the 1980s, many others across the USSR. They were attended by hundreds of professionals from around the world, including those with strong scientific backgrounds, medical doctors, geologists, physicists and hydro-electronic engineers.

Professor Dubrov outlined the key achievements and the effectiveness of dowsing in Russia and the Commonwealth, which, he confirmed, were supported by certification and official documents issued by government organizations and institutions. He highlighted the successes of dowsing in prospecting for valuable resources – oil deposits, gold-bearing zones, diamond pipes, platinum zones, lead, silver and palladium – and in the detection of leaks in underground municipal heating, oil pipelines, gas pipelines and electric cable networks, in the identification of cracks in a dam at a hydro-electric station that could not be detected by *any known means*, in geological mapping and engineering, and in the search for water.

All this had culminated in the establishing of training schools with qualifications and certification for dowsers, some at post-graduate level, the course of study in the school in Siberia being 'officially permitted' in 1973 by the USSR Ministry of Higher Education. They created the position of 'operator trainer for dowsers' – someone with at least 20 years of dowsing experience who was qualified to teach dowsing, give examinations and award certificates.

For a world superpower to *officially* progress in this direction is quite something. But then with dowsing, along with other fields of research into psi capabilities or the 'paranormal', the Russians don't mess about. They take it very seriously. Apart from the financial benefits (Professor Dubrov alluded to the savings made by the use of dowsing in his full address), the USSR has a long and substantial history of applying the extra-sensory powers of the mind in military intelligence activities. The authors of *Psychic Discoveries Behind the Iron Curtain* point out that 'Psychical research in the USSR is regarded as a new field in the natural sciences linked with bionics, physiology, biology etc… Psi laboratories in communist countries are in universities, technology institutes, colleges. Psi research is generally done by pure scientists… The Soviet government supports parapsychology research to the tune of an estimated *20 million roubles* a year.' At that time, in the late 1960s, the United States' government budget for this type of research was understood to be zero.

A considerable proportion of this expenditure was allocated to investigating *remote viewing*, a means of accessing information about a specific location or unseen target by the extending of the mind or consciousness. In his autobiography, Ingo Swann, one of the most talented remote viewers in the world, and one of the first participants in the early CIA remote-viewing experiments, also alludes to the vast amount of money allocated by the Soviet Union to what we can generally define as 'super-sensory perception'. He suggests that in the late 1960s American intelligence analysts 'guesstimated' that the Soviet annual budget for psychical research was 500 million dollars.

It was the sheer size, scope and funding of the Soviet work in the field of *distant viewing* or *mind control via distant influencing* that, according to Swann, pushed all the American panic buttons and eventually culminated in the training, and using, of remote viewers for intelligence purposes by the US Army, including Project Star Gate. This was an American government-sponsored remote-viewing research exercise that ran from 1978 until 1995, and its archive was released by the CIA in 2004. Although much of the operational material of the various projects remains classified, its existence and the successes of the individual remote viewers are well documented. One remote viewer trained by Swann, Major Paul H. Smith, confirms that dowsing was used to *support* remote viewing for American intelligence operations, specifically in the detection of contraband.

Apart from the financial investment in dowsing, there is one other factor that sets the former Soviet Union apart. While much of the world seems to be disposed towards amassing statistical evidence on dowsing in an effort to *dis*prove its efficacy, Russia and its neighbours have done the opposite and focused on the empirical evidence and practical uses *for* it. Rather than investing their resources in establishing *if* dowsing works, they appear to have put their energies into *how* it works and what are the most effective and beneficial applications.

In a subsequent paper published by Professor Dubrov, 'Modern Achievements of Dowsing: Brief review of scientific research

1990–2000', he goes on to state, 'This period has seen a substantial growth in the application of dowsing for research and practical work conducted in geology, mining, architecture, town-building, and ecology' and, very promisingly, 'It should also be noted that the scientific world has changed its attitude towards dowsing.'

Fantastic – it looks like we're making progress.

An article published in the *Sunday Telegraph* on 10 August 2003 tells of how the motorway authority in Austria turned to dowsers to help reduce the number of accidents on one of the worst stretches of autobahn. After inspecting a 300-yard section of the autobahn by dowsing and identifying anomalies in the Earth's magnetic field below it, the dowsers restored the balance of the field simply and effectively with pillars of white quartz. A secret two-year trial followed and during this time the number of fatal accidents fell from an average of six per year to zero. Harald Dirnbacher, an engineer from the motorway authority, said, 'I admit that when we first looked at [the energy lines], we were doubtful. We didn't want people to know in case they laughed at us, so we kept the trial secret and small-scale. But it was really an amazing turnaround.'

But, just when we think we're getting somewhere…

In the same article Dr Georg Walach, a geophysics professor at Leoben University in southern Austria, ignored the dramatic fall in deaths and responded by saying, 'Natural sciences need evidence. Whatever cannot be measured does not exist. These energy lines and their flow cannot be grasped or measured, and their existence is therefore rejected by scientists.'

How can this be?

The dictionary definition of 'science' (*Chambers Concise 2004*) is 'the systematic classification and observation of natural phenomena in order to learn about them and bring them under general principles and laws (from Latin *scientia* knowledge, from *scíre* to know)'. Science is the search for knowledge. For truth. And scientists would be the first to admit that the universe is full of unsolved mysteries – the ongoing applications for millions of dollars of research grants and the current Large Hadron Collider project would attest to that. The universe is not a 'done deal' and science is a work in progress. Where it comes unstuck is when some factions of the scientific community dismiss unsolved mysteries because they do not fit into a prevailing paradigm. Rejecting the existence of unsolved phenomena on the grounds that you haven't (yet) quite worked out how to measure them doesn't seem to be in accord with the definition of science. Amit Goswami, PhD, theoretical physicist and Professor Emeritus of the University of Oregon Institute for Theoretical Physics, highlights this very point in his book *God Is Not Dead*, stating, 'Every new paradigm of science brings along some modifications of the old standards of measurement.'

The obvious irony is, of course, that condemnation by religious groups and ridicule from orthodox authorities and institutions are not the exclusive territory of the dowsing community: science and scientists throughout history have had a rough deal – from the same authorities and institutions, from theologians, from their own peers and from those who espouse the dogma of current received wisdom. Yet hindsight, context and new scientific discovery have modified, and will continue to modify, our assessment of historical figures – and there have been giants among them.

And at the very heart of the matter is the *same shared search for truth and knowledge.*

Galileo Galilei simply spoke the truth of what he saw through his telescope about the order of our solar system, putting the sun rather than the Earth at its centre. It earned him condemnation from the Catholic Church for contradicting the Holy Scriptures, accusations of heresy and eventually house arrest. It was not until 1992 – over 300 years after his death – that Pope John Paul II officially expressed regret over how he had been treated and conceded that, subsequent to a study by the Pontifical Council for Culture, the Earth did indeed move.

Similarly, Nikola Tesla was a brilliantly minded genius, visionary and lifelong inventor who, despite a catalogue of discoveries extraordinary in its extent and magnitude and 700 patents to his name, died penniless and largely forgotten. In more recent times AC electricity, neon lights, radio transmission, the electric motor, remote control, hydraulics, basic laser and radar technology, X-rays and the means for tactical warfare have all been attributed to him. The controversy in Tesla's story surrounds his claim of having invented a free form of energy harnessed from the ionosphere that would benefit the whole world. A humanitarian, he was determined to make electricity equally available to all people on the planet – as his gift. Free electricity with no opportunity for commercial gain – or control – rendered him a potential threat to the world energy economy and the project was brought to an end. He became astutely aware of the vested interests of commercial enterprise, and his refusal to compromise his ideology did nothing to further his career. Throughout his complex life he was ostracized by many and dismissed as mad, and his work was discredited by those who simply could neither understand a man so advanced in his thinking nor rationalize his altruistic principles.

In the medical arena, Dr Ignaz Semmelweis was an Austro-Hungarian physician who made great contributions from which we still benefit today. In 1846, whilst working in the maternity wards of Vienna General Hospital, he concluded that the high mortality rate was due to 'particles' being carried on the hands of doctors and medical students, years before the link between microorganisms and disease was discovered. He introduced hand washing with chlorinated lime solutions and the death rate significantly reduced. But as his deductions came from astute observation rather than scientific proof, they were rejected by established medical opinion. His colleagues objected to being told to wash their hands and dismissed his hypothesis outright. Forced to resign from the hospital, Semmelweis tried to continue his research elsewhere, but was ostracized by the medical community. Such was his frustration at the non-recognition of the truth that his mental health quickly deteriorated and he was committed to an asylum, dying only 14 days after admission. The excruciating value of his message is being replayed in hospital wards around the world today as the battles against MRSA and *Clostridium difficile* continue.

Nor can the kind of dismissive thinking faced by these men be excused by poor education or medieval superstition. As recently as the 1980s, French immunologist Dr Jacques Benveniste made the profound discovery, initially from a serendipitous laboratory error, of the *memory of water*. Despite his work being replicated by four independent laboratories, he suffered the indignity of his methodology being checked not by top-flight scientists but by, amongst others, a stage magician for sleight of hand. Thirty short years later, his results have been replicated and verified by prestigious institutions worldwide, but at the time Benveniste was discredited, his reputation destroyed and his career in institutional science effectively terminated.

The *principle* of these examples is not about science versus dowsing. Anyone, whatever their discipline or field of study, who has the courage to stand up and speak their truth in the face of received wisdom will encounter detractors. Throughout history, the search for knowledge and truth has been stifled or impeded by those with hidden agendas, vested interests or egos that prevent them from keeping open hearts and minds. Those, like Father Jean Jurion and Dr Semmelweis, who walk their path of truth with passion and integrity, at the cost of their own reputations, their health and often their very lives, deserve our admiration and respect.

In the scientific world today a similar situation to the Catholic paradox exists. Despite the reluctance of institutional science to acknowledge dowsing, let alone consider it a subject worthy of research, some of the most talented dowsers turn out to be those qualified in scientific fields. I know dowsers who are doctors, physicists (quantum and nuclear) and aeronautical engineers. They all believe totally in the validity – and reliability – of dowsing and achieve some remarkable results. It would seem that, irrespective of the general condemnation by theology and science, ultimately it comes down to each individual's personal belief system. And if in the course of writing this book I have opened just one mind to our innate power to connect through dowsing to an infinite field of information, the book will have served its purpose and the journey will have been worthwhile.

One of the world's foremost water and oil dowsers, George Applegate, who enjoys close to iconic status in the dowsing world, is a qualified engineer and geologist. Dowsing for over 55 years, his track record is formidable: over 2,500 successful boreholes (including several finds yielding up to a million gallons a day) with a *less than 1 per cent failure rate*. The diversity of his client list reflects his professional success and gives an interesting insight into those who consider dowsing to be both genuine and beneficial to their needs: the Department of Environment, the Ministry of Defence and HM Prison Service, water authorities, the Coal Board, hospital boards, hotels, country clubs and racecourses, Elton John, the Prince of Wales and Madonna. Mr Applegate takes the conundrum one step further, actually considering dowsing to be a science. In his book *The Complete Guide to Dowsing: The Definitive Guide to Finding Underground Water* he writes:

> *Science means the knowledge of laws and principles. It means systemised and coordinated knowledge that can be applied. In an address given to the American Society of Psychic Research, Professor Henry Margenau, Professor of Physics and Natural Philosophy at Yale University, declared: 'Today we know there are many phenomena on the fringe at the periphery of present-day science, which are not yet understood, which are still obscure, but will nevertheless be encompassed by a scientific method and by scientific understanding in the future.' I conclude that dowsing is one of these fringe scientific phenomena. For we have reached a*

very strong position today where we no longer need to have our position as dowsers confirmed – the facts speak for themselves.

In Mr Applegate's case, they certainly do.

In conversation with this exceptionally skilled but totally unpresumptuous dowser, I raised the issue of the viewpoint of institutional science. His response was: 'I haven't got the problems of a scientist criticizing me – I've overcome all those problems. I'll say to a scientist, "If you want to drill a hole, drill your hole, and if you get more water than me, I'll pay you. If I get more water than you, you pay for my hole."'

He added wryly, 'And nobody takes me on.'

He acknowledges: 'It is easy to criticize something that you don't understand … scientists have got to deal with facts, and it's very difficult to explain to a scientist the facts of what is going on in the mind of a dowser.

'I've seen some very wonderful things done by dowsers. I used to know a gentleman down in Devon called Mr Burgoyne. Police used to employ him to trace missing bodies and I witnessed him find a body of a woman in a lake. Now a scientist would have a job to go along with that. The only thing that counts on this Earth with regard to dowsing is results – results that can be proven – and a track record.

'It's possible to teach people. If you can teach them, and they become accurate then I contend that dowsing becomes a science. Really and truly, the aim should be the *science of dowsing*.'

That's the view of a dowsing icon. What about the general public?

Apart from the handicap that approximately 60 per cent (as suggested by professional feedback) of the public have *never heard* of dowsing, the remaining 40 per cent have mainly come across it on television as 'entertainment'. Not wishing to become camera fodder, I myself have kept television appearances to the bare minimum. But on one occasion, appearing in a television series about health and measuring, on camera, the health readings of one of the unhealthy participants, I was subjected to her look of disbelief and the immortal words, 'I'm not having someone telling me about my health with a pair of *coat hangers*.' Needless to say, for its pure entertainment value, this was the bit that sadly *wasn't* left on the cutting-room floor.

The existence of dowsing and its general acceptance are also hindered by the reluctance of organizations and authorities to admit they employ dowsers *and* enjoy the benefits of successful results. Invariably, my corporate clients ask me to work discreetly, outside normal office hours, and usually during evenings and weekends, but … in the middle of the night?

The Prologue is a true story that occurred in the late spring of 2009. The witness is known to me; she is a credible and professional woman and certainly not given to flights of fantasy. Her neighbours had an ongoing problem with a water leak, which was confirmed by their escalating meter readings. Three times the local water authority had tried to locate the leak, three times they had dug up the pavement and three times they had replaced the Tarmac, yet the leak persisted. After the nocturnal visit of the water dowser, the water authority returned a fourth time, dug at the spot he had marked with the blue paint, located and repaired the leak, replaced the Tarmac and, on this final occasion, also the paving slabs. Problem solved.

The water authority in this area is Thames Water. It took five telephone calls, ten emails and three months of trying to elicit a comment on their use of water dowsers. Their eventual response – 'It isn't Thames Water policy to use "diviners" in leak detection … we prefer to use a number of "scientific" ways such as listening rods and radar' – raises more questions than it answers. Who employed the dowser? And why was he dowsing at 3:15 a.m? And if Thames Water doesn't use dowsers, why did they dig at the very spot he identified? Surely a success story such as this, with its proven benefits, saving untold man-hours and expense, could only enhance the reputation of the employers?

For those members of the public who *have* heard of dowsing, I would be the first to admit that it still has an image problem.

That traditional figure of the grey-haired bearded male still persists, but add to this a kaftan, sandals and a flaky New Age demeanour and you will come close to what is expected. For this very reason, when I co-founded and ran a dowsing/geopathic stress consultancy, dress code was on the top of my list. Smart, designer and invariably black was the attire of choice – important for our corporate clients.

Etched on my memory is the day we attended a private client in London at a friendly community of terraced houses just off the South Bank of the Thames. Whilst waiting for the client, we stood in the street and chatted to neighbours, who had been apprised of the novel event to come.

'We're waiting for the dowsers,' said a friendly woman in a conspiratorial tone. 'They should be here soon.'

'Um, *we're* the dowsers,' I ventured, indicating my colleague and myself.

'*You're* the dowsers?' she said, taking a step back and, very slowly, looking me up and down with an expression of incredulity. '*You're* the dowsers? But … you don't *look* like dowsers.'

Image problem aside, dowsing in the 21st century is, in fact, enjoying a huge resurgence of interest and massive global success in the commercial field. Thriving communities and societies of dowsers are flourishing around the globe. One of the largest, founded by Colonel A. H. Bell, DSO, OBE, MRI, is the British Society of Dowsers. Just 43 members attended the society's first meeting in 1933. Today it has over 1,600 members and over 80 members are on its professional dowsing register in categories as diverse as: water sources for domestic, commercial and agricultural needs; locating pipes and drains, blocks, leaks and breaks and other concealed features; finding natural resources, including minerals, oil and gas, and 'missing things', including objects, people and animals; archaeological features; agriculture; health; site energies, including sick buildings, geopathic stress, sacred spaces and ghosts.

Equally, in the USA, the American Society of Dowsers, based in Danville, Vermont, has in excess of 3,000 members. America also has a century of well-documented and formidable achievements in the fields of water, oil and gas dowsing.

To most professional dowsers with proven track records it is therefore all the more inconceivable that the authorities, institutional science, medicine and technology can possibly dismiss dowsing. What actually is it that renders it beyond rational discussion – or even consideration? And why? Is it because dowsing is a full-on challenge to core belief systems about how the universe works? Is it that if it were proved to be valid it would undermine the basis of *mainstream* science? The sheer weight of empirical evidence briefly summarized in this history would, in any other field, merit serious research, as it has done in Russia. But, as former science editor of the *Daily Telegraph* and now its consulting editor Adrian Berry wryly comments:

> *How many times in history has 'mainstream scientific opinion' turned out to be wrong? If the judgement of experts had been accurate, then the Earth would be flat, the Atlantic would be infinite and unnavigable, the stars would be equidistant from us; and radio communication, photography, nuclear energy, motor cars, aviation and space travel would all be impossible.*

If, therefore, we were to examine the authenticity and validity of dowsing solely through the eyes of Newtonian physics, with its limiting linear perception of space and time, I suspect we would fall flat on our face, only adding to the chorus of scepticism and derision.

But as dowsing *transcends* currently understood physical laws of space and time, it is to the pioneering developments in advanced theoretical physics that we must look for answers.

CHAPTER THREE

WHO CAN DOWSE?

Do not hesitate to know that you can be a successful dowser.
You can if you know that you can and not until then. Your
ability to dowse will be in direct ratio to your belief.

George Applegate, *The Complete Guide to Dowsing*

Don't believe what your eyes are telling you. All they show is
limitation. Look with your understanding, find out what you
already know, and you'll see the way to fly.

Richard Bach, author of *Jonathan Livingston Seagull*

So, who can dowse?

Anyone!

Everyone has the innate ability to dowse. It is not the exclusive territory of the gifted few. But, as with any other inherent human potential, the importance of training is paramount. And in fairness to all the fantastically skilled professional dowsers, to make a career of dowsing takes years of learning, hard work, trial and error, the complete absence of ego, studying one's field in absolute depth and detail, and weeks … months … years of practice.

Dowsing is not just about making the dowsing instrument *move*. Hand most people a pair of dowsing rods and they will almost immediately start to turn in their hands. When giving a weekend workshop, my experience is that, almost without exception, everyone has learned the rudiments of dowsing and can demonstrate basic dowsing skills by the end of the first day. But there is more to the practice than this. It is about understanding and perfecting the processes that prompt the movement of the dowsing rod. It is also about belief.

Or perhaps *suspending disbelief*.

The best dowsers are children, without half a lifetime of inherited prejudices and cynicism. They have never been told that they can't dowse or that it is *not* possible. They don't have conditioned belief systems to get in the way.

There is a wonderful piece of film footage showing a group of young children being taught dowsing by Michael Bentine. Michael, who could definitely be termed a one-off, lived a fascinatingly diverse life. Although best known for his role along with Peter Sellers in *The Goons*, he was not only an internationally known comedian, actor, scriptwriter and author, but also a military intelligence officer in the RAF, a veteran parapsychology researcher, psychic, talented dowser and honorary member of the British Society of Dowsers.

In the film, Michael is shown walking slowly, with approximately eight young children abreast, across a large field. They are all holding dowsing rods and they have been told that somewhere in the field there is an underground watercourse. Suddenly, at a point midway across the field and at precisely the same second, nine pairs of dowsing rods spontaneously cross. Their location of underground water was subsequently revealed to be totally correct.

In my own experience, some of the most delightful tales of children dowsing come from parents who attend my weekend dowsing courses. On the Saturday evening they proudly take their new dowsing rods home to demonstrate their skills and their children pick them up and – effortlessly and spontaneously – dowse. The parents return to the workshop on the Sunday morning shaking their heads with bemusement.

As Henry Ford said, 'If you think you can do a thing or think you can't do a thing, you're right.'

But, like any skill or craft – playing the piano, learning a language, driving a car – in order to dowse with competency and reach any level of proficiency it is essential to practise, practise, practise. The results achieved are proportional to the amount of time, effort and commitment devoted to the craft. The innate ability may be there, but the mind needs to be trained in the specific techniques. In dowsing, as in music or learning a new language, I'm afraid there are no short cuts. But the more you practise, the more you observe your reactions and are reassured by your results, the more your confidence will build. And, like the piano, you can choose whether you apply your dowsing skills for personal use, to enhance and enrich your life, or whether you train to be a professional dowser in a specialist field. The choice is absolutely, indisputably yours.

In Part II of this book we shall look at the fundamental tenets and methods of practical dowsing – and how to be the best dowser you can possibly be.

PART II
PRACTICAL DOWSING

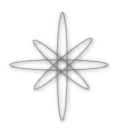

Chapter Four

PREPARATION FOR DOWSING

All things vibrate, and they vibrate at their own frequencies. When you understand this, you will significantly broaden your understanding of the universe. With this understanding, your eyes will open to things you have never seen before – things previously pushed to the back of your consciousness – and these discoveries and feelings will give new life to your soul.

Dr Masaru Emoto, *The Hidden Messages in Water*

I've led such a little life ... when inside me there was so much more. Why do we get all this life if we don't ever use it?

Shirley, *Shirley Valentine* by Willy Russell

A shift in our frame of reference is needed. So let's *get used to* several things:

- *Get used to* living in a universe of awe-inspiring magnitude and majesty.
- *Get used to* seeing the world in terms of energy, rather than matter.
- And *get used to* being an integral part of a cosmos of pure consciousness and potential, where *everything* is inter-connected.

All of us spend so much of our time in a world of the mundane and minutia, bogged down in the everyday grind, isolated and disconnected in our closeted lives, that we lose sight of the breathtaking extraordinariness of our existence.

So, step out from the ordinary ... and *get used to the extraordinary*.

Reach out and recapture the wonderment that absorbed your childhood, that filled every waking moment with the sheer fascination of new discoveries, however simple. Rekindling this frame of mind is a very good beginning.

Then immerse yourself in anything that uplifts and inspires you, that reminds you of the extraordinary potential and raw power of the human spirit and moves you to your very soul – nature, a good book, fine art, music, the gentle powers. (We will explore why this is so vitally important in Chapter 8.)

And then remind yourself of the astonishing order and design underlying all life. Consider the animal kingdom – the remarkable migration of the tiniest bird over thousands of miles and the fact that it can repeat that exact same journey the following year; the complexity of ant colonies, often up to a million ants synchronizing their work and social lives, and their ability to carry up to 20 times their body weight; the mysterious magic of the dolphin species, with their exceptional communication abilities and evident support when humankind is in need of rescue and healing; the humbling honey bee, beating its wings over 11,000 times per minute, visiting up to a 100 flowers each collection trip, but needing the collective effort of over 500 bees visiting 2 million flowers to make one single pound of honey. Or the plant kingdom, where a single plain black pinprick-sized seed inconceivably contains the potential and *information* to form vigorous and vital lifeforms, breathtaking in their beauty, exquisite in their scent and miraculous in their sheer diversity of size, shape and colour.

Life *is* extraordinary.

And although at times we may feel battered and careworn from the trials of our past, or may experience trepidation about the challenges of the future, we have the distinct privilege of being part of this mind-boggling world today. Consider the fact that we can lie on our backs on the grass on an exquisitely peaceful summer's day, marvelling at the stillness where not a single leaf or blade of grass around us is moving, and then try to contemplate that our Earth is hurtling through space at 66,000 miles per hour and *at the same time* spinning on its axis at 1,000 miles per hour. And still not a blade of grass moves (relatively speaking).

Contemplate the on-the-face-of-it-absurd fact that our bodies are 99.9999999999999 per cent space, so far apart are the nuclei of each and every single cell. Logically, we shouldn't even be able to see one another! Rationally, you'd think we'd fall apart.

Consider that there are in the region of 100 trillion bacteria in our digestive system, more than the total number of cells that make up our body, all working away for our benefit without our having to give them a single conscious thought or even know that they are there.

Reflecting on these facts, and countless more like them, will not only remind us of the sheer miracle of being alive on this planet but also, by perspective, help nudge dowsing back into the arena of the possible.

Get used to the idea that scientific research has established, beyond all reasonable doubt, that the power of our directed thoughts – *intention* – affects our current and future physical manifestation and expression. And hold on to your hats… Recent scientific research now suggests the barely imaginable concept that our thoughts can reach back in time to influence our past *as it unfolds as the present*, causing scientists to conclude that our conventional understanding of sequential time needs to be completely re-examined in terms of cause and effect. In this context, dowsing is suddenly placed firmly in the realms of 'this world' rather than 'otherworldly'.

If you had a microscope powerful enough to magnify matter down through all the levels of its intrinsic structure – down through its constituent molecules, then atoms, then subatomic particles and quantum packets – you would not be viewing its basic building block components as solid *matter*. Matter is not composed of matter. You would see oscillating, spinning, flickering and fluctuating *energy*. And this characteristic is not limited to a rock, or a tree, or the chair that you are sitting on. This also applies to the human body.

So *get used to* living in a world where everything is energy… Including you.

The following description of the complexity of the energies that are us and surround us is one of the most potent I have ever come across. It is taken from *Conversations with God: Book II* by Neale Donald Walsch:

> …built into all things [is] an energy that transmits its signal throughout the universe. Every person, animal, plant, rock, tree – every physical thing – sends out energy, like a radio transmitter. You are sending off energy – emitting energy – right now, from the centre of your being in all directions. This energy – which is you – moves outward in wave patterns. The energy leaves you, moves through walls, over mountains, past the moon, and into forever. It never, ever stops.
>
> Every thought you've ever had colours this energy. (When you think of someone, if that person is sensitive, they can feel it.) Every word you've ever spoken shapes it. Everything you've ever done affects it. The vibration, the rate of speed, the wavelength, the frequency of your emanations shift and change constantly with your thoughts, moods, feelings, words and actions.
>
> Now, every other person is, naturally, doing the same thing. And so the ether – the 'air' between you – is filled with energy; a Matrix of intertwining interwoven personal 'vibes' that form a tapestry more complex than you could ever imagine.

This weave is the combined energy field within which you live. It is powerful, and affects everything. Including you...

The Matrix – the combined current energy field within any given parameter – is a powerful vibe. It can directly impact, affect, and create physical objects and events... Your popular psychology has termed this energy Matrix the 'Collective Consciousness'. It can, and does, affect everything on your planet: the prospects of war and the chances for peace; geophysical upheaval or a planet becalmed; widespread illness or worldwide wellness.

Get used to the idea that you are part of this Matrix, and that your mind – subconsciously, consciously and super-consciously – quintessentially drives and is driven by this process. Whether you like it or believe it, or not!

And what about this *consciousness?*

This is not the consciousness that is referred to as a product of the brain, of being in a waking state. Instead, the brain itself is a product of consciousness. Consciousness is the absolute state of being. It is present everywhere. Everything that exists, as matter or non-matter, is expressed from a pre-existence of consciousness. It is the *ground state of all being.*

Consciousness has infinite levels of expression, from a simple amoeba to the more complex states of human existence. Its supreme state is God-consciousness. It is an infinite, immeasurable field of continuously communicating intelligent information. It exists beyond the limitations of space and time, without division or separation. It is the Oneness of all that has ever been, is or will be.

In its individuated state, it is the essence of our divine spark. It is consciousness that gives expression and form to our physical body. Our bodies exist as a result of consciousness – not the other way around. And it is what *continues to exist* after our physical bodies have expired.

Collectively, it is the energy Matrix as described previously, where all our individuated states of consciousness are fundamentally interconnected to form the whole – the *collective consciousness*.

Are you still with me? If these are new concepts to you, please bear with me. Neither concepts nor language can capture what is ultimately the essence of the infinite. Any description of consciousness will always be, by definition, an incomplete approximation. How can All That Is be encapsulated or illuminated by something that is not All That Is? The spoken or written word can only be signposts pointing in the general direction. But the nitty-gritty here is to *get used to* the idea that we are not, after all, disconnected beings – we are all *interconnected expressions of a conscious whole*.

Perhaps the perspective of David R. Hawkins, MD, PhD, author, teacher and Director of the Institute of Advanced Theoretical Research, will help. He says of collective consciousness:

> *We may think of it as a vast, hidden database of human awareness, which is characterized by powerful, universal organizing patterns. Such a database, comprised of all of the information ever available to human consciousness, implies stunning inherent capabilities; it's far more than just a giant storehouse of information awaiting a retrieval process. The great promise of the database is its capacity to 'know' anything the moment it is 'asked', for it's able to tap in to all that has ever been experienced anywhere in time.*

So, everything is consciousness.

And all consciousness communicates.

So *get used to the idea* that we are all consciousness and therefore we all have the ability to communicate with everything that has consciousness.

All we need is a means of access. And that is where dowsing comes in.

CHAPTER FIVE

THE DOWSING INSTRUMENT

The great English astronomer Sir Arthur Eddington had anticipated inter-connectedness by saying, 'When the electron vibrates, the universe shakes.' Physicists now accept inter-connectedness as a ruling principle, along with many forms of symmetry that extend across the universe...

Deepak Chopra, MD, *Quantum Healing*

Recent research demonstrates that living things are constant transmitters and receivers of measurable energy.

Lynne McTaggart, *The Intention Experiment*

There are myriad dowsing tools that have been used throughout history and many that are still in use today, their shape, size, design, material, complexity and flamboyancy being limited only by humankind's inventiveness, ingenuity and, occasionally, one-upmanship. Those tools in more common usage include:

The 'Y' or 'V' Rod

The traditional forked stick, also known as the 'Y' or 'V' rod, is probably the most widely recognized. These were historically

chosen from hazel or willow branches, or any trees that had flexibility, strength and availability, and were conveniently taken fresh
from the nearest hedgerow. Today, the modern version of the
'Y' or 'V' rod is usually made from plastic, nylon or carbon fibre,
primarily because of their greater flexibility and sensitivity, but
also because, unlike wood, they don't dry out, become brittle and
have to be regularly replaced.

The two shorter ends of the 'Y' are held in the hands, with
the long part of the 'Y' pointing forward (see Fig. 1) and the palms
(usually) facing upwards, under slight tension. The rod's dowsing
response will be for the long part of the 'Y' to rise, or dip or turn
in a complete revolution, twisting and distorting the wood – quite
something to watch in the hands of an experienced dowser.

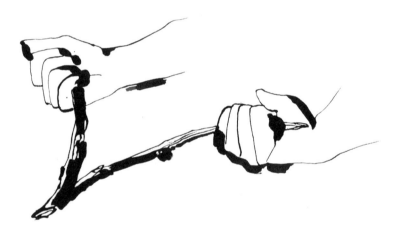

Figure 1: 'Y' or 'V' rod.

The 'L' Rods

Perhaps the most commonly used dowsing rods are the angle
rods, also known as 'L' rods. These consist of two separate rods,
bent into 'L' shapes. The shorter length of the 'L' is held one in
each hand, with the longer length projecting forwards, parallel
with the ground (see Fig. 2). The rods are held approximately
body-width apart, with the arms extended but with the elbows

comfortably bent. They are then free to swing to and fro, or fully rotate, on the horizontal plane.

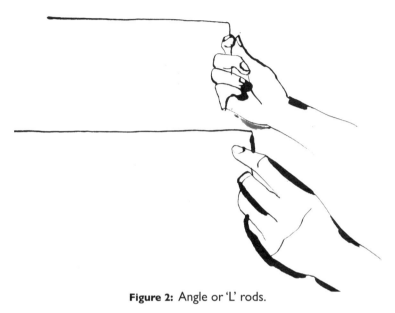

Figure 2: Angle or 'L' rods.

Angle rods are generally made from thin but sturdy metal – brass, aluminium, iron or copper. More often than not, wire coat hangers serve the purpose admirably! (*See Figs 3 and 4.*)

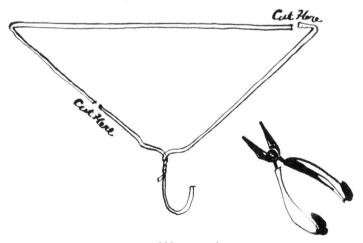

Figure 3: Wire coat hanger.

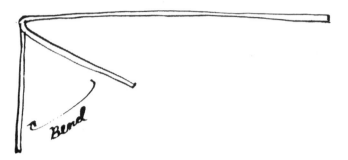

Figure 4: Wire coat hanger rods.

The length (of both the shorter and longer parts of the 'L'), the weight of the rods and the diameter of the metal are very much down to personal choice. Factors to consider include the size of the dowser (particularly their hands), the type of dowsing to be done and the environment in which the rods will be used. Spending hours a day, indoors, in the practice of information dowsing requires lightweight rods (otherwise you build the biceps of a heavyweight boxer); outdoor dowsing where there is the possibility of gale-force winds requires heavier rods and a firm grip. Lighter and longer rods have more sensitivity. Shorter rods will have more difficulty gaining momentum.

Handy 'telescopic' 'L' rods are also available (see Fig. 5), which do look as if they have been made from old-fashioned car aerials but are highly useful in that they are both discreet and easily portable. Until you are used to them, dowsing rods do have a tendency to poke you in various parts of your anatomy!

You will also see 'L' rods with a tube or sheath over the shorter part of the 'L', the part that is held in the hands. Again, this is a personal preference – some dowsers like to feel the rods turn in their hands, while others prefer not to have any contact with the rod in order to gain the psychological reassurance that they are not influencing the turning of the rod in any way. The sheath can be made of wood, plastic or metal. The outer plastic tube of an old biro can be used and, when circumstances have

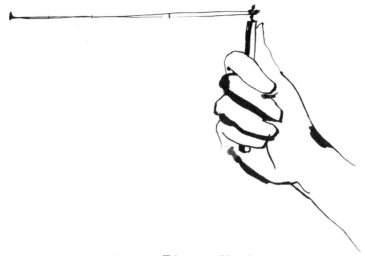

Figure 5: Telescopic 'L' rods.

demanded in impromptu teaching sessions, I have found even cut-down drinking straws work well. There is nothing like the resourcefulness of a dowser!

As the long part of the 'L' rod is then totally free to swing to and fro, it may be necessary in anything other than absolutely still conditions to lightly 'damp down' with the thumb, i.e. rest it, on the bend of the rods. This will give the dowser the benefit of increased control (see *Fig. 6*).

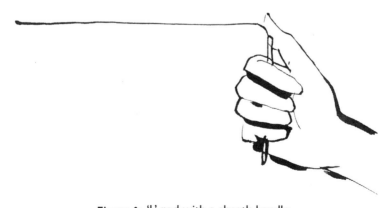

Figure 6: 'L' rod with a sheath handle.

Hamish Miller, the author, blacksmith and veteran dowser who enjoyed an international reputation in the field of Earth energy dowsing, forged handsome custom-sized and personalized dowsing rods in iron with slightly flattened handles. This gave the added tactile benefit, he explained, of 'a great sense of *feel* for the strength of the energy' when the rods moved and turned in the hands.

The Bobbing Stick

The bobbing stick or wand is a single long slender stick (*see Fig. 7*). It can be made of fine wire, plastic or nylon – again, there are many versions, depending on the requirements of the dowser. Often there will be a spiral of wire at a point partway along the rod, to provide extra spring.

Such is the flexibility of this rod that while it is held in the hand its end will 'bob' up and down or describe circles.

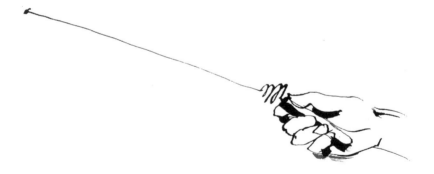

Figure 7: The bobbing stick or wand.

The Double-'V' Rod

The double-'V' rod, invented by top UK water dowser Clive Thompson, is an ingenious device primarily designed for use in water dowsing (*see Fig. 8*). Looking like two 'V's, this consists of three lengths of flat nylon or plastic (the type that can be bought from DIY stores for edging kitchen cabinets, I am reliably informed!) attached together at two points. The ends of the outer part of this rod are held in the hands, palms facing upward, and slight tension is put on the rod.

When crossing a watercourse or line of electromagnetic disturbance, the 'points' of the double 'V' will alternately dip down, indicating the beginning, middle and furthest edge of the course or line. More challenging to master than a 'Y' rod because of its fine balance, the double-'V' rod has the benefit of a remarkable level of sensitivity.

Figure 8: The double-'V' rod.

The Pendulum

With pendulums, it is safe to say, the sky is the limit. A pendulum is simply a weight attached to a short cord, thread or chain. The length of the cord is adjusted to suit personal preference.

The cord is held in the predominant hand between forefinger and thumb, ideally with them pointing downwards (see *Fig. 9*), so the pendulum is free to swing in any direction – to and fro, in clockwise or anti-clockwise circles, or in a figure of eight.

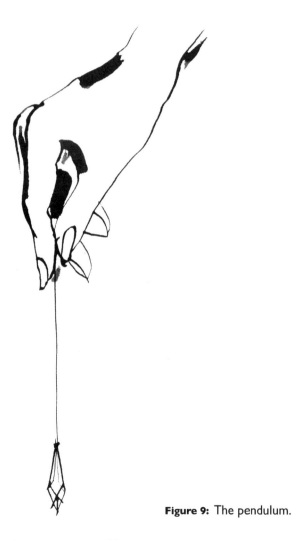

Figure 9: The pendulum.

The 'weight' or 'bob' can be made of wood, metal, glass, plastic, various types of crystal or stone, or even an article of personal significance such as a ring or other piece of jewellery. The shape and design of the pendulum is again down to personal preference, with two or three exceptions. Some dowsers find it advantageous to have a pendulum bob that tapers to a point, as in a cone or traditional crystal shape, as this gives more pinpointing accuracy whilst chart or map dowsing. A weight will trace a smoother path when it is well balanced, therefore choosing a pendulum that is symmetrical will be an advantage.

Pendulums are also available with a small cavity to hold a representative sample of the substance for which the dowser is looking. This small sample is referred to as a 'witness' and can help with focusing the mind on what needs to be found.

As with dowsing rods, the other factors to consider with the pendulum are the weight and sizing. If the cord is too long it will be unwieldy; too short and it will be limiting and hamper the dowsing response.

Experimenting with different types, styles and sizes of dowsing tool is the best way forward. The aim is to feel relaxed and balanced. Ideally, you should feel so comfortable with your dowsing rods or pendulum that you are barely aware of their physical presence, therefore minimizing any intrusion on the more important processes of focus and directed thought. Ultimately, a dowsing tool needs to be almost a natural extension of the human body – not unlike a musician and their instrument, or a conductor and their baton.

A certain amount of trial and error and road testing of size and proportions over a period of time will be necessary to achieve this. Some dowsers own assorted types, sizes and styles of dowsing tools for use in different applications. My own personal choice for everyday use is 'L' rods, for their flexibility and versatility, properties that we will explore in Chapter 7. They are approximately 27 cm by 11 cm, although I was dowsing for a while before I realized that longer rods (40 cm by 15 cm) were not necessary and were somewhat cumbersome for my small hands. My rods are also extremely lightweight, appropriate for the hours a day I spend information dowsing, weighing in at a feather-light 14 grams each. And although I spent many years very happily using brass rods (and the occasional doctored coat hanger), my current rods are made from sterling silver – a gratefully received but extremely indulgent gift. Having said that, I have a further dozen pairs, of varying sizes, secreted in handbags, shoulder bags, briefcases, suitcases, my car, my Filofax, my desk, my bedside table … I like to be prepared for all eventualities!

As Father Jean Jurion discovered in the last century, the most important thing to remember about your dowsing tool, comfort and practicality aside, is that you can dowse with *anything* – the only limitations are the human mind and its preconceived ideas. Affectionate familiarity or sentimental value notwithstanding, apart from the very rare exception, dowsing tools are not imbued with special powers. The dowsing tool is simply an amplifier of the *real* dowsing instrument.

Namely, you.

Yes, *you* are the transmitter-receiver. The sole purpose of any dowsing tool is to amplify the minute involuntary neuro-muscular reactions of the human body to a stimulus. Once your body-mind has received the prompt, involuntary muscular reactions move your arms and wrists, which subsequently and unconsciously then move the rods (or the pendulum) in a given direction. A good analogy would be a transistor radio. Without an antenna, a radio will still pick up a weak signal, depending on the location of the radio and the source of the broadcasting waves. Once the aerial is extended, however, the signal becomes clearer and louder. What you are doing by holding a dowsing tool is *extending your antenna* to receive a clearer, more pronounced, physically observable signal.

That the human body-mind is an extremely sensitive receiver and transmitter – or transceiver – of information is beyond any doubt and happily over a century of research exists to support this. Well-designed, replicable, rigorously controlled laboratory experiments have been carried out by highly qualified scientists from respected institutions.

In 1929, in the United States, the Duke University Para-psychology Laboratory was established. This was headed up by the biologist J. B. Rhine, PhD, who pioneered the use of ESP or Zener cards – one of the original mainstays of research into telepathy and extra-sensory perception. The strength of this experiment was in its simplicity: a deck of 25 cards, made up of five different and simple designs (square, circle, wavy lines, star and cross) was shuffled and, one by one, chosen by a person (the transmitter) who then would try to mentally 'send' the image to a distant person (the receiver). The person could be in another room, another town or another country. Perhaps the most ambitious Zener card experiment was that of astronaut Dr Edgar Mitchell: on his return from the moon on board Apollo 14, at a prearranged time, he 'transmitted' images from the Zener cards to colleagues at home. As the results significantly exceeded chance expectation, they suggested that the transceiver effect is not limited to the confines of the Earth.

Over a period of 60 years, 188 experiments, consisting of millions of trials, were carried out under controlled conditions. A recent meta-analysis (an analysis of a collection of all previous experiments) showed that even the most highly controlled extra-sensory perception studies had *odds against chance of 375 trillion to one.*

And that was only the initial groundwork. The second half of the 20th century saw scientific researchers in America, followed by others from prestigious institutions around the world, take the simple model of the Rhine cards experiment and run with it, translating it into sophisticated tests utilizing computers and other modern technology. Experiments were carried out to determine if it was possible for one human being to affect the *autonomic nervous system* of another human being, at distance, by directed thought, the outcome being measured by monitoring the response and activity of the sweat glands, or what is known as *skin conductivity*. The answer was a resounding *yes*. Further experimentation in America and Europe was carried out using EEG (electroencephalogram) correlation of brain activity to determine whether it was possible for a person to distantly influence the *central nervous system* of another. Once again the answer was a very resounding *yes*.

Perhaps the most compelling evidence for the capacity of the body-mind to transmit and receive information comes from the study and application of *remote viewing*. Essentially, this is the ability to sit quietly and focused in one location and, by extending the mind or *consciousness*, remotely 'view' a scene in a distant or remote location. 'Distant' could mean 100 yards or 10,000 miles – or more. What, and how much, can be observed is dependent on the innate ability and training of the viewer, but this can range from fleeting images and impressions to highly complex and technical details. The images can be static or moving and may be accompanied by further sensory feedback such as sound or smell.

What is not in question is the fact that remote viewing has been used successfully by various government bodies and agencies throughout the world for intelligence purposes. The evidence for this is well documented and the skills of the pioneers and main protagonists are detailed in various biographies like *Memoirs of a Psychic Spy: The Remarkable Life of US Government Remote Viewer 001* by Joseph McMoneagle, who received the Legion of Merit for his work in this field.

The term 'remote viewing' itself was coined by the American physicist Harold Puthoff, PhD, and the pioneering and extensive experimentation officially began at the Cognitive Science Laboratory (CSL) at Stanford Research Institute in California, although it seems more plausible that the USSR began their research prior to this, and there are reliable reports that the British utilized remote viewing during World War II. The US remote viewing research was funded by, amongst others, the CIA and the Defense Intelligence Agency, and CSL went on to provide support for intelligence operations, including the now declassified Project Star Gate. As previously touched on, the majority of the operational material remains classified, but it stands to reason that it would be inconceivable for the US government to spend 24 years sponsoring remote-viewing research if it hadn't been in its best interests.

Having been trained in the process of remote viewing and participated in experimental work, I can testify to its authenticity and potential to be startlingly accurate.

Device-less Dowsing

Further illustrating that it is indeed the human body rather than the dowsing tool that is the transceiver is the method of dowsing known as 'device-less dowsing'. Dowsers who are able to do this have no need of dowsing rods – their bodies are powerful receivers that are tuned highly enough not to need an extended aerial to amplify a signal.

This is actually quite easy to do and you can have fun with it. One way is to use your arm as a pendulum. Standing up, shift your body weight to one side so your corresponding arm is hanging free; imagine it being 'detached' from your shoulder and let it swing loosely by itself (see *Fig. 10*). Ask your arm to show you a *yes* response and observe what it does. Then do the same, asking for a *no* response.

You now have your very own portable and discreet pendulum to use in public situations where brandishing a pendulum (say, to dowse over the vegetables in the supermarket or check the food on your plate in a restaurant) might be seen at the very least as pretentious or at worst as flaky. I made the mistake of using a pendulum (just once) over a meal on a flight to Australia, causing a panic amongst the flight attendants, who immediately assumed that something was wrong with the food and envisaged some *Airplane*-movie food-poisoning scenario.

Another device-less method is similar to the clicking of the fingers. As your thumb slides from the middle to the forefinger,

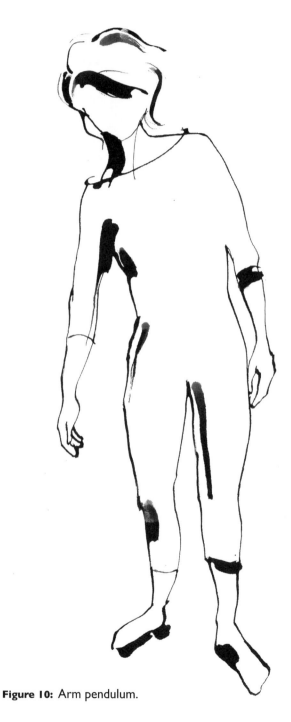

Figure 10: Arm pendulum.

ask a question. Generally if the thumb 'sticks' to the middle finger, the dowsing response is a *no*. If it slides easily to the forefinger, this is a *yes* response.

A friend of mine uses her whole body as a dowsing tool. Standing tall and upright, she crosses her forearms over her chest, balances her body and closes her eyes. She then asks her questions and finds that her whole body will fall slightly – forwards for a *yes* response and backwards for a *no* response.

My husband uses a method which will be more familiar to practitioners of muscle testing: he forms a circle by pressing together the ends of his thumb and the little finger of his right hand and forms a hook with the forefinger of his left hand which he then hooks through the circle at the point where the thumb and little finger join. He then exerts medium pressure with the hook to break the circle. If it remains unbroken and strong, then the dowsing response is *yes*; if it weakens and breaks, then the dowsing response is *no*. The key is to keep the pressure consistent with every question asked.

These methods blur the distinction between dowsing and muscle testing, but it doesn't matter. They are all techniques that demonstrate the *physical body's response to a stimulus or connection to a source of information*.

There are countless other methods involving extending the arms, feeling the vibrations in the hands or linking the hands together to form pressure until they flutter or vibrate. In her moving and powerful book *Mutant Message Down Under*, American author Marlo Morgan describes how she was trained by Australian Aborigines to dowse. She was shown how to determine whether vegetables that grew underground were ready to harvest by simply moving her hands over the plants and intuitively listening. She says: 'Ultimately they taught me to dowse by asking plants if they were ready to be honoured for their purpose of being. I asked permission from the universe and then scanned with the palm of my hand. Sometimes I felt heat, and sometimes my fingers seemed to have an uncontrollable twitch when I was over ripe vegetation.' Significantly, the Aborigines told her that dowsing was a *natural ability* given to all humans.

One of the most truly impressive displays of device-less dowsing I have witnessed was by David Ashworth. At a dowsing conference, to show the different energy fields of a willing participant, he literally ran backwards and forwards across the stage, indicating a radius of energy at 20, 30 and 40 feet. He was not holding dowsing rods but determining each field with the palms of his hands. When I asked him to describe what this *felt* like, he explained, 'There are a number of things going on at the same time. You may perceive a temperature change, or a pressure or change of pressure when you touch that energy, or you may feel a tingling, which is actually the electromagnetic energy of the human body. Or a combination of all three.'

Now that we have established what (or who) is the true dowsing instrument, we need to do some tuning of the transmitter-receiver.

CHAPTER SIX

IN THE MOOD TO DOWSE

We, and all things in the universe, are non-locally connected with each other and with all other things in ways that are unfettered by the hitherto known limitations of space and time.

Dr Ervin Laszlo and Dr Jude Currivan, *CosMos*

Have you ever noticed that if you are in a bad mood you quickly affect the mood of everyone around you? The same is true when you are in a good mood... If you affect a person's mood then you also affect their biology, given that the body and mind are intertwined.

David Hamilton, PhD, *It's the Thought That Counts*

In order to be the best possible dowser you can be, your transmitter-receiver needs to be relaxed and balanced, with a freeflowing charge of energy. And, just as importantly, you really do need to be in the mood.

Playing a transistor radio with flat batteries gives a weak and distorted signal – or no signal at all. Playing a transistor radio that is incorrectly tuned to a station weakens the signal, making it difficult to hear and the information broadcast open to possible misinterpretation. A radio tuned into the wrong station can give totally unwanted information. Dowsing is just the same. You cannot dowse if your batteries are flat or if you are *incorrectly tuned*. Dowsing cannot be done if you are tired, stressed, angry, upset, unwell, fearful – or in any heightened negative emotional state. Well, it can; but don't expect to get accurate or meaningful results.

Neither is it a good idea to 'drink and dowse'. Drinking and dowsing is a bit like drinking and driving. You think you are a better driver, but only because your perception is distorted. Out of respect for what I do, I never drink when there is the slightest possibility of dowsing. Having said that, when a genuine emergency situation arises, it is gratifying what the universe will allow you to override.

The more relaxed and balanced you are – both physically and mentally – before commencing dowsing, the clearer, stronger, more accurate and factually correct your information will be.

Every professional dowser has their own way of preparing to dowse and 'getting in the mood'. Some begin with a short meditation, others by 'asking permission' of the universe to dowse, some by repeating an affirmation of their intent or giving a commitment of what they want to achieve with their dowsing. Yet others have more novel ways of focusing their energies. Water dowser and ex-President of the British Society of Dowsers Clive Thompson, a veteran dowser in his eighties, swears by playing Abba at full volume on his car stereo on the way to the site – *Mamma Mia!* He says it lifts his mood to the positive and joyful state of mind that he feels is conducive for dowsing. Which is exactly what we are all trying to achieve.

So, before we pick up the dowsing rods for the first time, I have included a short relaxation/visualization exercise for you. I am not suggesting you do this every time you dowse, or that you even do all of the exercise – you may want to just use the parts of it that feel comfortable to you. In time, depending on your requirements, you will develop your own way of clearing your mind and finding your focus. The aim is to take a few minutes before you dowse to calm the conscious mind/brain, put aside the chattering voice in your head and arrive at a place of stillness and positive anticipation. The following is simply one suggestion of how it might be done. And you never know, it might just put you in the mood...

Choose the quietest space that you can find. Sit comfortably in a straight-backed chair, with your feet flat on the ground. Place your hands comfortably in your lap and feel the weight of them resting there. Loosen and relax your fingers, wrists and arms. Close your eyes. Ensure that your back is straight and your head in correct alignment with your spine. Make a conscious effort to drop your shoulders as far as you can and relax.

Slow your breathing. Take the focus of your breathing down to your abdomen and just breathe. Breathe slowly and gently, aware that when you breathe in, your abdomen expands, and when you breathe out, it flattens towards your spine. Just ... breathe.

Now check your shoulders, and ask your mind to drop them two more inches. Tell your body to relax. Say, 'Body, relax,' and observe all the tension flowing out of you. The only part of your body that remains structured is the straight-ness of your head, neck and spine, as if there is a string going from the crown of your head pulling upwards. Everything else is totally relaxed.

Keep breathing...

Now go inside and have a good look around. See where there might be areas of tension and make a conscious effort to let go of that tension: breathe into that area and, as you breathe out, see the tension dissolve away. Tell any tense parts to relax. Say, 'Knees, relax,' or, 'Forehead, relax,' and feel them letting go.

Now become aware of your energy body or auric field. Move your attention around and experience what your energy body feels like. You might feel a tingling sensation or perhaps very fine pins and needles. Have a look at its colour. Feel its energy.

And keep breathing…

Now move your attention to deep within your solar plexus (in the centre of your body just below where your ribcage joins). See or visualize (it does not matter) a ball of pure white light there. Take this light from the solar plexus and see it travelling in a constant stream of light down your legs, down your thighs and your calves and out through the soles of your feet. See it travelling down into the ground and deep into the Earth.

As it travels through the Earth, see it gather momentum. At the same time, it changes colour, from white, to pale yellow, to gold, to dark gold, to orange, to amber to red. At the point it turns to red, your energy stream has reached deep into the core of the Earth. Feel it anchor into the Earth.

Now it starts to travel back, the colour sequence reversing from red, to amber, to orange, to dark gold, pale gold, pale yellow and, at the point it re-enters your body through the soles of your feet, it is once again pure white.

The white light now travels back to your solar plexus and continues up your spinal column and out through the crown of your head. The beam of light travels upwards and upwards, gathering momentum and speed. Keep pushing its boundary until it reaches *the very highest point that it is possible to imagine*, and when you have done that, see it reach *just a little bit more*. Firmly anchor it there.

Now see it stream back, through the crown of your head, down your spine, to re-enter your solar plexus. See yourself suspended, firmly, safely and securely balanced on the beam of light between Earth and the furthest point in the universe.

Your feet are firmly anchored to the Earth, while your crown is accessing the highest level of light.

And breathe.

Visualize the light in your solar plexus expanding outwards, further and further into infinity.

And breathe…

When you are ready, slowly open your eyes. You are now poised and ready to pick up your chosen dowsing tool(s).

The importance of a relaxed body cannot be overstated, and is confirmed by energy consultant and healer Dan Kahn. Dan has played an active role supporting me whilst I am giving UK workshops. When we have the occasional student whose dowsing rods simply will not move, he can be observed gently placing his hands on their shoulders. After a minute or two of his calming intervention, the rods in the student's hands can be seen to slowly move into action. Dan explains:

The movement of the dowsing rods is the reflection of micro-muscle movements in the body – it is a whole-body response. If someone is tense, their muscles are going to be quite rigid and they will get less of a response. I send energy in with the intention to relax them. When they are relaxed, the micro-motor action can better be magnified by the dowsing rods.

When you're relaxed, Qi [energy] flows better. Energy likes to move through a relaxed and happy person. The human body is an amazing and high-tech piece of equipment – the amount of processing that goes on down to the molecular level is astounding. The energy field is a product of that, but it is also an information medium that is able to communicate information to all parts of the body.

In other words, achieving a relaxed and happy state will give you the optimal environment for dowsing.

And now that you're in the mood, let's do a little tuning…

CHAPTER SEVEN

TUNING YOUR DOWSING

Do the one thing you think you cannot do. Fail at it. Try again. Do better the second time. The only people who never tumble are those who never mount the high wire. This is your moment. Own it.

Oprah Winfrey, actress and television talkshow host

*How do you know but every bird that cuts the airy way
Is an immense world of delight, closed by your senses five?*

William Blake, *The Marriage of Heaven and Hell*

The feel of dowsing rods independently moving in your hands for the first time is a remarkable sensation. For many, it is a moment they will always remember, because it verifies, on a tangible level, the existence of an invisible world of energy outside the one that we see and feel and smell and hear and touch. A world other than the one we perceive with our five senses.

In reality, the experience can also be quite daunting.

So where do you start? As we have previously discussed, your choice of dowsing tool is entirely down to comfort and practicality. In this instance, for the purpose of practical dowsing instruction, we will be working with 'L' or angle rods. Experience suggests that they are the most immediately *visually* responsive, with the broadest range of application. They can be used as a *finding tool*, by asking them to 'point' and indicate a direction, as a *calibrating tool*, by asking them to determine a number or an amount, or as an *information* or *communication tool*, by asking questions and receiving *yes* and *no* answers.

When you pick up your 'L' rods for the first time, one of several things will happen:

They will swing wildly all over the place.

They will do nothing, then slightly, just slightly, creak into action.

They will spin round in circles.

They will swing round and point at you.

They will swing round and point at another person.

One rod will swing to the left or right and the other will remain stubbornly still.

They will do nothing at all.

The *very important* thing to remember is that all these responses are perfectly normal. If your rods have moved, congratulations, you are now beginning to dowse. If they haven't, take a deep breath and persevere.

There is a lovely and very reassuring story told in *The Art of Dowsing* by Richard Webster about Albino Gola, a highly intuitive and widely skilled dowser who went on to become the president of the New Zealand Society of Dowsing and Radionics. When Albino started to dowse with a rod, he couldn't make it move. For over a month he tried desperately hard, with no success. But as soon as he made the decision to give up, the rod started working for him. By surrendering, he unconsciously gave up *willing* the rod to move by a process of sheer determination. By surrendering, he also relaxed, consequently allowing the process to work spontaneously through him. You cannot will a dowsing rod to work, straining with gritted teeth! Just *know* that you can dowse, step aside and let the process flow.

Let's take stock.

Sit in a comfortable chair (one without arms, to give you freedom of movement), with your back straight, your shoulders relaxed and your feet flat on the floor.

Hold your 'L' rods in your hands with a relaxed grip. Do not clutch them. If your 'L' rods have a sheath or handle, hold your rods in the most comfortable way for you. If you choose rods without handles, one of the easiest ways to hold them is to 'thread' them through your fingers (see *Fig. 11*). They are now lightly supported, but free to move easily. With or without handles, keep the bend of the 'L' slightly proud of the forefinger (see *Fig. 11*), so your fingers do not restrict the movement in any way. Your thumbs should be free to enable them to be used to 'damp' (rest lightly) on the bend of the rod for greater control. Look upon your thumbs as the brakes.

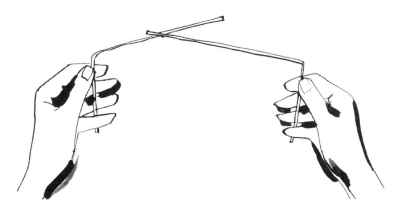

Figure 11: Threading the 'L' rods.

Observe what the rods do. Let your dowsing instrument (you!) get used to interacting with the matrix of energies that surround you.

Now stand up and slowly walk around, watching how the rods react. Remember to do the following:

Drop your shoulders.

Relax your upper body.

Keep your arms approximately body-width apart.

Keep your arms extended.

Bend your arms slightly and comfortably at the elbows.

Keep the rods parallel to the floor.

Relax your grip.

Oh, and walk at the same time.

Do I hear you say, 'You've got to be joking!'?

For those of you who drive, this process is going to feel reminiscent of the learner-driver process. You never, ever believe that you will be able to look in the mirror, push the foot pedals, change gears, steer the car, press the indicator and avoid hitting anything all at the same time. Relax. You've done it. And you will dowse. It just takes practice.

The reason why we hold the rods body-width apart is that if you hold them too closely together, they have 'nowhere to go' – you reduce their potential momentum and are inhibiting the energetic resonance between them. If you hold them too far apart, they become unwieldy, you decrease their cohesion or ability to work 'in synch' and you increase your chance of hitting something or poking someone in the eye. In both cases, you potentially reduce the strength of the dowsing signal. And you increase the risk of upsetting someone!

The reason why we keep our arms extended (whilst holding them comfortably bent at the elbows) is that by putting slight muscular tension in our arms we increase the potential of the maximum dowsing signal.

There are two reasons why it is important to keep the rods parallel to the ground. If you allow the ends of the rods to drop down (so they are pointing to the floor), when you get a dowsing response (the rods either moving to the left or the right) they will struggle to work 'uphill', thereby once again reducing the signal. If you hold the rods with the ends slightly pointing upwards, it is likely that they will fall backwards towards you, giving you a false signal.

And, as with driving, it is important to start with good habits, although as you progress and gain confidence, you will discover short cuts and ways to suit your style. Remember, there is no right or wrong way with dowsing, just whatever you are most comfortable with. Everyone develops their own style over time. Having now dowsed for a very long time, while spending many hours a day information dowsing I allow myself the comfort of supporting my elbows on the arms of my office chair. My dowsing response is sufficiently strong for this not to reduce the dowsing signal. Those who have occasionally heard on the other end of the telephone the smashing of my water glass as my rods spin round and hit it will attest to this!

So now you have mastered walking around with your dowsing rods, allowing them to react freely to all the energies around you. These might include energies from the fabric of the building you are in, from the people who surround you, from any plant or animal life in the vicinity, from the vacillations of the Earth's magnetic field or energy streams and from the myriad of electromagnetic fields – appliances, electrical cables, computers and wireless systems, mobile phones, communication masts and underground transport – in the area. No wonder the rods don't know which way to turn. Literally.

But what does it all mean?

At this point, you can look upon your dowsing rods as a couple of unruly children who haven't been out to play for a long time. They have to be disciplined and managed, and a framework of agreed communication has to be put in place. But, above all, it is important to know that *you* are in control. Or, to use our car analogy, in the driving seat.

You Are in the Driving Seat

One of the most frequently asked questions of dowsers, when they are looking for facilities hidden from sight, is how they distinguish between the many different factors that may be present. For example, if they are looking for an underground water pipe, how do they know they have not identified a gas pipe or an electricity cable? The answer is that they *weren't looking* for a gas pipe or electricity cable, they were looking for a water pipe. They had formed and posed a very specific question and directed their intent to identify the water pipe.

In the simplest of terms, you need to tell your dowsing rods *what you want them to do*.

To practise this, let us use our rods to measure something. It is best to start with something that has a strong energy field, for example a person or a tree.

Assume the relaxed posture, with your arms and rods in the optimal position. The rods should be in 'neutral', with both of them pointing directly forward.

Say (at this point in your dowsing training) out loud, 'Please show me the radius of the energy field of this person [or tree].'

Walk slowly towards your subject, focusing your mind on your request. At a given point, you should find that the rods will respond, doing one of two things: they will either open outwards on a horizontal plane or cross inwards in front of your body. Neither way is right or wrong; whichever happens is just your individual dowsing response. Over time you may find that this alternates or occasionally changes and finally settles to one way or another.

If your rods are not yet moving, don't worry, you are still gaining invaluable practice learning to walk whilst holding the rods parallel to the ground. Relax your shoulders and keep trying.

At this point in your dowsing practice it is important to approach your subject slowly. If you walk too fast, *you will not allow your dowsing rods enough time to react* and therefore you may over-shoot your target and obtain a false result. Approach slowly and steadily, giving sufficient time for the dowsing response. As you become more adept, and your dowsing response more immediate, you can increase your speed.

Once you have a result that satisfies you, you can be a little more adventurous.

Working with another person, establish the radius of their energy field.

Then ask them to focus on something that makes them unhappy or distresses them in some way.

Measure the radius of their energy field once again. You will be surprised: depending on how strong their thoughts and emotions are, you will find that their energy field has diminished considerably.

Now ask them to clear their mind and then focus on something that brings them great happiness or joy.

This time, begin your measuring process from at least 20 feet away. Once again, walk towards them stating your request. You will find that their energy field has considerably increased.

Doing this exercise in a workshop, we take it further. The whole class focuses on sending joy and unconditional love to the subject. Due to the collective intent and power of thought, I usually have to leave the room and go halfway down the adjoining corridor to identify the outer perimeter of their vastly increased energy field.

Not only will these exercises help you to practise your dowsing but they will also demonstrate the sobering reality of how much our thoughts affect our own energy field, and consequently our health and well-being.

By now, your enthusiasm should be fired!

Practical Applications

One of the foremost practical applications of dowsing is to enable you to increase the quality of your life. You will more rapidly understand the benefits of dowsing when the results impact you, your environment or the life of your family and friends. You may want to survey your home, identifying anything that might be non life-supporting or detrimental to your health and well-being. In this instance, you might say, 'Please show me the radius of the harmful emissions from this...' and you may want to measure your television, alarm clock radio, computer or microwave oven. Try the microwave when it is switched off (but plugged in) and then see the difference when it is switched on.

Using a family member or friend as your subject, measure the radius of their energy field, then measure it again while they are carrying a mobile phone in their pocket on standby. Then measure their energy field again whilst they are actively engaged in a telephone call. The results should – at the very least – prompt them to curb their mobile phone usage or alternatively fit a protective device to the mobile to reduce the level of harmful emissions. The results will be even more sobering if the family member is a child.

When I was first taught to dowse it was by a method of finding things. My teacher took me to the library of his home, which had a plentiful array of objects and artefacts. He began,

'The object I am holding in mind was given to me by my father in 1962 and is of great sentimental value. Now find it.' My immediate thought was, *How on Earth can anyone do that?* Followed quickly by, *Oh well, what have I got to lose…?* I focused on his words and watched, fascinated, as the rods began to turn to my left. I faced the direction they were indicating and followed the course they traced, veering slightly to the left and right as they turned. As I reached a bookcase on the far side of the room, they crossed in an X directly over a small ornament. 'Correct,' my teacher said and, without giving me a moment to recover from my astonishment, we started the process all over again.

You can practise dowsing by recruiting a willing friend to help you with the same process; alternatively, they can actively hide previously identified objects. A coin under a rug, a book behind a cushion, an item of jewellery under a pot – the list is only limited by your imagination. While you are still in the early stages of learning, however, I would advise keeping the potential hiding places to a fairly limited area!

The *Yes* and *No* Response

Information dowsing is dowsing in order to obtain information by asking questions, as opposed to using your dowsing rod as a directional tool to locate something. The basis of information dowsing is establishing a *yes* and *no* response from your dowsing tool. Mastering this will give your dowsing the widest possible application because you can employ information dowsing in *any* field.

> Sit in your chair, feet flat on the floor and upper body and shoulders relaxed. Extend your arms slightly, with your elbows gently bent, and put the rods in the neutral position. Ensure that your rods are body-width apart. Then say, 'Show me a yes response.'

One of three things will happen: the rods may cross inwards, they may open outwards or they may do nothing. The first two are perfectly natural responses.

If nothing happens, persevere and ask again. Remember to stand aside and observe what happens, letting the process work through you. This is not about willing the rods to move through sheer determination!

An alternative method is to obtain a *yes* in a more indirect way by asking a question that you already know (without any doubt) has a *yes* answer. If your name is Michelle, ask, 'Is my name Michelle?' If you have blue eyes, ask, 'Are my eyes blue?' Make the question relevant to you.

If a response is still not forthcoming, move your upper body until your arms (still approximately body-width apart) and rods are centred over your right knee. Holding them there, ask for a *yes* response again. By doing this you will gain extra benefit from the flow of male or yang energy on the right side of the body. (We will explore the role of yin and yang energy more fully in the next chapter.)

Once you have established a *yes*, ask for a *no* response. Or again you can ask a question that you already know has a no answer. This time, to enhance your response, shift the centre of the rods over to the left knee to benefit from the female or yin energy.

As a novice dowser, it is important that you recheck your *yes* and *no* responses every day you choose to dowse. In the beginning, you may find that your responses occasionally change or even alternate. In due course this usually settles down and a consistent response will become apparent.

You may find obtaining a *yes* and *no* response more challenging than asking the dowsing rods to react to an energy field or object.

Initially it is not uncommon to find that your rods move only very slightly – perhaps an inch or two. This is entirely expected. When we are information dowsing, we are using a slightly different energy process (we will look at this in more detail in Chapter 10). However, patience, practice and perseverance will eventually bring about a more pronounced response.

As dowsing is all about finding the most effective way to amplify your body's inherent response to an energetic field, for information dowsing you may want to experiment with using a pendulum. Often those who are initially unable to obtain a response from dowsing rods are able to use a pendulum quite successfully. The reverse also applies.

Pendulum Dowsing

The choice of pendulums is vast. When choosing your first pendulum, one of a medium weight is a good place to start. Other than that, it can simply be one of which you like the look or feel.

It is important to make the pendulum work for you in the most effortlessly comfortable way possible. As with the 'L' rods, an agreement has to be established between you (or your subconscious mind) and the pendulum in order to establish which response will be your *yes* and which response will be your *no*. I say 'your' *yes* and *no* because, again, although the tendency is for *yes* to be clockwise and *no* to be anticlockwise, it does vary from person to person. *Yes* or *no* could even be a simple swing backwards and forwards or side to side.

And again, there are several ways to establish your response – and none of them are either right or wrong.

Start by determining the optimal length of chain or cord for you.

Hold the cord of the pendulum in the predominant hand between forefinger and thumb. Ensure that the tips of the forefinger and thumb are pointing downwards so as not to impede the swing of the cord in any way.

Begin with about an inch of cord extended. Gradually lengthen the cord a half-inch at a time until you observe the pendulum start to swing with its own momentum.

Continue to extend the cord until you feel you have reached a comfortable length where the bob is making a natural easy movement. If you continue extending the cord after this point, you will generally find that the movements become unwieldy.

Decrease the cord again until you reach the optimal length. As a general guide this will be at a point between a short one-and-a-half inches and a relatively long six inches.

Of course, you may have extended your pendulum cord the whole way and not experienced any movement whatsoever, just an obstinate stillness. Don't worry – just experiment with another way.

Hold your pendulum cord between finger and thumb with an extended length of about four inches.

Gently swing the pendulum to and fro, towards you and away again, so it gains some momentum.

Now, with the momentum going but with your hand now still, say to the pendulum (as we did earlier with the 'L' rods), 'Show me a *yes* response.'

Relax and watch what the pendulum does.

If it doesn't respond the first time, try again. Be patient – you are training your body-mind in a completely new process. Try the process holding the pendulum over the right knee, as we did with the dowsing rods.

Once you have received a discernable response, do the same asking for a *no* response.

Again the key is patience, perseverance and practice.

After a time, if you are still not experiencing any response, you can try yet another way. In this method, we are actively training the subconscious mind, in the same way that you might, for example, train it to touch-type. Successful touch-typing means that, without looking at the keyboard, just by thinking of a letter, your fingers go automatically to that key; your subconscious mind has been previously programmed in a physical response.

Hold the pendulum in the same way, with approximately four to five inches of cord extended.

Now gently swing the pendulum in a clockwise circular motion. Whilst you are swinging the pendulum, say to yourself, 'This is a *yes* response.'

Do this several times.

Now swing the pendulum in an anticlockwise movement and say to yourself, 'This is a *no* response.'

You may have to do this a few times, but once you are comfortable with the response you are getting, you can start to ask questions.

Practise ... with Fun

Keep the questions simple at first. We will look at questioning in more detail in a separate chapter, but the key is to ask questions that are simple in structure, unambiguous and precise. You can always practise by asking questions that you know the answers to in order to check your *yes* and *no* responses. And, as with the dowsing rods, in the early days of your training, check your pendulum's *yes/no* responses on a regular basis to ensure the direction in which it moves hasn't changed. Eventually this will settle and you will become confident about which is *yes* and *no* without having to check.

Practice will help to refine this process and build your confidence and comfort level with your dowsing tool. You can invent your own ways to test your dowsing. Some dowsers use playing cards, trying to identify first the colour of the suit of a downturned card, then the suit and finally the card itself. Alternatively, you can make your own symbols: on small pieces of paper, draw simple symbols, for example, a circle, a heart, a square, a triangle and a cross. Fold up the papers and, using your pendulum or your rods, identify what is on the folded paper. Keep a tally of your scores and then compare your dowsing progress over time.

You might like to enlist the help of a friend to assist in your dowsing practice. Ask the friend to take three cups and secrete an object like a paperclip, coin or key under one of them. Your job is to identify which cup the object is under. Hold your dowsing tool over each of the cups in turn and ask, 'Is the key under this cup?' Or have your friend put one of the objects under each cup, so you have to identify which object is under which cup.

Take it a step further: ask your friend to place a number of paperclips (or keys or coins) under a cup and then you identify how many items are there by counting up: 'Is there more than one paperclip? More than two? More than three…?' Placing photographs of friends or family members in envelopes is another way to practise. You can then dowse whether they are male or female and then dowse again to identify who they are.

But do ensure that the friend that you choose to help you is interested, or at least inquisitive, rather than sceptical of dowsing. Their critical input might inadvertently or subconsciously put pressure on you, resulting in you feeling tested and having to 'perform' to prove that dowsing works. It is best to avoid this sort of negative input until you have developed enough confidence and experience to detach yourself from any distracting or unwanted influence. Above all, have fun while you are doing this. *Enjoy* the process.

After what you consider to be sufficient practice, what if your dowsing is proving to be hopelessly inaccurate or, worse still, hasn't responded at all? We will look at some possible obstacles to dowsing in the next chapter, along with some fine-tuning of the dowsing process.

CHAPTER EIGHT

FINE-TUNING

The important thing is not to stop questioning. Curiosity has its own reason for existing. One cannot help but be in awe when he contemplates the mysteries of eternity, of life, of the marvellous structure of reality. It is enough if one tries merely to comprehend a little of this mystery every day. Never lose a holy curiosity.

Albert Einstein

It is always true that the message, even from the highest levels, is coloured by the person who receives it, by that person's beliefs, vocabulary, subconscious...

Dorothy Maclean, co-founder of the Findhorn community, *To Hear the Angels Sing*

Many years ago, English visionary, author and spiritual teacher David Ashworth learned to dowse on a week-long dowsing course. At first, he wasn't successful in getting his dowsing rod to move *at all*, so the teacher intervened. In a similar way to Dan Kahn's assistance in my workshops, David's teacher put her hand on his back. David felt a surge of energy move through his body – and he immediately began to dowse.

The effect was short-lived. A week later, on his return home, he fashioned a pair of dowsing rods from coat hangers and found he couldn't dowse. He told me:

> *I walked around with them for weeks and weeks and weeks, every minute of every day, and couldn't get them to do anything. Eventually, they just started to pick something up, just started to creep round, but even then I didn't know what I was finding, so I just kept on and kept on. And because I was never sure of what I was finding in those early days, I developed a different way of finding out. I used to just listen so intently with every sense of my being that eventually I reached a point where I didn't need any of the dowsing tools anymore because I could see, feel, hear, sense. I could find what I was looking for at any level.*

At one of the first workshops I gave in Ireland, in the closing minutes of the weekend, one of the students approached me. With a look that managed to encompass both apology and desperation, he explained he just simply couldn't get his dowsing rods to move. 'But I can do this,' he added hopefully, thrusting his hands forward and giving an extraordinary demonstration of measuring energetic fields by device-less dowsing.

These anecdotes illustrate two very important points:

1. When you first start to dowse, you may be lucky enough to just pick up dowsing rods or a pendulum and dowse. On the other hand, it may take weeks and weeks of perseverance and tenacity. In your moments of doubt and frustration, be heartened by the initial experience of David Ashworth and the success he has gone on to achieve.

2. And, like both David and the Irish student, it may take some thinking outside the box. It *simply doesn't matter* if you find your own way forward, your own unique method. But never, ever be stymied or stifled by others' teaching methods or

have ideas forced upon you that go contrary to your own intuition.

Remember, the process of dowsing is a natural, innate ability that you will give expression to in your own unique way.

Having now established this, we can go on to look at some guidelines that may benefit you in honing your dowsing technique. These principles are applicable in any field of dowsing.

Focus Is Key

As your mind is the interface between a field of information and your final outward physical dowsing response, the ability of your mind to focus is key to your dowsing success. Your dowsing tool responds to the questions that you formulate with your mind, and whether you verbalize these questions out loud or not is immaterial. Your dowsing tool responds to the thoughts in your mind, *not what comes out of your lips!*

If, for example, you are *asking*, 'Is this the location of the mains water pipe?' and at the same time you are *thinking, Did I remember to lock the car?*, your dowsing will respond to the question that is in your mind – whether you locked the car. If you are *asking*, 'Is my body currently deficient in vitamin C?' whilst *thinking, Is the supermarket open late tonight?*, then your dowsing response will be in answer to the question about the supermarket. If you *ask* out loud, 'Has this shellfish deteriorated to a level where it might be detrimental to my health and well-being?' at the same time as *thinking, Did my team win the cup final today?* – well, you can see the potential for disaster.

Remember, the dowsing tool will respond to your predominant thought. So you simply cannot afford to let your thoughts wander at any point. As your dowsing will respond to even the most fleeting thought, the everyday minutiae of life have to be put aside to give you your best chance of accurate and apposite results. Learning to focus on the questions you are asking is crucial.

Anyone who has attempted to meditate knows how difficult it is to silence the intellectual mind and to dispense with the chattering and constant commentary going on inside all of us. Although practice has to be at the top of the list, the following suggestions may help when you are formulating and asking your questions:

- First, put aside the busy analytical mind. Be absolutely present in the moment. It may help you to close your eyes.
- You can ask questions out loud or ask them silently in your mind, whichever you are most comfortable with. In the beginning, however, doing both simultaneously will give the words more force.
- Really focus on the meaning and the intent of the words. Actually see them traced out, or printed out, word for word on the visual screen of your mind's eye. The movement of the dowsing tool should be almost incidental as you totally focus on what you are asking.
- *Feel* the meaning of the words by creating a picture from them. If you are asking about water, see or feel the nature of water; if you are asking about your dental health, visualize your teeth; if you are asking about the well-being of a person, see or feel the essence of that person, whatever that might be to you.
- So now you are visually seeing the words, speaking the words, hearing the words and feeling the words, and visually creating a picture from them. By doing all of this – or even just some of it – you will increase the energy, potency and clarity of the question, and therefore the accuracy of the answer.

By applying as many senses as possible, you will add emphasis to the *intent* of the words, your *attention* will be fully engaged and you will minimize the potential for wandering thoughts.

And remember that your ability to focus will be impaired if you are tired, upset, unwell, angry, resentful or emotionally involved. If you are feeling this way, either find a way to change your thoughts or totally centre yourself physically, mentally and emotionally: read an uplifting book, take a walk in nature, find a way to laugh deeply and genuinely with joy or do a selfless deed for someone with no expectation of any reward. By doing something completely different you will change the resonant frequency of your thoughts to one that is more conducive to working with consciousness. If this is not possible, leave dowsing until another occasion.

A Witness

In some circumstances it might also be appropriate, and helpful to the process of focusing, to use a *witness*. A witness, as mentioned earlier, is a small representative sample of the item or substance you are looking for. It can be held in the hand, placed nearby or carried in the hollow of a pendulum specially designed for the purpose.

A leading UK water dowser, Peter Taylor, tapes a small phial of water to the end of each of his 'L' rods when he is working. Archaeological dowsers frequently carry a small piece of bronze, or gold perhaps. Health dowsers might use a sample of their subject's hair or blood. The thinking is that a witness can help connect the mind energetically to what needs to be found. But determining the right witness is important and sometimes this can be difficult when what you are dowsing on is more abstract or nebulous, such as electromagnetic pollution or a causative factor behind a negative emotional state. My personal feeling, certainly in the causative health field, is that the directed and focused *intention and attention* of the human mind is equally, if not more, powerful. So, if an obvious witness does not present itself for your purposes, do not worry, simply concentrate your intent and move on.

When you first start to dowse, you will also find it easier to focus in a calm, quiet location without the ringing of telephones or interruptions from family and friends. In the real world, however, this will not always be possible – you may be out on site with invasive noise or challenging weather conditions, or you may be responding to a client or situation in crisis. Nevertheless, you must find your focus no matter what the conditions and you will become more immune to a distracting environment over time and with practice. In my own experience, just trying to read a book with any background noise is a challenge, but when circumstances have demanded, I have managed to dowse in the presence of a client's booming television, a gale-force wind with driving rain, the attentions of an over-amorous dog, swarms of flies and – for me, the ultimate test – in front of a screaming infant.

Emotional Detachment

Once you have learned to focus, the next stage is to master complete mental and emotional detachment.

Having emphasized how crucial it is to focus when you are dowsing, it might appear to be a contradiction in terms to now assert the importance of detachment, but one question that I am asked more than any other is whether it is possible to mentally or emotionally influence the dowsing tool and the resulting answer? This question is usually accompanied by a hopeful look that pleads, 'Please say you can't.'

The answer, I'm afraid, is a definite, unambiguous, unequivocal yes. You *can* absolutely influence the dowsing tool. Anyone who has held a pendulum, said with intent, 'Move in an anticlockwise motion,' and observed it do just that will know how easy it is to will the outcome with the force of the mind.

After countless experiments, Professor William Tiller, PhD, in his book *Science and Human Transformation* states:

> *The motion of the wand [rod] can also be influenced by the operator's conscious mind through voluntary muscle action... It is not at all surprising that this should happen and that mentally generated voluntary muscle signals could swamp out the sensor signal-generated involuntary muscle movement ... it is relatively easy to*

let voluntary muscle control slip in if we are looking for a preconceived result.

The key is to develop total mental and emotional detachment. *You cannot have any vested interest in the answers to the questions you ask. Only a vested interest in truth.* Let me say it again, *the pursuit of truth, on every level, is the only way to become a successful dowser.*

What we are trying to accomplish with dowsing is a form of *switching process.* You begin by focusing with clarity and intent on forming an unambiguous, precise question and then you must immediately put aside the strictures of the mental processes and switch to being the *observer of the outcome.* It sounds almost impossible at the start, but practising these steps will lead you there:

- Detach from the analytical mind. Observe what happens. Do not engage the mind in speculation or judgement.
- Focus on the question, not the answer.
- Keep focusing on the question, then *stand aside* and let the response unfold.
- Let go of any preconceived ideas or beliefs – these have no place in dowsing. The most you can allow yourself is open-minded curiosity.

Our beliefs colour what we do on a daily basis, moment to moment, forming the context within which we live our lives. To give an example, say from an early age you have been told by your parents that drinking fluoridated tap water is beneficial for your teeth. This is then confirmed and reinforced by your dental surgeon. With the information coming from credible and professional sources and not hearing anything to the contrary, you will not question its validity. Then if the occasion arises when you need to dowse on your dental health, you will simply *not consider the need to question* whether the fluoride you are being exposed to is beneficial or not. It will probably not even occur to you. Your dowsing questions will be based on an assumption. On a belief.

Then one day you read an article by a qualified medical professional. It states that the three compounds most commonly used to fluoridate drinking water are highly toxic to the body. In fact, two of them are the waste products from the wet scrubbing systems of the fertilizer industry and are classified as hazardous waste. In addition, a highly respected medical journal states that fluorides are general protoplasmic poisons that change the permeability of the cell membrane by certain enzymes. These chemicals are also linked to bone cancer, brain damage, genetic disruption and dementia. On top of that, it states that *pro-fluoridation* dental researchers from the University of Adelaide in South Australia have been unable to demonstrate any difference in the permanent teeth of children who have lived all their lives drinking fluoridated water and those that have drunk rain or bottled water. Suddenly half a lifetime of beliefs is turned on its head.

Will you be prepared to reconsider long-held presumptions and convictions? If you will, your dowsing questions will then be formulated on a wholly different basis.

With dowsing, you have to be prepared to question *all* preconceived notions, even accepted wisdom imparted from those you trust, love and respect, maintaining a totally open mind and objective stance, *devoid of all emotion*. Sometimes the truth can be shocking, sometimes unpalatable, sometimes simply inconceivable. Sometimes it might force you to question your whole life-view. You have to be prepared to re-evaluate and reflect on everything you know or believe in order to arrive at the absolute untainted truth.

After years of practice and application, I am pleased to have established a reputation for a high level of accuracy. Nevertheless, there have been a few occasions when I have been wrong, and these occasions have always been in personal circumstances where I have been emotionally involved and therefore unable to detach. And when it goes wrong, it has the potential to go horribly wrong.

I would rather forget the morning when, late for an important meeting, I dropped, and apparently lost, a contact lens. After an initial cursory search, *in a panic* (note those words) I picked up my dowsing rods and, trying to maintain a calm I wasn't feeling inside, searched for the lens. My fruitless hunt led me from room to room and back again: bathroom to bedroom to hall to bathroom. First the dowsing rods said the lens was not in the bathroom, but was definitely in the bedroom, and then, on finding nothing there, I checked and rephrased my question. The dowsing rods then indicated the hall. When I found nothing there, dowsing then suggested they were in the bedroom. Now very late, I rechecked and rephrased my question in an effort to make some sense of it all. Watching the ticking clock and close to despair, I gave up … only to find, on my return to the bathroom, the offending contact lens brazenly stuck to the top of my toothbrush.

In contrast, arriving one morning at an office where I was a part-time consultant, and therefore emotionally uninvolved, I found everyone running around in a state of mild hysteria. The managing director was away, but she had left instructions that a critically overdue tax demand be paid – and the deadline was at the end of that very day. This was unfortunate for the staff, as they had mislaid it. I was pounced upon to help, which was a challenging task because even at the best of times the office was in a state of chaos. After a few pointless moments of sifting through the disorder, I decided to use the rods I carry in my briefcase. As my dowsing was, at best, tolerated, I asked if anyone minded – but by this point they were beyond caring. Asking for the location of the mislaid documentation, I found the rods firmly swinging towards the secretary's desk, and after following their orientation, I watched them cross in an X over one of the piles of papers.

She eyed me with disdain. 'I've been through *that* pile three times. It's not *there*.'

Rebuffed, I retreated to my desk. But after a further half-hour of watching the fruitless search and rising panic, and with the secretary's attention distracted, I somewhat daringly decided to have another go. The rods crossed over the same pile of papers.

I surreptitiously started to go through the pile. The tax demand appeared, the third sheet of paper from the top. 'Is this what you're looking for?' I asked breezily.

I was a heroine – for a few minutes, anyway. But oddly, no one seemed very interested in my methods.

There is a long-held dowsing myth that says you cannot dowse on questions that involve yourself. This is not strictly true: you *can* dowse for yourself, but only once you've mastered the skill of mental and emotional detachment. If you are not sure if you have reached this level, there are two ways around this. Either write the options concerned on pieces of paper, secrete them in envelopes and dowse on which envelope gives the truthful or most beneficial option. Alternatively, make a note of your questions and their answers, then ask a fellow dowser in whom you have confidence and can trust to verify your work.

The Art of Questioning

Mastering the art of forming precise, unambiguous and explicit questions is probably the most important aspect of dowsing you will ever learn. Remember you are dealing with what is effectively a binary system: yes/no, truth/non-truth. The field of information you are accessing is never, ever wrong. It is the dowser's *interface* with the field that is potentially the weak link.

Poor questioning ability is actually the most common factor behind why those learning to dowse consequently give up. They attribute their confused, unintelligible and seemingly incorrect responses as an inability to dowse and believe they have failed. Not true. If the dowsing tool moves, you can dowse. What needs to be mastered is the skill of the *questioning*.

In the early days, as a novice dowser, I attended the British Society of Dowsers' annual conference. At the President's dinner on the first evening, I watched rows and rows of the attendees dowsing over their food with their pendulums. I was marvellously impressed! Not wanting to be left out, I had a go myself. Having been taught dowsing with rods, the pendulum was fairly new to me. Holding it over a small dish of salt, I asked, 'Is this salt bad for me?', surmising that this should be easy enough, as everyone knew salt was bad for you.

The pendulum moved hesitantly, almost as if it was not sure what to do, making a movement in a shaky figure of eight, and then finally settled for what I interpreted to be a *no* answer.

I was devastated. Everyone knew that salt was bad for you – and my pendulum said that it wasn't. I felt hopeless. Discouraged by this one incident, that night I nearly gave up dowsing. What I hadn't understood, of course, was that the fault was not in my dowsing – the pendulum had quite clearly given me a response – but in my *questioning*.

My mistake was in asking an ambiguous question – and therefore receiving a misleading answer. In fact, salt in and of itself is *not* bad for you; it is a necessary requirement for life. The impact consuming it will have on your system does depend, however, on the type of salt, the additives in the salt, the amount of salt consumed and the individual needs of the body. How on Earth was one dowsing question going to take into account all of the above?

Generalized questions such as this rarely have definitive all-encompassing *yes* or *no* answers. And the context of your question is just as important as the question itself. Perhaps, *in the context of this occasion*, a more apposite question might have been, 'Would it be in my best interests, for my best health and well-being, to add *this* salt to my food this evening?'

A novice water dowser once told me of being employed by a farmer to locate a leaking water pipe in one of his fields, which was causing considerable expense. The job was booked for a Sunday, and the farmer, a JCB and various hangers-on were on standby. The dowser asked of his rods, 'Show me the site of a leak in the water pipe.' He set off across the fields, the others trailing in his wake in eager – if not sceptical – anticipation of witnessing this feat of dowsing. After some time, the dowsing rods responded, the location was identified and they begin to dig.

Nothing.

They dug further and further down, the dowser biting his fingernails and the digging team delighting at the prospect of double time on a Sunday.

Quite suddenly, many feet down, a pipe revealed itself. Unfortunately for the dowser, it *was* a water pipe with a leak – but one that had been repaired by the farmer several years before.

The dowser was given the answer to the imprecise question he had asked. He actually found the site of a water leak quite correctly, but what he would have been advised to ask for was 'the site of the *current* water leak in need of repair'.

Realizing his error, he set off again and eventually located the site of the currently leaking water pipe.

Some years ago a client of mine, a young woman living in London, asked if I would do a health consultation for her father. He was flying in from his home in Australia. His daughter wanted to give him the opportunity of restoring his body to optimal metabolic balance. She was concerned about his overall heath as he had suffered a heart attack some eight years before, was experiencing digestive problems and was a born worrier – not a good combination!

Working with him in person over a couple of hours, I was able to establish the root causative factors in his current imbalance of health. Although an incredibly physically active man – his routine included sailing, golfing, cycling, walking daily and yoga – his body was carrying an extremely toxic load from his previous profession as an industrial chemist, including heavy metals, asbestos, solvents and polyvinyl chloride (PVC). The presence of this wide range of toxins was massively compromising his body's absorption and bioavailability of key minerals, the very building blocks for good health. He was severely deficient in all the major minerals. Towards the end of the consultation, he asked me if I would give a reading, as a percentage, for the overall health of his heart. Not the usual sort of request, but I did – and it was 80 per cent. A checklist of all the factors he needed to address for his return to optimal health was prepared and he flew back to Australia.

A few weeks later, a message came from his daughter. Her father had been rushed into hospital as an emergency case and the surgeon had proceeded to undertake open-heart surgery lasting five hours for a *quintuple* heart bypass.

How did I get it so wrong?

A month later I received an invitation from his daughter for dinner in a London restaurant. It was not without trepidation that I went, unsure of what my reception might be.

'How is your father?' I managed to venture.

She replied that he was doing really well and the hospital was very pleased with his progress. There was a pause. Then she said, 'Of course, you were absolutely right.' Too astonished to speak, I gazed at her in confusion. 'Oh yes,' she continued, 'after the operation the surgeon visited my father in intensive care and told him that they were very pleased with the way that the procedure had gone and the good news was that his heart was absolutely healthy, undamaged and in good condition. Just what you said.'

I gaped.

Everything began to be clear. His *heart* was healthy – it was the arteries leading from the heart that were not. And we had already addressed the underlying causative factor for poor blood vessel health in his consultation: the significant toxic load that, in turn, was resulting in severe mineral deficiencies – the very minerals that keep the arteries clear of scale build-up. And as he had been mineral deficient for so many years, this had built up to an alarming level – 90 per cent blocked, according to the surgeon.

In this instance, due to the client's extremely long-term metabolic imbalance, it is highly unlikely that the underlying factors could have been addressed and measures put in place to rectify the blocked arteries swiftly enough to prevent the heart attack and resulting surgery. Nevertheless, by omission, I had given my client incomplete information.

Unless you know your field or are prompted by an expert in their field to ask *all* the questions and cover *all* eventualities, the potential is there for basing assumptions on misleading or incomplete information. So the degree of success of your dowsing will depend not only on the questions you ask, but also *the questions you don't ask*. Everything that I had dowsed was absolutely correct – but incomplete. The dowsed information simply wasn't enough to give the all-encompassing picture.

Failure to acknowledge the undoubted existence of a bigger picture has the potential to take us to our most misleading answers and assumptions. In short, this is one of the biggest pitfalls in dowsing.

Thankfully, our greatest mistakes usually provide us with our most profound learning experiences and, as long as we are able to view these instances through the eyes of humility rather than defensiveness and dejection, they offer invaluable opportunities to refine our dowsing techniques.

To avoid assumptions made on or through incomplete information, it is important to put in place a set of double-check questions. Depending on the circumstances, the following may be appropriate:

'Have I misinterpreted the information in any way?'

'Have I misunderstood the information in any way?'

'Have I made any assumptions based on incomplete information?'

'Do I have all the information to give a complete picture of...?'

'Am I missing information that might prevent a full and total understanding of the whole picture?'

'As a result of the information dowsed, have any assumptions been made that might not be correct and true?'

'Taking everything into consideration, is there any additional key information that might benefit (the person)?'

And in this particular case…

> *'Does the information given through dowsing provide an accurate and true reflection of the overall health of the client?'*

Perhaps now, from these examples, you are beginning to understand the critical importance of good questioning ability…?

Clarity of Detail

We also need to remove from the equation the potential for *misinterpretation* of the dowsing response.

The pendulum figure of eight movement I spoke of before (in the salt anecdote) is actually a helpful response. Although I was unaware of it at the time, the figure of eight was my *yes and no* response, indicating one of the following answers: 'Possibly', 'Maybe', 'Borderline', 'Sort of' or 'It depends.' Or even 'Your question is not clear!' If using the rods, the equivalent movement is likely to be a swinging to and fro of the rods between your *yes* and *no* responses.

This is the point where you need to persevere – do not give up. This dowsing reaction is potentially helpful because it signifies *a prompt to clarify your question*, to go on and ask further questions or to break a complex question down into simple unambiguous one-answer questions.

This is of huge importance. Dowsing beginners often make the error of asking more than one question at a time and expecting one definitive answer. No wonder the rods are confused! An example might be, 'Should I sell my house next week for £100,000?' This is in fact three questions. For better results, try:

> *'Would it be in my best interests to sell my house?'*

> *'When would be the optimal time to do so? This month? Next month? Within the next six months? Within the*

next year?' (Work up the scale until your dowsing tool responds.)

'What would be the optimal price to market the house at? More than £90,000? More than £100,000? More than £110,000?'

Further accuracy, and assurance that you have covered all bases, would be gained from prefixing your questions with: *'Taking everything into consideration*, would it be in my best interests to…?' It might be in your best interests to sell your house for financial gain, but not necessarily for your emotional well-being or perhaps for the well-being of your partner or children. Remember, the bigger picture is often hidden from us and by not breaking your questions down into simple facts, you run the risk of making assumptions and erroneously pre-empting answers.

It is also crucial not to base your *first* question on an assumption. If you are waiting at a bus stop with a looming appointment, you might find reassurance in dowsing on the punctuality of the bus. 'Is the 8.30 a.m. bus from Beaconsfield running late this morning?'

Wrong!

If your dowsing gives you a *no* response to this question, you might, in your blissful ignorance, assume that the bus was therefore running on time. But what if the bus had been cancelled and wasn't running in the first place? Your dowsing would still give a (very accurate but literal) *no* response to your question, because it would be true that it was *not* running late. The fact that it was not running at all might not be deduced from the literal dowsing response. Instead try:

'Is the 8.30 a.m. bus from Beaconsfield running this morning?'

'Is it running on time?'

'Is it running late?'

'How late will the bus be in reaching this bus stop? More than 5 minutes? More than 10 minutes? More than 15 minutes...?'

It will serve you well to think very carefully about basing your first question on an assumption. The fewer short cuts you take, the more accurate your dowsing will be and the more you will remove the margin for misinterpretation. Patience and practice are your greatest allies.

The Literal Universe

You may have noticed in the examples that the phrase *'Is it in my best interests…?'* has repeatedly been used. This is as opposed to the phrase 'Should I…?' Why?

The information field is objective, not subjective. Using the question 'Should I?' suggests that you require an opinion, not facts or truth. Should I? In whose opinion? For what reason? For what end? Whose opinion are you asking? It might appear a little harsh, but the universe doesn't have any opinions about the choices you make. It doesn't have any judgement about *what* you do – only that you have the free will to do it. In our existence on this planet, free will is not only paramount, it is also our greatest gift. If you want an opinion, ask your mother, father, partner or friend – not the universe. If you want accurate facts and the highest level of truth, banish 'Should I?' from your vocabulary.

But remember, if you form and ask a literal question, you will receive a literal answer. At best (and inadvertently) this may not necessarily be what you want; at worst it may lead you to make important decisions based on misinterpretation.

Read on…

Be very aware of how you formulate your questions. Recently, after much time spent agonizing over the choice of a birthday gift, I decided to ask for some guidance. I dowsed, 'Would it be a good idea to give a hamper as a gift?' Fortunately, after dowsing a very strong *yes* response, a niggling doubt made me realize my error. What the enthusiastic but literal response was really indicating was, *yes*, it would be a good *idea* to give a hamper. There was nothing wrong with the *idea* at all. But the second part of the unsaid answer was 'But taking into account the practicalities of lead-time and delivery, in practice, *no*.' In reality you can have many good ideas, but this is not the best way to phrase a dowsing question. Perhaps a better question would have been 'Taking everything into consideration, which of the following gifts would be the optimal choice?' and then identify the best option from a list.

If you are looking for an alternative to the phrase 'in my best interests' in order to ask if something is the 'right' or beneficial thing to do, ask if something is 'in the best interests of all parties concerned' or 'in the best interests of the higher good'. Or formulate your own phrase that works for you within your spiritual belief system.

Calibrating

Once you are familiar with your dowsing tool, you may start to observe subtle changes in speed and emphasis in its movement. This is probably easier to discern using dowsing rods as opposed to a pendulum. If you asked a question, for example, 'Taking everything into consideration, would it be in my best interests to take a holiday?', you might observe the rods moving very slowly, perhaps even reluctantly, to a yes response. (An equivalent move by the pendulum might be an elliptical rather than a circular motion.) Alternatively, you might observe dowsing rods moving confidently and swiftly to a yes position, or even spinning around at speed in the yes direction. What you are now getting is a qualified response. In order to interpret that qualified response and maximize the potential information, we need to put in place a scale of analysis. This therefore leads us to calibration.

Calibrating the scale of the response will enable us to obtain more sophisticated, defined, broad-reaching and constructive information. If, for example, you asked, 'Would it be in my best interests to attend the committee meeting this morning?', you have the potential of several answers:

- A *yes* response, with varying degrees of speed or emphasis by your dowsing tool.
- A *no* response, with varying degrees of speed or emphasis by your dowsing tool.
- A *yes and no* ('possibly, partly, maybe') response.

None of which is particularly helpful in making an informed and definitive decision.

If, however, you asked the question, 'On a scale of one to ten, *how much* would it be in my best interests to attend the meeting this morning? More than one out of ten? More than two? More than three…?' and up the scale, you would then receive a *quantified answer*. As you work up the scale and get a *yes* response to each number, keep going until you are given a *no*.

If the answer is two out of ten, you will know it is not in your best interests; conversely, if the answer is nine out of ten, you will know it definitely is.

If the response is five out of ten, this is your prompt to ask further questions. You could perhaps then prefix your question 'On balance, is it in my best interests…?' or 'Taking everything into consideration, is it in my best interests…?' Or obtain further information, for example, 'Would my time devoted to the meeting be spent more productively elsewhere? Would it be in my best interests from the chairman's perception to put in an appearance? Would it be in my best interests to attend one part of the meeting? The first part? The second part?' Your personal circumstances will dictate the questions.

The more intelligent and defined your questions, the more intelligent and defined will be your answers. The more information you can gather, and the greater the breadth of knowledge, the better placed you will be to make well-informed decisions.

Another key benefit of asking for a calibrated response is that it will significantly help you to distance yourself from the answer. As we have discussed, when asking a dowsing question that emotionally involves you, it can be challenging to remain sufficiently detached to prevent yourself from influencing the response. Focusing your attention on a scale of numbers will help in doing this.

In workshops, I suggest to the students that they visualize a digital counter or clock – similar to the (annoying!) ones seen whilst queuing in supermarket delicatessens. Really see in your mind's eye the numbers clearly forming or ticking over. Or use your powers of visualization to trace the numbers as they form, as if they are being written out in front of you. Placing all your attention on the scale of numbers rather than the outcome will help prevent you from exerting any inadvertent influence.

And as long as you *establish a clearly defined scale*, anything can be measured.

It does not have to be a scale of 1 to 10. It can be a scale of 1 to 100 (or a percentage) or 1 to 1,000 – whatever is most practical in the circumstances. You could just as easily use a ratio. For health readings, I normally use a percentage scale. Then you are consistently comparing like with like and you have a broader scale with more scope than 1 to 10.

David R. Hawkins, MD, PhD, is an internationally known teacher, author and speaker on advanced spiritual states and consciousness research. He is also one of the greatest pioneers of establishing a scale of measurement. Years ago, whilst attending a lecture on Behavioural Kinesiology, he had a light-bulb moment. He realized that the practice of muscle testing had the potential for a greater application, that it was more than simply a mechanism in establishing what is life-supporting or non-life-supporting, with the body going weak when exposed to harmful stimuli. He suddenly recognized that muscle testing was also an indicator of the body's response, at a protoplasmic level, to truth and non-truth – a powerful tool to tell the truth or falsehood of any situation. Rather like dowsing. Moreover, by applying a scale, he realized that he could assess the *level* of truth or consciousness (he maintains that they are one and the same) of anything that exists, be it a person, sentence, book, symphony, film, corporation, concept, organization, country – *anything*.

Many years of research followed and after countless tests with thousands of people, Dr Hawkins developed what is now known as the *Map of Consciousness*. The Map calibrates levels that are specific processes of consciousness – emotions, perceptions, attitudes, world views and spiritual beliefs – with numeric values, on a scale of 1 to 1,000, that reflect the inherent energy of each. And, just as the body becomes weak when exposed to harmful stimuli, he found that anything that calibrated under the level of 200 also rendered the body weak, was an *energy-drainer* and non-life-supporting. Anything above 200 was life-supporting or enhancing. Therefore, 200 became the pivotal level of truth or integrity.

To fully understand Dr Hawkins' work, reading one of his many books is essential. However, what we as dowsers can take from this is the process of calibrating. In the same way that Dr Hawkins uses muscle testing to calibrate the level of consciousness, we can use *dowsing*.

As always, the wording is vitally important. We must establish that we want to know the level of consciousness of something specifically using Dr Hawkins' scale. Therefore we might say, 'What is the calibration, on Dr David Hawkins' Map of Consciousness, of this [person, book, film, etc]? More than 100, more than 200…?' and work up the scale. As long as you get a *yes*, go to the next level. If you get a *no*, go back and break down the scale further. For example:

'*What is the calibration, on Dr David Hawkins' Map of Consciousness, of this film?*'

'*More than 100?*' *Dowsing tool says yes.*

'*More than 200?*' *Dowsing tool says yes.*

'*More than 300?*' *Dowsing tool says yes.*

'*More than 400?*' *Dowsing tool says no.*

'More than 310 ... 320 ... 330 ... 340 ... 350?' Dowsing tool says no.

'More than 341 ... 342 ... 343 ... 344?' Dowsing tool says no.

'Is the calibration of this film then 344?' Your dowsing tool should confirm a yes.

As we discussed before, you will find it easier and be more able to remain objective if you visualize a digital counter in your mind and see it clicking over rather than focusing on your dowsing tool and its response. If you still find it challenging to distance yourself from the question, put the name – or picture or description – of the item or concept you want to calibrate in an envelope and do the dowsing 'blind'.

Not only is this process a beneficial way to practise your dowsing, it also gives you a powerful tool to assess the consciousness, truth or vibrational level of everything you surround yourself with on a daily basis. To understand more comprehensively the implications of this, it is necessary to read Dr Hawkins' work. But on a fundamental level, it begs the question why anyone would want to surround themselves – or their family or children – with anything that calibrates below 200? That is, anything that is below the level of truth or that is non-life supporting. Because – and here's the crux – just the act of being in higher-energy consciousness has a profound effect on *your* energy. And, as we briefly touched on in Chapter 4, the more you expose yourself to beauty, truth and profound love, the more you will raise your own energetic resonance and the more you will evolve through the levels of consciousness.

As Dr Hawkins says, 'The greater the alignment with truth, the higher the calibration.'

And truth is what dowsing is all about.

You now have an invaluable tool to help you improve the quality of your life. But remember to have fun with it. You may be shocked by the calibration of your daily newspaper – or maybe not! Calibrating party political broadcasts to establish their level of truth is usually a source of much hilarity. Calibrate books before you read them, films before you see them, television programmes before you watch them – and you may become more discerning and revise your plans.

When you become assured of your dowsing, you might want to calibrate an employment opportunity before you take it, an accountant or lawyer before you instruct them, a practitioner or healer before you consult them or a potential romantic partner before you embark on a committed relationship.

Dowsing gives you a tool to help you make *choices*. Just remember to be mindful of your questions and then the sky is the limit.

Male/Female Balance

A frequent dowsing conundrum is why, when using two rods, they often either move out of synchronization – one rod sluggishly following half a beat behind the other – or one rod simply and stubbornly refuses to move at all. To address this, we need to go back to looking at the male/female energy balance in the body.

Energy consultant Dan Kahn explains,

> *The left and right sides of the body can have different energy signatures. Generally the right side is considered the Yang or male aspect, and the left side the Yin or female aspect. This is not necessarily in terms of sexuality, but an indication of certain qualities. On the right-hand side the energy is generally easier to emit, say from the right hand, and on the left it is easier to take in. If there is an imbalance – and this can be physical, mental or emotional – then that can be reflected at the energy level, leading to certain tensions within the body that would inhibit the micro-motor muscle response of the dowser.*

Certainly in my own experience, the perfect synchronization of my dowsing rods was preceded by several years of imbalance: the movement of my right-hand rod was much stronger than the left-hand rod, giving the appearance of that being the 'leading' rod. Sometimes, when I was measuring environmental energies, the left-hand rod did not move at all. However, after learning how to freely express the feminine side of my personality and achieve an overall balance of male/female energy within, I found my dowsing rods began moving in perfect synchronization and with a power and speed I had not experienced before.

During the early stages of dowsing, allow time for your dowsing tool and body to attune themselves and for any idiosyncrasies to settle down. After that, if you are still experiencing a disparity in the movement of your dowsing tools, this may be indicative of an energy imbalance in the body, whether of physical, mental or emotional origin. A visit to a practitioner specializing in the energetic fields of the body – perhaps cranio-sacral therapy, Reiki, shiatsu or Bi-Aura therapy – would determine if this was so. And, of course, this would benefit more than just the fine-tuning of your dowsing.

Maire Dennhofer, founder of the Bi-Aura Foundation, explains:

> Good health is about balance, mentally, emotionally and physically. A healthy person has a balance of female Yin energy (intuition and inspiration) and male Yang energy (the will to take action). If we have good ideas but fail to take action, then we have insufficient Yang; if we are active without inspiration, then we have insufficient Yin.
>
> When we allow the Yang to support the Yin, our heart's desires, emotions and feelings are supported by our actions. We take care of our own physical, mental and emotional needs as well as those of others, and work, rest and play in balance. Bi-Aura therapy has

*helped many clients to achieve this equilibrium and
find joy and harmony in their lives.*

So dowsing, as a process, can provide a further benefit: the
revealing of subtle imbalances in our energy body. And acting
on this information will give us an opportunity to restore and
maintain optimal balance – a necessary prerequisite for the best
possible health.

Finally ... a Gentle Warning

You might be surprised to discover that dowsing can be extremely
tiring. Why and how will be revealed in Chapter 10. However, at
this point (hopefully in your enthusiasm!), you need to be mindful
of how tiring dowsing can be.

A straw poll of experienced though not full-time professional
dowsers recently revealed that most of them draw the line of
dowsing *continuously* at about two hours. I would absolutely agree
with this. I know I can dowse comfortably and accurately for a
continuous period of two hours. When circumstances demand,
I can dowse for three-and-a-half hours without a break. But
anything over four hours has resulted in complete and sustained
exhaustion for several days.

With experience, you will find your limits. Please be mindful,
however, of the many and complex faculties of the mind and body
that are involved in the process of dowsing. The focus required
alone is akin to taking a major written examination. Whatever
your state of health, fitness and age, don't underestimate how
tiring dowsing can be. Take regular breaks, keep well hydrated
and never, ever, dowse on anything of critical importance for
yourself – or anyone else – while in a state of exhaustion. Far
better to sleep on it, literally, and wait for another day.

CHAPTER NINE

INTENTION AND ATTENTION

Intention appears to be something akin to a tuning fork, causing the tuning forks of other things in the universe to resonate at the same frequency.

Lynne McTaggart, *The Intention Experiment*

What is inside you is the power of intention. No microscope will reveal it. You can find the command centre with X-ray technology, but the commander in the command centre remains impervious to our sophisticated probing instruments. You are that commander.

Dr Wayne W. Dyer, *The Secrets of the Power of Intention*

During the last 20 years, as we climb to a pivotal point in the development of human consciousness, volumes have been written on the subject of intent and intention.

Intent in this context does not mean something that you *intend* to do. It could be better described as *directed thought or purpose* – but it is yet more than that. It is a way of being, or state of mind, and the application of that state of being-ness. It is a dimension of *consciousness*. And if consciousness is awareness, intention is the activation of that awareness.

In his work *The Secrets of the Power of Intention*, international expert in the field of self-development Wayne W. Dyer, PhD, describes intention as 'an all-pervading force in the universe that allows the act of creation to take place'. He explains that intention is not something that you *do*, but 'an energy that you are a part of' and – of the utmost importance – that it can have nothing 'to do with ego'. The power of intention is 'the power of being able to reconnect ourselves to the source energy from which everything emanates' and with which everything is connected.

Crucially, your own personal intent will also *attune* itself with other similarly resonating fields of intent. When you are dowsing you are essentially asking the universal information field to reveal the truth of any situation. If your intention is truth, and you unfailingly hold that intent or *resonance* of truth, then your state of being will lead you to truth. Rather like a tuning fork. If your intention when you are dowsing is for a specifically desired outcome, you may jeopardize your ability to connect with truth. If you want something strongly enough to override your intent for truth, you may get the dowsing response you hope for – but it will not necessarily be the truth.

If your intent stems from powerful emotions of the ego – greed, fear, revenge, need or self-aggrandizement – you will by the same token align yourself with, and attract, corresponding fields of energy. As all the great spiritual teachings say, you *attract what you focus on*. Driven by personal agendas, your emotions will compromise your integrity and self-deception will take over. Diligence, a regular reality check and a brutally honest examination and continuous re-definition of your intent are essential.

And vitally important, whatever your expression of intent, is to ensure that it is in alignment with the *highest possible vision of yourself*.

Comprehending the fundamental meaning of intent may be something you suddenly grasp or that gradually unfolds for you. Reading or listening to the works of Dr David R. Hawkins, Dr Wayne Dyer and Lynne McTaggart are good places to start, but understanding can equally come about through the awareness of the simple tasks we all have to tackle on a daily basis. For me, this extract from *To Hear the Angels Sing* by Dorothy Maclean, co-founder of the Findhorn community, perfectly illustrates intention. She is talking about her spiritual teacher:

> *Once, when I was dusting her furniture and thinking that chore boring and time-wasting, she gave me feedback on how upsetting my thoughts were, and asked me to leave. I was annoyed at having been so accurately caught out in my thoughts, but after that, whenever I found myself doing something without love, I remembered that incident and tried to change, aware that my surroundings were affected by my frame of mind.*

Perhaps some of the most tangible evidence of how our very way of being, *our intent*, influences our environment and the matrix of energies around us is physically visible in the captivating work of Dr Masaru Emoto. Dr Emoto pioneered a method of freezing water to form ice crystals, which he then photographed. First by chance and then in controlled experiments, he discovered that crystals that formed in frozen water revealed changes when *specific concentrated thoughts were directed at them*.

For example, he found that high-quality water from clear springs and water that had been exposed to positive or loving words formed crystals that were complete, complex and stunning in their beauty – similar to the exquisite structure of snowflakes. By comparison, low-quality water from polluted sources or water exposed to negative or hostile thoughts formed asymmetric, incomplete or deformed crystals. He conducted many experiments and the dazzling photographs have been published in his books, one of which is *The Hidden Messages in Water*.

In the experiments where water was exposed to the influence of words, these were either written on pieces of paper and taped to bottles of water or directly spoken to the water. When the words 'love' and 'gratitude' were taped to the bottles, the resulting crystals were striking in their symmetry and beauty.

Conversely, bottled water that had the word 'fool' taped to it produced crystals that were deformed and fragmented.

One experiment involved children from a Japanese elementary school. They were asked to tell a particular batch of water, 'You're beautiful.' When the water was told this several times, it produced crystals that were better formed than those of water that was only told this a few times. By contrast, crystals formed from water that was *ignored* were the least complete.

Unsurprisingly, Dr Emoto has attracted criticism from some who accuse him of pseudo-science and say that his experiments are unscientific and devoid of the necessary protocol of double-blind testing and rigorous controls. However, although he is clearly a man who has retained a child-like awe and wonderment at life and the universe, his discoveries are not fanciful notions. They are backed up with solid research from reputable scientists and institutions. In her book *The Intention Experiment*, journalist Lynne McTaggart reports:

> *I discovered a body of scientific evidence examining chemical changes caused by intention. Bernard Grad, an associate professor of biology at McGill University in Montreal, had examined the effect of healing energy on water that was to be used to irrigate plants. After a group of healers had sent healing to samples of water, Grad chemically analysed the water by infra-red spectroscopy. He discovered that the water treated by the healers had undergone a fundamental change in the bonding of oxygen and hydrogen in its molecular makeup... A number of scientists confirmed Grad's findings; Russian research discovered that the hydrogen–oxygen bonds in water molecules undergo distortions in the crystalline microstructure during healing.*

The Russian research was published in the *Journal of Scientific Exploration*. And the title? 'Human Consciousness Influence on Water Structure.'

Ms McTaggart refers to a further study where experienced meditators sent an *intention* to affect the molecular structure of water that they were holding during a meditation. When later the water was examined by spectrophotometry, many of its essential qualities, particularly its absorbance of light at a specific wavelength, had been significantly altered. She concludes, 'When someone holds a focused thought, he may be altering the very molecular structure of the object of his intention.'

Dr Emoto tells of a family who, after reading his magazine, conducted an experiment based on his water-crystal work, but instead they used rice. They put it in two glass jars and every day for a month they said, 'Thank you,' to one jar and, 'You fool,' to the other. They then monitored how the rice changed. After a month the rice that was told 'Thank you' started to ferment with a mellow smell like that of malt, but the rice that was told 'You fool' rotted and turned black.

As a result of Dr Emoto publishing this anecdote, hundreds of families throughout Japan conducted this experiment for themselves – with everyone reporting the same results. Overall, he came to the conclusion that the resonance of positive words or the 'energy of human consciousness' has the power not only to change water but other substances too.

And other substances include *living organisms*. Lynne McTaggart concludes:

> *The largest and most persuasive body of research has been amassed by William Braud, a psychologist and the research director of the Mind Science Foundation in San Antonio, Texas, and, later, the Institute of Transpersonal Psychology. Braud and his colleagues demonstrated that human thoughts can affect the direction in which fish swim, the movement of other animals such as gerbils, and the breakdown of cells in the laboratory.*

These examples illustrate the importance of your attention and intention – and how you direct them. Wherever you place your awareness, dynamic energy follows. This energy can either be life-supporting or fragmenting and destructive. As we have already seen with dowsing, whether the words are spoken out loud or formulated in the mind makes no difference – what is crucial is the focus and intent, and the resulting resonant energy. Your dowsing results will be compromised if your intent is questionable, your focus fuzzy and your thoughts vague and ambiguous.

As a discipline, by its very definition as a tool to discern truth, dowsing necessitates a considerable element of self-analysis and understanding. It forces you to examine who you are, where you are going, your most fervently held dreams – and your inner moral compass. Whether self-knowledge is a prerequisite for effective dowsing or becoming proficient at dowsing leads to self-awareness is up for debate. Personally, I believe it is an unfolding, hand-in-hand journey, and one leads to the other. David Ashworth agrees, saying, 'I see dowsing very much as a tool to open your perception and your sensitivity. As your perceptions and sensitivities continue to open as long as you don't limit them, you just keep moving and evolving into field after field.'

As you develop your dowsing skills, suddenly at your (metaphorical and literal) fingertips you have a very powerful tool. Initially this can be quite a heady experience and it is frighteningly easy to delude yourself that it is *you* that has this unique and exclusive power, rather than *what you are able to connect with*, and that somehow *your* truth is the only truth. George Applegate's pronouncement on this is:

> *Ego is a terrible thing when it comes to dowsing. It controls the whole process of dowsing – you get a swollen head, you can do this and you can do that, and you suddenly become very humbled by a failure. So ego, in my view, is out of the book. You've got to discount your ability and put it down to something greater inside you.*

Every professional dowser that you care to speak to will underline the importance of humility and the complete absence of ego. Dowsing from ego can result in the worst of all trip-wires: overconfidence. This potentially leads to carelessness, short cuts, imprecise questioning and false conclusions. Conversely, when your intent is to always use dowsing for the highest purpose, the highest possible vision of yourself, humankind or the universe, its power will increase exponentially.

Both Neale Donald Walsch's description of the energy Matrix and Dr Masaru Emoto's inspiring water crystals serve to illustrate the power innate within us. We are not intended to be the flotsam and jetsam of life, floating around buffeted and helpless, but rather the *commanders and co-creators* of our destiny.

And, as we will see, the very power of our focused, directed, coherent thoughts to change the expression of energy at its most basic quantum level is a fundamental component of the dowsing process. Deliberately focusing our attention and intention kick-starts a chain of events. And this chain of events is the very one that underpins the whole process of the phenomenal mechanics of dowsing.

PART III
THE MECHANICS
OF DOWSING

CHAPTER TEN

THE PHENOMENAL MECHANICS

*All matter originates and exists only by virtue of a force
which brings the particles of an atom to vibration and holds
this most minute solar system of the atom together. We
must assume behind this force the existence of a conscious
and intelligent mind. This mind is the matrix of all matter.*

Max Planck, Nobel Prize-winning physicist and quantum theorist

*With an understanding of vital energy phenomena and how
vital energy works, one can formulate a theory to explain
dowsing. Conversely, our theory construction enables us to
claim that dowsing is a very convincing proof of the potency
of vital energy. Dowsing also may direct us to new ways of
harnessing downward causation and other fruits of the new
science thinking.*

Professor Amit Goswami, PhD, University of Oregon Institute of Theoretical
Physics, *God Is Not Dead*

So, what do these men of science actually mean? And how do we
get to grips with what this implies for us all?

As we have seen, it is the very misunderstanding of what
dowsing is and how it works and the misinterpretation of

where the information comes from that leaves it so wide open to accusations of occultism and witchcraft, condemnation and denouncement from religious groups, and disbelief and derision from classical science.

Quite surprisingly, many dowsers have a peculiarly relaxed, *laissez-faire* attitude to it all. Some are not sure how dowsing works or, more blatantly, confess to simply not having a clue. Others insist that no one really knows how dowsing works. Yet others even feel they don't *need* to know and just resign themselves to accepting that dowsing is 'a gift from God', a clairvoyant ability that shouldn't be questioned and for which a fee should definitely not be charged!

If the dowsing community itself is so diverse with regard to dowsing's fundamental mechanics, then blame for its misinterpretation cannot be totally apportioned elsewhere. As dowsers, if we are at all serious about changing the perception of our craft, it is simply not enough to say with a shrug that nobody really knows how it works or that it is a mysteriously bestowed gift. We need to establish a credible explanation, perhaps even a theory.

In centuries past, any event, occasion or happening that could not be explained and was outside the grasp of a superstitious and uneducated populace was variously dismissed as magic, a miracle or the work of the devil. In the 21st century, however, this breathtaking narrowness of thinking would do little justice to the unprecedented resources of information and education now accessible to the global community. With the recent discoveries and observations by scientists of how the very building blocks of energy behave and function, it is simply no longer appropriate to reject dowsing as some New Age flaky nonsense or a phenomenon that has zero evidence to support it, or to proclaim that nobody knows how it works.

Nor is it acceptable to pronounce it the work of the devil!

Sadly, this limited thinking continues to prevail for many whose only sources of guiding wisdom are the popular press, television entertainment and anachronistic religious ideals based on unworthiness and/or fear. But for others whose enquiring minds allow them to dig a little deeper, outside the confines of media manipulation, a whole new world of extraordinary and spellbinding discoveries presents itself.

An explanation of how the process of dowsing works is already out there *for those who wish to find it.* If you are one of them, read on.

The *source* of the information accessed by dowsing is so fundamental to its credibility that we will explore this in depth. And then we will examine and define the *phenomenal mechanics* of dowsing across a broad spectrum by looking back to the wisdom of the ancients and forward to the pioneers of quantum physics.

Movement

As we have already explored, the dowser holds a dowsing *tool* in their hands – either rods of various designs or a pendulum – but the actual dowsing *instrument* is the human body. So it is the human body – or human body-mind – that is the receiver or antenna and the dowsing tool simply amplifies that signal. Those skilled in device-less dowsing, with no need for a dowsing tool, demonstrate that this is so. In reality, for its very survival, the human body-mind is constantly picking up millions of environmental signals and prompts *every second* of which the conscious mind is unaware. The act of holding a dowsing tool to magnify this feedback simply reminds us that we are already finely tuned transceivers.

So, the physical momentum to move the dowsing tool comes from the dowser. The dowsing tool moves because you physically (but involuntarily) move it!

In the 1970s, the Czech scientist, psychologist and inventor Jan Merta, PhD, undertook research into the movement of the dowsing rod. Author Christopher Bird writes of his findings:

From knowledge gained in his experimental work at McGill University in Montreal, Dr Merta suspected that the movement of the dowsing device had to be directly connected to muscular contractions in the body — specifically in the arms or hands — of a dowser. He therefore reasoned that if he could build an apparatus that could simultaneously record both the movement of the dowsing device and any muscular contraction, he would be able unambiguously to determine which came first.

Dr Merta constructed a measuring instrument called an accelerometer which, when attached to a pocket-sized Y-rod held in his hands in the dowsing mode, could record the rod's every movement through an extremely sensitive built-in crystal, including movements so slight or minimal that observers, unable to measure or detect them visually, believed that the rod was motionless. When the rod was under tension and moving in the hands of the dowser, its imperceptible motion was recorded on a strip chart as a wiggly line. When it lay still upon a table, the record on the chart flattened out into a perfectly straight line. This was clear proof to Jan that the dowser's muscular contraction could move the rod even before he went searching for a target.

In a further test, Dr Merta electrically wired the *flexor carpi radialis* muscle in the wrist area of the forearm to his apparatus. Both the movement of the rod and the contraction of the muscle were then recorded by the chart when the dowser was exposed to a dowsing stimulus. From this he was able to determine the interval between the muscle's contraction and the subsequent movement of the dowsing rod: it was approximately half a second.

William Tiller, Professor Emeritus at Stanford University, later confirmed Dr Merta's findings in his own experiments. He describes securing a dowsing rod in a fixed vice, with the fingers of the dowser wrapped around the handle. When exposed to dowsing stimuli, no movement of the rod was observed. When the vice, still holding the dowsing rod, was detached from the workbench and placed on a supportive surface, again with the dowser's fingers on the handle, a dowsing movement started to build up.

Christopher Bird concluded: 'Dr Merta believes he has unquestionably proven that dowsing devices react only after human beings operating them pick up a signal, which stimulates a physiological reaction.'

So if, when dowsing, you are gleefully accused with 'I saw your hands move!', the answer is a very definite 'Yes, of course you did.' The prompt, however, as to which *direction* the dowsing tool moves in, is a completely separate issue.

The Subconscious Mind

Every morning, in the same old routine, you leave your house, step outside and into your car, turn on the engine and drive to work. Just down the road, you pick up a colleague and share the journey. To pass the time, your conversation covers an eclectic and broad range of topics: the latest economic crisis, the dubious merits of last night's reality-TV programme, the best café for lunchtime sandwiches…

The potentially tedious journey passes quickly with your conscious attention focused on the exchange of information and gossip. You reach your place of work, navigate the car park, collect your belongings and, *as you lock the car door, realize that you remember nothing of the journey.*

So who – or what – was driving the car?

Your subconscious mind was driving the car. The same subconscious mind that whilst touch-typing thinks the letter 'A' and prompts your fingers to move *automatically* to key 'A'. The same subconscious mind that controls the involuntary physical functions of the body: heartbeat, blood circulation, digestion, absorption of nutrients, cell regeneration and, most important of all, breathing. In the same way that you don't have to *consciously* think about driving the car, you don't have to *consciously* think about breathing. It happens all by itself!

In fact, we don't even need a travelling companion to distract us or occupy our conscious minds, thus rendering us unconscious of routine tasks or learned behaviour. We can simply be *lost in our own thoughts*.

The processes of the subconscious mind are both complex and very powerful. The subconscious mind is not a totally separate mind, but a dimension of the overall mind. Whereas the *conscious* mind is the reasoning mind – it distils and processes information accessed by the five senses, makes decisions and reaches conclusions based on input – the subconscious mind is very different. It does not form opinions or make decisions but is receptive to programming. It does not engage in reasoning, but accepts orders, responding to suggestions and instructions. It also responds to your thoughts and *takes direction from your beliefs*. It is *highly receptive to the nature of your conscious thinking*.

Biologist Bruce Lipton, PhD, succinctly sums up:

> *In reality the subconscious is an emotionless database of stored programmes, whose function is strictly concerned with reading environmental signals and engaging in hard-wired behavioural programmes, no questions asked, no judgements made. The subconscious mind is a programmable 'hard drive' into which our life experiences are downloaded.*

It is said that, at some level, we all have the ability to *know* everything. One of the ways of accessing this knowledge is when we are able to put aside the chattering, intellectual conscious mind, thereby gaining access to the subconscious realm of information. This is demonstrated in the police authorities' use of hypnotism: when a key witness is unable to remember vital details about a crime scene, accessing their subconscious mind by hypnosis often reveals a wealth of information not immediately available to their conscious memory.

The information-processing capability of the subconscious mind is staggering: Dr Lipton indicates it is in the region of

20 million environmental stimuli per second as compared to 40 environmental stimuli interpreted per second by the conscious mind. I remember once reading about a lecture given by a hypnotist. People had travelled from various destinations to attend the meeting; one woman had driven 40 miles. Whilst she was in her normal conscious, waking state, the hypnotist asked her how many telegraph poles she had passed on her journey there. Of course, she had no idea. Under hypnosis, however, she was able to state exactly how many telegraph poles she had passed, and probably how many traffic lights and telephone boxes too…

The subconscious mind has a key place in the phenomenal mechanics of dowsing for two reasons:

1. It is the subconscious mind that we are programming when we give instructions for our dowsing tool to move in a pre-agreed direction to indicate a *yes* or a *no*. Please understand that this does not mean that you are instructing your subconscious mind to *answer* the question with a *yes* or *no* response, only that you are programming it to physically and consistently move the body in a given direction that indicates a *yes* or *no*.
2. The way you program your subconscious mind with your *beliefs*, and indeed your self-beliefs, can either make you a skilled and successful dowser or effectively scupper your chances from the start.

If you have any doubts about how crucial your self-belief is, please read *The Power of Your Subconscious Mind* by Joseph Murphy, PhD. With the help of this compelling but user-friendly book, you can change negative conditioning and reprogram your subconscious mind with powerful and life-affirming beliefs. Constant affirmations like 'I am a skilled and successful dowser' and 'These abilities are applied for the benefit of humankind in restoring balanced health and well-being' worked powerfully for me. Within weeks my dowsing career dramatically changed: I attracted more work than I could comfortably manage, received consultation requests from clients throughout the world and was approached to give lectures and seminars, write articles and make television appearances.

Programming your subconscious mind with positive beliefs will consequently lead to a change in your field of consciousness. And the stronger your directed *focus and intent*, the more powerful the results will be. Every successful athlete, actor, politician and captain of industry knows the power and value of positive belief. And, as George Applegate so appositely sums up, 'Just remember that your subconscious must be convinced of the reality of your *belief in your ability* to dowse.'

The Sixth Sense

In 2003, conference attendees at the US Institute of Noetic Sciences (founded by the astronaut Dr Edgar Mitchell) took part in a survey asking for their feedback on their experience of *gut feelings* about people or events. Of the 500 that responded, 89 per cent of females and 72 per cent of males indicated they had often or frequently experienced such feelings. Even 78 per cent of those who considered themselves 'highly sceptical of unconventional claims' confirmed they had experienced the feelings. Often we refer to these gut feelings or intuitive hunches as a 'sixth sense'.

Scientific research into sixth-sense occurrences reveals quite staggering statistics: in 1989 psychologists conducted a meta-analysis of precognition studies. They looked at articles published from 1935 to 1987 concerning nearly 2 million individual trials by over 50,000 subjects. The combined results produced 'odds against chance' of precognition of *ten million billion billion to one.*

In truth, most of us are accessing, with varying degrees and frequency, a field of information that gives us our so-called sixth-sense hunches or inspirational moments. We do it on a regular basis, albeit in an apparently random or unconscious way. How many times, just prior to the telephone ringing, have you known not only that it is about to ring but also who is telephoning you? How many times when you are driving have you had a sudden but overwhelming premonition to slow down or take avoiding action, only to be proved heart-stoppingly correct? How many times have you just known *with every fibre of your being* a course of action to take or the concealed truth of a particular situation?

Often, when working with clients during consultations, I find my role is to simply confirm their intuitions and hunches. I am there only to verify their strongly held gut feelings about events or circumstances, rather than to give them information of which they were previously totally unaware. Although this sort of confirmation is empowering for the client, if we all had total belief in our sixth sense my work might soon become redundant!

The key difference with dowsing is rather than the process being haphazard or unconscious, we are accessing the information in a structured, methodical and deliberate way, where the intellectual analytical mind is first disengaged and then the questions are *intentionally* directed. So the information is discerned in an ordered fashion as opposed to via random moments of insight or intuition.

We have seen that the conscious mind, which is disengaged, is the domain of *sensory* perception. Aside from forming the initial clear and concise question, we do not employ these senses whilst dowsing. We can therefore conclude that dowsing is in the realm of the *extrasensory*. But which *is* the extra sense? Is it the so-called *sixth* sense? And how do we correlate it with the process of dowsing?

In one of the dowsing experiments Dr Jan Merta conducted and participated in, his technician blindfolded him. Although he could not see the dowsing stimulus (which was a vial of water), his apparatus still recorded the contraction of the forearm muscle and the subsequent movement of the dowsing rod. The only conclusion that he could reach was that the presence of the water had been picked up *extrasensorially* – not using the five ordinary senses of sight, hearing, touch, taste and smell. And in total accord with David Ashworth's observations from his self-taught methods, Dr Merta explains, 'It's all a question of being able to pick up a signal, a symbol, an idea, or a thought extrasensorially. It doesn't matter in which form it's expressed. But it does require intensive training.'

So that effectively rules out the five known senses. But could it be the *sixth* sense?

At this point we need to distinguish between different categories of dowsing and which category might correlate with an 'extra' sense. We have previously identified:

Field dowsing, in which we are in the presence or vicinity of that for which we are searching.

Map dowsing, which entails using a map or plan as a means of focus to discern information.

Information dowsing, when the subject or object may be thousands of miles away or may be a concept, idea or theory that has no physical presence.

Field dowsing has been the subject of countless experiments over many years. That our bodies, and those of animals, are highly sensitive magnetic and electromagnetic instruments is beyond question and, as a result, many of these experiments have attempted to explain the process through the physical body's response to electromagnetic fields. Perhaps the best known of all is the work of physicist and scientific advisor Dr Zaboj V. Harvalik.

Dr Harvalik learned to dowse in his native Czechoslovakia, but it was only when he emigrated to America and was frustrated by the 'contradictory conclusions' put forward in dowsing hypotheses, that he began his experiments. Over several years during the 1960s and hundreds of hours of tests (with the help of either extremely tolerant or downright curious friends and colleagues!), he not only proved that a dowser had sensitivity to magnetic fields but also determined the *degree* of that sensitivity. He established that 80 per cent of his subjects could obtain dowsing responses to a magnetic field at a current strength of over 20 milliamperes. The rest of his subjects could continue to obtain responses down to 2 milliamperes and one or two obtained reactions at only half a milliampere. One supersensitive or master dowser consistently detected a magnetic field produced by a current in the ground at an astonishing one thousandth of a milliampere.

Harvalik posited that *minute changes in magnetic fields were responsible for the dowsing signal*. And that the changes in the Earth's magnetic field could be caused by variations in the properties of soil, by ground water or fast-flowing underground water, by subterranean cavities or tunnels and a variety of other anomalies, including waste sites, buried corpses and the root systems of trees.

Spurred on, he set up further experiments attempting to establish in exactly which part of the dowser's body the sensor or *receiver* for magnetic variations was located. He used a special alloy and also aluminium sheeting, wire and foil to shield various parts of the dowser's body, including the organs, in turn. He then determined whether the dowsing signal remained constant or was extinguished whilst the dowser was exposed to magnetic and electromagnetic fields. As a result of numerous tests, he concluded that the dowsing sensor(s) might be located in the vicinity of the adrenals (above the kidneys), the pituitary (at the base of the brain) or the pineal gland (at the front of the brain, commonly known as the *third eye*).

Dr Harvalik came to the conclusion that the *human being was a living magnetometer of incredible sensitivity*. Furthermore, that dowsers were potentially sensitive to *all kinds of natural or man-made electromagnetic signals, ranging from thunderstorms to radio and television waves, for which they should be able to serve as detectors*.

So, is this ability to respond to and detect magnetic fields a function of the so-called *sixth sense*? The world-renowned biologist Rupert Sheldrake, PhD, believes so. In his book *The Sense of Being Stared At*, he states:

The sixth sense has already been claimed by biologists working on the electrical and magnetic senses of animals. Some species of eels, for example, generate electrical fields around themselves through which they sense objects in their environment, even in the dark. Sharks and rays detect with astonishing sensitivity the body electricity of potential prey. Various species of migratory fish and birds have a magnetic sense, a biological compass that enables them to respond to the Earth's magnetic field.

Dr Jude Currivan agrees. She tells me, 'The sixth sense is actually a physical but very subtle attunement to physical electromagnetic fields. Our body is an electromagnetic instrument and therefore we attune electromagnetically on that physical level – often without being aware that we do.'

So field dowsing appears to be a function of the body's ability, through a sensory system, to tune into and detect magnetic and electromagnetic fields, whether they emanate from underground water, various minerals or fluctuations in the magnetic field of the Earth.

So far, so good. But this is only part of the story.

As it is scientifically proven that both magnetic and electromagnetic fields decline rapidly with increasing distance, and experience and experimentation show that there is no corresponding decline in the accuracy of dowsing over distance, this theory *doesn't even come close* to explaining map dowsing or information dowsing. It doesn't explain how a dowser sitting in London can *instantaneously* provide accurate information about the physiology, health or mental and emotional state of a person sitting in Sydney, Australia. It doesn't shed light on how a water dowser can accurately pinpoint the location of water from half a continent away. It doesn't demonstrate how dowsing can provide information about an abstract theory, or a concept, or a truth. And it doesn't account for how dowsing can provide clear-cut and detailed information about the past or the future – information subsequently proven in so many cases to be true.

Which is why we need to differentiate between the sixth sense and the *seventh sense*.

The Seventh Sense

Pivotal to understanding the premise on which the seventh sense is based is the re-examination of our definitions of the brain and the mind.

We have been trying to define the relationship between the brain and the mind for as long as … well, for as long as we have been aware that we had a brain *and* a mind. What have been the conclusions so far? It is accepted that the brain is an organ located in the skull, consisting of a highly developed mass of nervous tissue that co-ordinates and controls the behaviour of the body's cells. Prevailing thinking also purports that the brain is the seat of intellect and consciousness, so surely it is an accepted fact that the mind is located in the brain, and is nothing but the activity of it?

Not any more it isn't.

Undoubtedly the brain and mind are inextricably linked in a close relationship of brain–mind activity, but there is no existing evidence proving the mind is a product of the brain. Instead, quite the reverse: internationally renowned neuroscientist and pharmacologist Candace Pert, PhD, asserts that *your brain is not in charge* and that the mind is not just in the brain but distributed throughout the whole body, by and through a process of signal molecules.

In his book *The Genie in Your Genes*, Dawson Church, PhD, tells of a study by the Institute of HeartMath in America. The researchers examined 'where and when, in the body, heart and brain, intuitive information outside the range of conscious awareness is processed'. On the basis of the results and other research they concluded: 'It would thus appear that intuitive perception is a system-wide process in which both the heart and brain (and possibly other bodily systems) play a critical role.'

Dr Sheldrake goes further, not only suggesting that our minds are not confined to our brains but also that they extend throughout our bodies and *further*. He explains that this occurs through the *fields* of the mind, rather like the field effects of gravity or magnetism: 'The field of a magnet is not confined to the inside of a magnet, but stretches out beyond it... Likewise, the fields of our minds are not confined to the insides of our skulls, but stretch out beyond them.' He believes that it is this stretching out of the mind beyond the confines of the body that supports the idea of a *seventh sense*. This seventh sense encompasses a range of intuitive behaviour from normal perception to aspects of telepathy, in both humans and animals. Dr Sheldrake also believes that the seventh sense is part of our intrinsic biological nature.

Crucially, he goes on to say, 'Our intentions likewise extend beyond the brain... Through *attention and intention*, our minds stretch out into the world beyond our bodies.'

Dr Currivan concurs that it is this non-local effect of the extended mind – this 'extra'-sensory perception – that is the domain of the *seventh* sense. She told me, 'The seventh sense is a fundamental non-local effect.'

When we take on board the body of work of Professor Valerie Hunt, PhD, things get *really* interesting. Dr Hunt is an internationally recognized pioneer scientist of human energy fields and is known as a frontier thinker for her groundbreaking discoveries. She has had a distinguished 40-year career as a university professor and physiology researcher, is Professor Emeritus at UCLA, holds advanced degrees in psychology and physiological science and is the author of several books.

In a recorded interview in 2008, she spoke in detail about the mind, or what she termed the 'mind-field'. She also made a distinction between the brain and the mind, wryly observing that man had been trying to find the mind forever, looking for it within the brain, but it was something entirely different from the material substance of the brain.

The brain is a retrieval, receiving and processing system for information. And if the brain is the mechanical instrument, the mind is the dynamic element.

Going back to basics, Dr Hunt explained that everything that occupies space and has a molecule of a cell has an atom. In that atom an electron spins around the nucleus and creates energy. That energy radiates off from the cell and goes to the surface of the body, where it comes out – but instead of going off into space, it *hangs around*, creating the aura or bio-field of the body.

But you have already discovered that for yourself using your dowsing skills! When you carried out the exercise suggested in Chapter 7, measuring the radius of the energy field of a subject, you were measuring the field described by Dr Hunt. With your dowsing you were measuring the energy field, or bio-field, of the body. You were also able to demonstrate that it is possible to extend the field into the world beyond our bodies, as suggested by Dr Sheldrake. When your willing subject focused their *attention and intention* on great happiness and joy, the radius of their energy field increased accordingly.

The concept of a *field* is vitally important to grasp in understanding the truly phenomenal mechanics of dowsing. A field is a *region or zone of influence in space*. We are familiar with the magnetic field of a magnet – the region of influence that extends beyond the magnet, is invisible and yet exerts a force, and has the ability to attract and pull towards it magnetic materials such as iron filings. Likewise, we are familiar with the magnetic field of the Earth – on the same principle, but much larger. Gravity is also explained in terms of a field, and the influence of gravity around the Earth is referred to as a 'gravitational field'. Malcolm Hollick, PhD, in his book *The Science of Oneness,* states, 'Despite their elusive, mysterious nature, fields are very real. Indeed *fields are a more fundamental aspect of reality than matter* [my italics].'

Imagine that. Invisible fields that we know exist only by virtue of their *force or influence* are considered by a leading scientist to be more real than what is physically experienced with our senses.

Dr Hunt explains that the field consists of energy packages, or *quanta*, and those quanta are *informed*: they carry information. So, by its very definition, the field is an *information field*.

The bio-energy field, or aura, is the information from inside the body, a unique pattern of information that consists of all the experiences that a person has had. This radiates to and extends out from the surface of the body. It is in this field, lying between the denser substance of the physical body and the outer world, that energy transactions take place: *a dynamic, interactive exchange of information going both into and out from the field.*

And fields interact with other fields, and matter, in various ways. When they interact with matter, they create forces between objects perceived to be separated by space. The field around your body is a constantly resonating matrix transacting with other fields, and as a result of all your experiences it becomes a dynamic and special pattern of information. This information goes into the body via the thousands of acupuncture points and then goes to all the cells of the body via the connective tissue. Dr Hunt believes that because these transactions occur in the field, the mind is to be found there. This is why she terms it the 'mind-field'.

So, the *mind* is in the *field*. It exists as a pattern of information of all the experience that a person has had in the world. The mind is a field reality of information that is carried in quantum packages. Dr Hunt also believes this is where consciousness can be found – not in the brain, but in the mind-field.

But there's more.

The individual mind-field of your human body *makes contact with all the other energy fields in the universe.* We experience the patterns of other people, for example, when we feel their energy or their 'vibes', almost, as Dr Hunt says, as if we read their minds. But we *are* reading their minds – their mind-fields!

Fields within fields. So, imagine that your mind-field is a single drop of water in the ocean, then envisage that the mind-fields of all forms of life in the universe are the drops of water that make up the rest of the ocean. Individual *drops*, all linked, forming an ocean. Individual *minds*, all subtly linked, forming one interconnected mind, an ultimate intelligence, or infinite field of information.

In other words, Dr Hunt's *mind-field* is Dr Sheldrake's *extended mind*, stretching out into the world beyond our body. What is more, they are both remarkably compatible with the concept of the Matrix of Neale Donald Walsch:

> *You are sending off energy – emitting energy – right now, from the centre of your being in all directions.*
>
> *This energy – which is you – moves outward in wave patterns.*
>
> *Every thought you've ever had colours this energy.*
>
> *Every word you've ever spoken shapes it.*
>
> *Everything you've ever done affects it.*
>
> *Your energy ... is interacting constantly with everything and everyone else.*
>
> *A Matrix of intertwining interwoven personal 'vibes' that form a tapestry more complex than you could ever imagine.*

Are you beginning to see the powerfully consistent thread emerging?

Our individual mind-fields, personal information fields or individuated fields of consciousness reach out and stretch out into the universe, connecting, reacting to and interacting with all other fields. They *give out and retrieve information...*

Just like dowsing.

At the core of information dowsing is the ability to focus the mind, pose a question with attention and intention and consequently access non-local information. It would seem that the concept of the *seventh sense*, the non-local effect of the extended mind, is in perfect accord with this process.

So, if field dowsing is the body's response to electromagnetic fields, and information dowsing is our connection to an information field at quantum levels, where does map dowsing fit in? Are we using the sixth sense or the seventh sense here? Or both?

I believe that it depends on the dowser. A map (plan, drawing, photograph, diagram) is simply an *energetic representation* of what it depicts. It carries all the information of the components of the actual location, site, object or subject, in an energetic format. Health dowsers might use a sample of hair or blood in the same way. As dowsers, we can then access that information with our sixth and/or seventh sense. When we are using the seventh sense, the map simply acts as a focus or conduit to connect to the information field of what is depicted.

Co-authors of *CosMos*, Dr Jude Currivan and Dr Ervin Laszlo, say:

> *Our non-local abilities to access information beyond the limits of space and time (called by the biologist Rupert Sheldrake our seventh sense) and differentiate it from the localized but subconscious environmental awareness of our sixth sense, reveals our innate connection to the A-field – the all-pervasive information substrate that corresponds to our notion of cosmic mind.*

Time to look more closely at the A-field.

The Akashic Field

Understanding the concept of a universal field of invisible energy that pervades all that exists and connects everything to everything else is fundamental to understanding the phenomenal mechanics of dowsing.

World-renowned systems theorist and twice nominated for the Nobel Prize Dr Ervin Laszlo states:

> *At the roots of reality there is an interconnecting, information-conserving and information-conveying*

cosmic field. For thousands of years, mystics and seers, sages and philosophers maintained that there is such a field; in the East they called it the Akashic Field. But the majority of Western scientists considered it a myth. Today, at the new horizons opened by the latest scientific discoveries, this field is being rediscovered.

And vitally:

The effects of the Akashic Field are not limited to the physical world: the A-field (as we shall call it) informs all living things – the entire web of life. It also informs our consciousness.

Sometimes we feel that we *just know* something or *just feel* something so strongly that we simply know it to be true, without knowing how we know. Other times, when undertaking a creative task, we find that whatever we are creating, perhaps a book, a painting or a piece of music, takes on a *life of its own* – all we need to do is get out of the way.

I remember once hearing Sir Paul McCartney, formerly one half of perhaps one of the greatest songwriting partnerships in the history of music, saying that he didn't write any of his songs. Instead, he said, they were all *hanging in the air*, waiting to be plucked out – all he did was copy them down. Mamdoh Badran, the strikingly talented Egyptian artist, once told me that when he paints his Turner-esque creations, it is akin to a process of meditation: he puts aside his conscious mind and allows the process to flow through him. If, at any time, he interrupts the reverie with conscious thought to analyze what he is creating, the link is broken. And one of the greatest of all creative geniuses, Michelangelo Buonarroti, believed that the figures of his sublime sculptures were *already present* in the blocks of marble that he carved. As a sculptor, his task was simply to chip away at the superfluous stone to reveal the form hidden within. Through the creative process, and in their own unique ways, all three artists were connecting to an inspirational source of information intrinsic to our universe: the Akashic Field

I am fortunate to own an 1892 edition of the *Working Glossary for Theosophical Students*, in essence, a handbook of Sanskrit words. The entry for *Akasha* reads: 'The subtle fluid that pervades all space, and exists everywhere and in everything, as the vehicle of life and sound.'

Akasha has given its name to the Akasha Chronicle or Akashic Records, a 'library' or database of all knowledge of human experience and the history of the cosmos, a storehouse of individual and collective memory. One of the world's most extraordinary and prolific psychics, American Edgar Cayce, is said to have accessed the information from the Akashic Records for the 14,000 or so readings he gave whilst in a trance state. A colleague who worked with Mr Cayce, Dr Wesley Ketchum, stated in 1910:

> *Cayce's subconscious ... is in direct communication with all other subconscious minds, and is capable of interpreting through his objective mind and imparting impressions received to other objective minds, gathering in this way all knowledge possessed by endless millions of other subconscious minds.*

Dr David Hawkins brings Cayce's experience bang up to date:

> *The individual human mind is like a computer terminal connected to a giant database. The database is human consciousness itself, of which our own consciousness is merely an individual expression, but with its roots in the common consciousness of mankind.*

The ancient Rishis or seers of the Vedic tradition speak of a similar concept: a field called *Atma*, an infinite, eternal field of pure intelligence, pure consciousness, an ocean of pure wakefulness responsible for creating and maintaining the infinitely diverse universe. Sir Isaac Newton believed there to be an invisible substance that permeated the entire universe, referring to it as *ether*. And the scientific genius and visionary Nikola Tesla wrote of an 'original medium', a kind of force field that filled all of space and to which he compared Akasha.

It was in honour of the ancients' concept of Akasha that Dr Ervin Laszlo named this field the A-field. He says:

> *The unified field is a space-filling medium that underlies the manifest things and processes of the universe... It carries the universal fields: the electromagnetic, the gravitational, and the strong and the weak nuclear fields. It carries the ZPF, the field of zero-point energies. And it's also the element of the cosmos that records, conserves and conveys information. In the latter guise it's the Akashic field, the rediscovered ancient concept of Akasha.*

Consciousness, the A-field, the universal database, the collective unconscious, the quantum hologram, nature's mind, the divine matrix, the mind of God, the unified field, universal mind or simply 'the field' – whichever name you choose, whichever words comfortably fit your belief system, one thing is abundantly clear: the ancient seers and the pioneers of cutting-edge science are in total accord. The very essence of our universe is an intelligent information field, a cosmic memory field that contains all information past, present and future, and encompasses all space – what we perceive to be solid matter and all the vast spaces in between.

Once we have put aside the censorship of our normal waking consciousness it is possible to access field information in creative endeavours, when we perceive danger and in random moments of intuition. But more than that, it is possible to access this field with focused and deliberate intent. Whether you realize it or not on a conscious level, you are in constant conversation with the universal mind, but it is also possible to *intentionally* retrieve information with astonishing accuracy.

And this is where dowsing comes in.

The Science

So what *is* the science that correlates with the phenomenal mechanics of dowsing?

Over the last century scientists have been exploring the world of the very, very small, the essence of our reality. This strange and enigmatic world has proved to be intriguing, perplexing, frustrating and enthralling. These scientists are the pioneers of a new world that has turned the previously understood rules of classical physics on its head. The new world is quantum physics.

The advancement of sophisticated technology has allowed the exploration of quantum theory to progress from the very, very small to the infinitesimal. It is the exploration of the stuff that makes up our universe, our perceived physical reality – and all the spaces in between. And although quantum theory has famously been referred to as a 'work in progress', there are certain discoveries that have been scientifically established – and that we need to grasp in order to illuminate the phenomenal mechanics of dowsing.

As we look at some of the basic findings of quantum physics, it is worth considering the words of Dr Malcolm Hollick:

> If the concepts of relativity are mind-bending, then those of quantum physics are almost beyond belief. Yet, once again, they are experimentally well-proven and rapidly being incorporated into new technologies. So open wide the doors of your imagination...

Hold on to your hats, here goes:

• What we perceive to be empty space is not empty at all. Far from it – it is brimming with spinning and fluctuating energy in a field that connects everything to everything else in the cosmos. The 'space' that you see around you is absolutely filled with energy.

- Although this field is invisible, its existence has been determined by the scientific measurement of its effects, in line with the other known fields in physics.

- The energy in this field comes in distinct packets, quanta or subatomic particles, such as electrons, photons and neutrons. Everything in our world is made up of these units of energy including you, this book, the physical reality of your life and all the spaces in between. It permeates the entire known universe.

- It is the enigmatic behaviour of the quantum world that has so intrigued science of late, not least because it transcends the Newtonian laws of space and time.

- Nothing is as it seems. What might at first be observed as a particle, a photon for example, can also behave as a wave, can be in both states at one time and sometimes can even be in collective states. Current scientific thinking suggests that the very act of observing or measuring a photon seems to determine the expression or potential of its state.

- Scientific experimentation has also demonstrated that quantum particles can appear to be in two places – separated by miles – at one time. They can be in instant communication and, once connected, can communicate instantaneously over vast distances, *no matter how far apart they are*, without force, expenditure of energy or even crossing space. If you find this spooky then you are in good company: Einstein referred to this 'non-locality', also known as 'entanglement', as 'spooky action at a distance' – instant non-local communication transcending the laws of space and time.

- The way quantum theory explains this being-everywhere-at-once-ness is by suggesting that the structure of the universe is holographic. In simple terms this means that all the information about the whole entity exists in every one of its component parts. The information about the entire cosmos is distributed throughout every constituent element.

- And, most critically for our purposes, the quantum field is intrinsically an information field. The scientific jury is still out as to how the information in the field is stored and conveyed, but it seems that the waves produced by quantum activity are information-carrying, and the node points where the waves interconnect embody the information.

So, we are talking here about the very building blocks that make up everything in our universe. But if that includes everything, *surely that means us as well?* If individual wave/particles at a microcosmic level behave in this extraordinary way and we are made of these same wave/particles, surely human beings function by the same rules? Surely we operate according to quantum processes? This would mean that we can be in two places at the same time, be in instantaneous communication over vast distances and exchange information about all things from anywhere in time.

A bit like dowsing, really!

At first quantum theorists thought that the bizarre behaviour of the quantum world applied only at microcosmic level. But recent cutting-edge experimentation suggests that our brains do in fact operate according to quantum principles. These principles not only apply at microcosmic levels but also at macrocosmic levels.

Scientific research suggests that we can access quantum holograms in the information field because our brain can function in the quantum mode. In very simple terms, access to the information field is gained when the quantum processes of the brain get into synch or resonate with the cosmic quantum hologram and a non-local form of communication is established.

If the universe, our brains, our minds and the embedded information are all holographic, this means when dowsing we are not actually doing the seemingly (according to classical physics) impossible by receiving instantaneous information from a location or subject hundreds of miles away; it is not being transmitted like a broadcast from a radio station, but rather we are connecting to a holographic information field where everything is everywhere at the same time. We are already intrinsically connected to *every part* of the universe as a holographic model. An exchange of information (the question and answer process) takes place when the dowser's brain/mind becomes tuned into or correlates with the quantum hologram that carries the information. And the combination of our attention and intention gives us the required *PIN and chip* to access the information required!

But how does the brain/mind-field navigate this cosmic quantum hologram? During the writing of this book I was given, through dowsing, a simple analogy for how this process might work. Translating the language of energy into the written word is always tricky, as it is filtered through subjective experience, but, with that caveat, this is how it was explained:

> *It is the consciousness of the mind-field that is actually the physical body's aerial. When we attune ourselves and direct our focus with intent, we manifest consciousness as a beam of coherent light. This beam or aerial is extended and acts as an attractor for the information required. This is an instantaneous process, created without energy or force. The more coherent you are as a human organism, the more coherent the beam and the more coherent the information. It is the coherence that establishes the communication line. At the most coherent levels you are able to access the highest or most coherent levels of consciousness.*

So how does this sit with reality? Quantum physicist Dr Jude Currivan explained to me:

> *Think of the difference between a light bulb, where the light radiates in all directions and on many different frequencies, and a laser, which is a beam of coherent light. And that's the difference: if you're radiating out in all directions then your energy field can only extend as a light bulb would, say, to light a room. When we deliberately attune ourselves to a particular set of vibrations, we have to be coherent with those vibra-*

tions – and the best description of that would be as a beam. The more coherently we align ourselves with those higher vibrations, the more we are able to connect to the A-field.

And the physiology? Dr Laszlo points to recent scientific research that indicates the key is to be found in the microtubule structures in the cytoskeleton of cells – the cytoskeleton being a system of filaments that form a cell's internal framework:

...The cytoskeleton's microscopic networks are the most likely structures to perform the computations that transform quantum level signals into information in the brain... Previously it was thought to have a purely structural role, but recent evidence indicates that it also conveys signals and processes information.

Dowsing suggests that this is not limited to the cells in the brain but is a *whole-body* process. And this correlates with Dr Bruce Lipton's assertion that receptor antennae in the membrane of cells throughout the whole body can read vibrational energy fields such as light, sound and radio frequencies.

Perhaps this is why we feel something with *every fibre* of our being?

The fact that we all possess the same communication equipment removes any excuse for not being able to dowse! We just need to familiarize ourselves with what we've got, take a little instruction in how to use it, apply a lot of practice and *believe* that we can do it. And, as we have seen, the more balanced or coherent our *total* body is, physically, emotionally and energetically, the better our dowsing will be.

The information discerned from either electromagnetic or quantum fields is conducted via the body's signalling system, which manifests in the physical body via the neuromuscular system and then prompts the minute unconscious physical responses that ultimately culminate in the movement of the dowsing tool; or, when device-less dowsing, as a part- or whole-body response.

This is not the full story, but it gives us a good start. To attempt a definitive theory of how and why dowsing works would be premature, bearing in mind the accelerating advancement of scientific discovery. But I am utterly confident in suggesting that dowsing is indeed a tangible manifestation of the human body's response to both electromagnetic and quantum fields. Or, in the elegant words of Dr Jude Currivan at the beginning of Chapter 1, 'Dowsing is a conscious attunement to the field of consciousness that non-locally connects each and every one of us with the cosmos as a whole.'

A gift that is given to us all.

CHAPTER ELEVEN

THE EVIDENCE SO FAR

All that happens in one place happens also in other places;
all that happened at one time happens also at all times
after that. Nothing is 'local', limited to where and when it
is happening. All things are global, indeed cosmic, for the
memory of all things extends to all places and all times. This
is the concept of the informed universe, the view of the world
that will hallmark science and society in the coming decades.

Ervin Laszlo, *Science and the Akashic Field*

I shall not commit the fashionable stupidity of regarding
everything I cannot explain as a fraud.

Carl Jung

Dr Harry Oldfield is a rare specimen.

Biologist, energy-field researcher and inventor, he qualified as a homoeopathic physician in 1982 and received an Honorary Doctorate (Citation of Honour) from the World Peace Centre in Pune, India, in 2000. He is a Professor Honoris Causa in the Department of Alternative Medicine, Zoroastrian College, Mumbai, India, a Visiting Professor of Energy Medicine, Holos

University Graduate Seminary, Missouri, and a Fellow of the Royal Microscopical Society, Oxford. He is also the recipient of the Alyce and Elmer Green Award for Innovation, the pre-eminent prize in new-paradigm science, which recognizes excellence, innovation and career achievement in subtle energies and energy medicine.

His journey began around the age of three when his grandmother observed him trying to capture, between his finger and thumb, the sunbeams spilling through the gaps in the dark curtains of her windows. It culminated with the inventions of Polycontrast Interference Photography (PIP), the Electro-Scanning Method (ESM) and Electro-Crystal Therapy (EleCT). In between times, he managed to fit in a good grounding as a secondary school teacher. Known as the 'mad prof', he was apparently the school's most popular science master – although he has a hunch that this had more to do with his blowing up the science lab than his actual teaching.

Originally a staunch Newtonian, he remains respectful of the protocols of science. However, like all good scientists, he has retained an open mind, a sense of awe and wonderment at the extraordinariness of life, and an irrepressible humour. He received the Green Award for 'allowing us to experience our multidimensional existence through his extraordinary images'.

Which is why he became involved in this story of dowsing.

Mind Mirror

In 1982 at a meeting of the American Society of Dowsers Dr Edith Jurka, a New York psychiatrist, measured the brain patterns of seven 'gifted' dowsers. She used a piece of equipment called the Mind Mirror, which is effectively two electroencephalographs (EEGs) boxed together in one instrument, one each for the left and right hemispheres of the brain. It was originally developed in 1976 by Dr Maxwell Cade and Geoffrey Blundell in order to measure what was going on in a person's brain, in the left and right hemispheres separately, at any given instant. It gives an instantaneous brain analysis of 14 frequency ranges from 0.75 Hz to 38 Hz, divided into the four basic brainwave frequencies; it also quantifies the amplitude of the signal from 1 to 160 microvolts. Dr Cade wanted to know how active (in terms of microvolts) each side of the brain was at many different frequencies, and how these combinations varied with different states of consciousness.

The four basic brainwave frequencies, or states of consciousness, are:

Beta waves *(13–30 Hz), which are associated with the normal waking states: organizing, computing and making sense of the outside world.*

Alpha waves *(7–13 Hz), which indicate an alert state with a quiet mind. Attention may be inwards or outwards, in focused concentration or inner calm.*

Theta waves *(3–7 Hz), which are produced with daydreaming, deep meditation and dreaming sleep. A theta state is associated with intuitive knowledge and deep creativity.*

Delta waves *(0.1–3 Hz), which are associated with the deepest levels of physical relaxation, sleep too deep for dreams, physical rejuvenation and healing.*

What Dr Cade established was a level of consciousness he called the '5th State'. This was characterized by a moderate amount of theta and beta, wide alpha and no delta, amplitude symmetry and, most importantly, stability. He discovered this state predominantly in practised yogis, people who had meditated for many years and effective psychic healers.

What Dr Jurka discovered was that all seven dowsers exhibited activity in *all four* brainwave states at the same time. They had all the elements of a 5th State, but with extra strong beta and delta, the slowest of all brainwaves, which are usually linked to a deep dreamless sleep state. But delta brainwaves are also said to provide us access to unconscious external material, the delta rhythms allowing us to tap into universal knowledge, or the 'mind beyond our own'. Dr Jurka writes:

> In other words, these gifted dowsers had the equivalent of a 5th State pattern, plus the delta frequencies of a search pattern, in their normal awake states of consciousness... It appears that the essence of the 5th State is familiarity in communication with the Universal Intelligence, and a constant realization of its presence and availability in a very practical way.
>
> Concerning the very high delta amplitudes in all the dowsers, Dr Cade said it correlated with higher levels of consciousness and a reaching out to the unknown. Certainly this is the essence of what a dowser does – reach out for information not available to the five ordinary senses. A confirmation of this interpretation is that the delta frequencies are absent in the 5th State of yogis, whose practice does not include a search.

Dr Harry acquired a Mind Mirror.

Wired to the machine via electrodes attached to my head corresponding to the left and right hemispheres, I underwent a session with him that was recorded both on video and still photography, whilst I was information dowsing at distance regarding the health of a client.

Dr Harry's findings exactly correlated with those of Dr Jurka: I went into the 5th State condition the moment I extended my consciousness in preparation for dowsing (what I affectionately refer to as 'logging on') and remained in the 5th State throughout the session, with almost total balance between left and right brain activity. There was also a constant and high level of activity in the delta frequencies.

A couple of very interesting anomalies were also observed. Dowsing on the causative factors behind my client's recent downturn in health, I determined there was only one – a critical factor that I would term an *absolute truth*. Whilst my dowsing rods were spinning at high speed in affirmation of the question, the readings on the Mind Mirror completely changed pattern and *went off the scale*, indicating an extremely strong increase in power – or amplitude output – from both sides of my brain.

The highest level of the beta range, 38 Hz, remained off the scale throughout the session. This frequency is the beginning of the gamma range, which unfortunately is not represented on the Mind Mirror. Gamma frequencies are associated with an enhanced overall perception of reality, increased compassion and the ability to be aware of one's consciousness. High levels are often found in advanced meditators, and the amplitude increases with the ability to go into deeper meditative states. Dowsing itself suggests that during Dr Harry's experiment my brainwave activity was peaking in the 70 Hz range.

The Cover Image

In one experiment whilst connected to the Mind Mirror, I focused on the image you see depicted on the cover of this book. At that instant, every frequency (apart from the 38 Hz beta, which remained off the scale) shut down, indicating a tranquil and serene state. The image had a totally calming effect on my brainwave activity. But what was it about this image that resulted in this effect?

Phil Argyle from Wholebeing had designed this image in response to my request. The only information I had given him was that I was writing a book about dowsing and I had included an abridged version of the introduction to provide some background. It was six months later that an email arrived with an attached image. Phil thanked me for my patience and the space I had given him to allow the image to 'emerge' and finished by saying, 'It embodies a powerful clarity that I feel relates to your intention when dowsing.'

I opened the attachment and, for a minute, I think my heart stopped beating. There in front of me on the screen was the *exact image I see every morning when I focus, extend consciousness and 'log on' for the day*. It is difficult to say exactly what energy the image embodies, but Phil's description of how he works will give you some idea:

> *There is an urge, a feeling of opening connections and communication with a sense of purposeful intent and integrity. The images are symbolic, representing the feel of the essential being of each soul, drawn down from that higher frequency. Sacred geometry, symmetry and light are the main components, and each of these elements allows the truth of the image to be displayed to its most potent and pure form.*
>
> *These images offer an open and direct channel for communication between dimensions.*

In placing this image on this book, I have made it my gift to you, to be used as a powerful shorthand alternative to the visualization process described in Chapter 6. Focusing on it before you dowse will help you centre your being, reach a place of stillness and facilitate the extending of your consciousness.

Polycontrast Interference Photography (PIP)

Our work with the Mind Mirror merely served to indicate that *something* was happening in the brain – the mechanism that processes the information. The most exciting findings arose, however, when I was filmed using the PIP technology whilst dowsing. The development of PIP was inspired by Dr Harry Oldfield's studies of Kirlian photography, a high-voltage, high-frequency system that can take electrical pictures of any object and the field around it. But instead of using electrons and electric fields, the PIP system uses light – photons – to show the same field effect. PIP technology is a real-time photo-imaging system that can distinguish between many different grades and qualities of light and shows variations in energy fields in three dimensions. These are the effects of photons passing in and out of energetic fields. The end result is an image on the computer screen of pulsating bands of colour and light.

PIP is used in health consultations. It is possible to see the graphical representation of energy vortices similar to the chakras described in Ayurvedic medicine and the meridian energy pathways central to traditional Chinese medicine. Even more riveting, in amputees it shows the presence of energy fields corresponding to the missing or 'phantom' limb. Something gave me an inkling that it might show some interesting results whilst a person was in the process of dowsing. In fact, in the words of Dr Harry, what we saw was 'quite spectacular'.

The film footage shows a sequence of energetic changes that took place whilst I was remote dowsing, accessing information about the health of a second client. The control footage, before any dowsing began, shows the bands of vivid colours – typically seen on a PIP scan – around my body and in the surrounding environment. Upon commencing dowsing, however, there is a progressive build-up of energy around my body, the original vivid colours gradually changing to paler and lighter hues – pale blue, pale yellow, then white. This eventually culminated in a vast area of pulsating brilliant white light, totally surrounding the full length of the left-hand side of my body, and extending halfway across the room. This luminosity was sustained whilst I was 'logged on' to the client, accessing key information. Concurrent with the build-up of the white light was an increase in chakra activity, most markedly of the heart chakra. At the peak of the white luminosity, the heart chakra remained fully expanded, pulsing in vibrant rapid waves of red, blue and indigo. At times this pulsing was so rapid that the appearance was virtually shimmering colour the length of my spinal column.

The white light was so remarkable that I asked Dr Harry if he had ever witnessed anything like it before. He confirmed that it had happened on one other occasion only, when he had been in the proximity of a giant quartz crystal (seven feet tall and four feet wide!), whilst undertaking experiments at the Monroe Institute in America.

Almost as striking was what happened when I 'logged off' from the client. The white light didn't fade, or shrink, or change appearance, but dramatically disappeared in a nanosecond, as if someone had thrown a switch. At the same instant, the pulsing of my heart chakra activity disappeared. This *switching off* fascinated Dr Harry perhaps more than anything. He remarked that it was as if I had gone to a lending library, taken out a book, retrieved the information I needed and promptly returned the book.

Dowsing later confirmed that I had indeed been accessing the client's personal Akashic Field. The permission to do this had been implicit in her request for my help.

Other observations were made: enormous energetic changes on the ground around my feet, where two foot-wide bands of scarlet and vivid pink pulsed across the floor; marked chakra activity in the crown area; and unusual white light configurations pulsing and fluxing over my right shoulder. Dr Harry's very positive report and endorsement of our pilot study can be found in Appendix I.

As fascinating as these images were, this was only the first step. We need to make many more on the journey to capture the mechanics of the dowsing process in image format. Fortunately, in the process of writing this book, an invitation was extended for me to be tested using highly advanced technology in a country where dowsing is taken *extremely* seriously.

Read on…

PART IV
DOWSING FOR HEALTH AND WELL-BEING

Chapter Twelve

HEALTH

There seems to be very little appreciation in mainstream medicine that actually many diseases are caused because the body has lost its ability to self-heal. What we need to be able to do is restore that balance in our bodies.

Robert Verkerk, PhD, Executive and Scientific Director, Alliance for Natural Health, *The Human Time Bomb*

It's supposed to be a secret but I'll tell you anyway. We doctors do nothing. We only help and encourage the doctor within.

Dr Albert Schweitzer, musician, philosopher, physician

The primary aim of this book is to present dowsing as a practical tool to enhance and enrich everyday life. The fundamentals of dowsing for personal use can be learned in a relatively short time. This part lays the foundation for the vast scope of personal dowsing, which you can develop to meet your own everyday needs. We'll start by looking at health.

What does the word 'health' mean to you? Do you awake every morning with the sheer joy of being alive, inspired to embrace the challenges of the day with vitality and enthusiasm? And in your inner core do you feel totally balanced, in harmony and coherence physically, mentally, emotionally and spiritually?

Or are you permanently exhausted, crawling your way through life with each day presenting a series of insurmountable hurdles? Do you suffer from disrupted or restless sleep? Perhaps you sleep through the night but always wake with a feeling of tiredness, lethargy and a fuzzy head, so simply getting through the day is akin to climbing the highest mountain peak. Do you suffer from constant headaches, frequent colds, aching joints, soreness and bloating, or viral, fungal and bacterial infections? Are you weary from an excess of allergic responses? Or do you put up with an all too regular recurrence of minor ailments? All these symptoms are indicative of an underlying metabolic imbalance in the body which, if left unchecked, invariably leads to more serious illness.

Alarmingly, we all too frequently resign ourselves to accepting these symptoms as normal and something to put up with when, conversely, *the natural state of the body is to be healthy and in balance.*

So what is 'healthy'? The dictionary definition, 'freedom from illness or pain', seems pessimistic – surely there is more to health than the absence of pathology? Our experience of family, friends and even famous personalities in the public eye certainly suggests there is. How many times have you heard of someone suddenly suffering a heart attack or unexpectedly being diagnosed with cancer, only for those who know them to say, 'It's so shocking, he was in perfect health…'

In *perfect* health? Is that how it really felt to the heart attack victim? In reality, for weeks, months, even years, he was probably living in a pre-symptomatic disease state and almost certainly being prompted by a still small inner voice that gently at first and then more loudly persisted: 'Take more of this, do more of that, drink less of that, drink more of this, take more exercise, get more sleep, let go of that anger, release that grievance, laugh more, get into nature, work fewer hours…' And he ignored and overruled the voice because there was always something more important to do. But how *important* can it have been for it to have taken priority over his health and eventually rob him of his life?

I was profoundly blessed to be taught the meaning and value of health by an extraordinary and gifted man whose insights transformed the lives of all those who consulted him. A naturopath and osteopath by training, he was, however, much more. I consulted him one day, body and spirit broken and battered by life. Six months later, skin glowing and hair shining, I had a newly gained zest for life and more energy than I knew what to do with! He was my physician from that day forward for nearly 20 years. During that time, he gifted me rare insights into what health really meant and inspired me to commit my life to sharing this knowledge with others.

His key to unlocking the vitality and dynamic equilibrium that embody true health was simply activating, supporting and reinforcing the innate healing ability of those he treated. In the words of Dr Albert Schweitzer, he encouraged 'the doctor within'.

The real crux of attaining and maintaining optimal health is understanding that the body in its primary state is an intelligent and self-organizing *field* – *not* physical matter. And this *mind-field* has an innate wisdom and unlimited healing capabilities.

It is how we treat ourselves – how we 'program' this field – that results in our well-being or in the manifestation of physical symptoms of ill-health. It is a choice we have, day by day, minute by minute. And all chronic metabolic imbalances and diseases result from the way we treat, or maltreat, our bodies – physically, mentally, emotionally and spiritually. A profound shift happens in our health and well-being once we realize that it is our responsibility to support this inner intelligence rather than interfere with or override such powerful innate wisdom. We ignore this doctor within at our peril.

But surely there are plenty of doctors *without*, in surgeries and hospitals, ready to take care of our health?

Think again.

The primary function of any health service is not to advise on good health but to respond to and treat the symptoms of sickness and disease *once they have already occurred*. The mission is not the prevention of disease and promotion of health, but addressing and alleviating symptoms – even though those symptoms might be critical indicators of an underlying metabolic imbalance that in itself needs addressing. Simply treating symptoms is a superficial way of looking at true healing, often resulting in a short-term fix rather than the long-term change required for a fundamental improvement in energy and well-being.

It is also why many of the most effective treatments are those that restore the coherence or balance of the body at *ground-state* level, addressing energetic patterns with *vibrational medicine*. Practices such as acupuncture, homoeopathy, bioenergetics, qi gong, shiatsu, cranio-sacral therapy and countless more work to this vitally important principle.

What is abundantly clear is that to enjoy optimal health, with all its life-enhancing benefits, you have to become an active participant in the process. It is not something that can be delegated to a third party. The simple, stark, sobering truth is that there is only one person ultimately responsible for your health.

You.

Sometimes, however, this responsibility can be overwhelming. And confusing. Trying to discern the still small doctor voice within can be almost impossible when shouting at the top of its voice is the constant stream of information and disinformation from the media and those who control it; from pharmaceutical companies with vested commercial interests; from governments whose impartiality is clouded by the benefits of vast levels of corporate taxation on those very pharmaceuticals, on tobacco, on mobile phones and a vast array of other industries; not to mention from some unenlightened and uninformed health professionals. Every week we are bombarded with conflicting new studies about miracle drugs, cure-all foods, must-have supplements. We are inundated with statistical analyses, scientific research, dietary warnings, experts' claims, health myths perpetuated, health truths exploded, and warnings, warnings, warnings. Three months later, new studies by new groups contradict those very claims, offering up new wonder drugs, new cure-alls. So we ricochet from regime to regime in the pursuit of good health.

And are these conflicting reports totally impartial and not sponsored in any way by the very industry or product being developed in the first place? My work only confirms that one cannot trust everything one reads. It is no wonder the general public is confused, frustrated and disillusioned by the advice of officialdom and finds it virtually impossible to discern the truth behind the hidden agendas of those who are so apparently concerned about our health.

Not anymore!

The real truth about your health is found in the wisdom that lies within. And now you have a way to access that truth and all the information you require. You have a tool to identify exactly what is potentially health-promoting for your own unique body, with all its individual needs shaped by lifestyle, hereditary make-up, conditioning and environment. This is not to suggest that you use dowsing as a tool to *diagnose* illness. But you do have a tool to assist you in optimizing your health, your well-being and your available energy.

By contrast, health recommendations are broad guidelines put together to apply to large groups of people, not individuals. So instead of delegating responsibility for your health to faceless committees generating conflicting and biased reports to the public at large, you now have the opportunity to access key knowledge about your own body and its unique needs. Ultimately, this will put you back into the driving seat and enable you to take control of – and responsibility for – your health.

To begin your new journey, let's look at six factors that underpin optimal health and how dowsing can be of real benefit.

Hydration

In early 2008 a provocative headline dominated the pages of the *Daily Mail*: 'Not a Drop of Evidence Eight Glasses of Water is Good for You.' This surprising piece of news seemingly contradicted previous beliefs that our bodies need regular and adequate water for optimal health and well-being.

The article was based on findings of a research project conducted by two doctors from the University of Pennsylvania in Philadelphia and published in April 2008 in the *Journal of the American Society of Nephrology*. The *Daily Mail* wrote:

> *The belief that we need eight glasses of water a day to stay healthy is a myth researchers say and concluded ... no studies showed any benefit to organs from increased water intake.*

Two other apparently informed statements appeared in the same article, this time from the British Dietetic Association:

> *Tea and the sort of coffee you get in Britain are fine for rehydrating – the diuretic effects of caffeine are massively outweighed by the fluids in those drinks. There are millions of people who get most of their fluids from tea without any ill effects.*
>
> *Most people can rely on their thirst to tell them when they need to drink.*

The article finished with a flourish:

> *The scientists concluded there was no clear evidence that drinking more water was healthy.*

If there is one thing I have learned in over 30 years of studying health, it is the fact that every time you hear the phrase 'there is no evidence' it means totally the opposite.

Without any shadow of a doubt, there *is* evidence.

Dr Fereydoon Batmanghelidj, affectionately known as Dr Batman or Dr B., was a world-renowned authority on the health benefits of water. His vast experience came about as a result of living through extreme circumstances. Born in Iran, he studied under Sir Alexander Fleming at London University, gaining his medical qualifications from St Mary's Hospital, London. He practised medicine in Tehran until 1979, when he was imprisoned, along with many other innocent Iranians, by revolutionary mullahs in the wake of the Shah's overthrow, and sentenced to death.

The prison conditions were horrific: often cells built for six to eight were crammed with up to 90 prisoners and sickness was rife. But Dr B. had no medical supplies. The only medication he was allowed to administer was water. So, for two-and-a-half years, on a daily basis, he had the opportunity of observing the extraordinary results of simply rehydrating his fellow inmates. He states, 'I knew I had witnessed a healing power of water I had not been taught in medical school. I found water could treat and cure more diseases than any other medication I knew about.'

During his time in Tehran's Evin Prison, he cured more than 3,000 ulcer cases with only water. He also saved his own life by presenting a research paper on water to the presiding judge, who rescinded the death penalty and decreed a shorter sentence so he could expand his study on the subject. He was released in 1982 and began a lifetime of research into hydration and health. His extraordinary story can be read in his book *Your Body's Many Cries for Water* and is essential reading for those who wish to truly understand the unquestionable necessity of a properly hydrated body and the certain role that dehydration plays in just about every major illness.

His observation 'There is no system or function of the body not pegged to the flow of water' gives us pause for thought. His assertions 'Dry mouth is one of the very last indicators of dehydration of the body' and 'Dry mouth is not a sign to rely on' directly contradict the statement from the British Dietetic Association that says, 'Most people can rely on their thirst to tell them when they need to drink.' Our thirst mechanism deteriorates with age, and even at a young age we often misread our promptings for water as a need for food.

Further, tea and coffee are not adequate substitutes for plain water. Dr John Ogden, DNM, affirms, 'It's very simple: the purer the water, the better for you it is.'

But how much water?

Dr B.'s rough rule of thumb was half one's body weight in ounces of water every day. For example, a child weighing 60 pounds would need 30 ounces of water (approximately four eight-ounce glasses) per day. But this guideline does not take into account your state of health, age, lifestyle and level of exercise and the climate temperature and conditions. So your water needs vary on a regular basis. It is also important to spread out your water drinking over your waking hours: guidelines say not to drink more than half a litre, or approximately one pint or two average glasses, per hour. Because, of course, it is possible to drink too much water...

And what sort of water?

Water drinking 21st-century style has become something of a minefield. Anyone wishing to avoid the ever-growing list of chemicals, pharmaceuticals, agrochemicals and mass medication (in the form of fluorides) in tap water now risks becoming a social pariah by expressing a preference for bottled water. Your designer bottle is no longer an accessory to be flaunted. Nor is it acceptable for the human race to contribute to the pollution of the land and oceans with plastic bottles: in 2007, the last year for which global statistics are available, more than *200 billion litres* of bottled water were sold around the world. Add to that the fact that a bottle that holds one litre of water requires *five litres of water to manufacture it.*

Supporters of tap water also point out that bottling water is no guarantee of its purity. About 40 per cent of bottled water is regular tap water that may or may not have received additional treatment. And take note of the potential ingredients not on the label which can be leached from the plastic in raised temperature conditions: bisphenol-A (BPA) (a hormone-disrupting chemical), pthalates (known to cause birth defects) and antimony (a toxic metal used in the plastic manufacturing process).

So, on balance, is tap water any healthier or more palatable? The average glass has the probability of containing one or more of the following, which are either added or not removed during municipal filtration: chlorine and disinfection by-products or DPBs (including trihalomethanes, which are known to cause cancer in animals); fluorides (including sodium fluoride and hexafluorosilicic acid, which are known to be highly toxic and carcinogenic); a coagulant, polyacrylamide (acrylamide is known to cause cancer in animals); aluminium (again used as a coagulant in water treatment and known to be neurotoxic and a suspected carcinogen); a variety of pharmaceutical products including painkillers, synthetic hormones, beta-blockers, cancer drugs, anti-cholesterol drugs, anti-depressants, anti-inflammatories, antibiotics and birth control drugs; artificial sweeteners; and a variety of pesticides and herbicides.

Confused? But perhaps the home filtration of water helps?

Filter jugs with a charcoal filter are a good start, but bear in mind that it is unlikely they will remove fluoride, pharmaceutical products and agrochemicals. Changing the filters regularly to avoid the build-up of bacteria and toxins that can then recontaminate the water is also critical.

A reverse osmosis system will remove more contaminants, but can be a wasteful system taking two gallons to make just one.

My own personal preference is a water purifying system from the company CIR, based near Plymouth and using *imploded water* technology based on the work of water engineer Viktor Schauberger. This system alters the composition of the water at molecular level, thereby rendering contaminants and toxins innocuous. There is no waste, even the most chlorinated water is left with a delicious creamy-like taste, replacement filters are not required and the added bonus is drinking water that has been re-energized.

But, ultimately, do not make the mistake of thinking you can tell if your water is safe by the way it looks, tastes or smells, or by what it says on the label. So how *can* you guarantee the safety and purity of your water?

Pick up your dowsing rods...

Suggestions for Questions

'For optimal health and well-being, what are my body's current daily needs for pure drinking water – more than half a litre? More than a litre...?' Check the amount on a regular basis or when any life circumstances change.

'Are there any significant levels of toxins in this water that might be detrimental to my best health and well-being? More than 10 per cent? More than 20 per cent...?' Check both tap and bottled water.

'How often would it be in my best interests to change the filter on this water jug, considering my average daily usage of water?'

'Have any harmful toxins from this plastic bottle leached into the water contained within?'

'Would my current health condition benefit from an additional intake of water?'

Sleep

Shortly after the water controversy appeared in the national press, a similar debate surfaced concerning the amount of sleep necessary for optimal physical and mental functioning. Rather than the age-old guideline of eight hours a night, it now seems that (in some quarters) this has been disproved. Professor Jim Horn from the Sleep Research Centre at Loughborough University said the 'fact' that we need eight hours was a myth and that it was perfectly possible for some adults to 'survive' on five, six or seven hours a night. Not only that, but too much sleep is now thought to be a contributory factor in diabetes, obesity, heart disease and back pain.

Although the role of too much sleep is still being investigated, there is well-proven evidence of the devastating effect of too little sleep. Like water, sleep is necessary for survival. For life.

Sleep deprivation is devastating to the human condition on many levels and is known as an effective form of disorientation in the process of torture. Sleep is necessary for maintaining a strong immune function, for our bodies to do their nocturnal housekeeping of cleansing and detoxing waste products, and for vital repair, rejuvenation and growth.

As with water, the amount of sleep needed is variable and determined by the individual needs of the person, which will take into account age, health and well-being, level of activity and demands of everyday life. Some researchers have stated that your body will not let you sleep more than you need to; others say that sleeping less may actually be healthier, especially if you have a tendency to oversleep. The best shot from yet others is to go for some arbitrary point in the middle!

It is not just about the amount of sleep – it is also the frequency and quality of sleep, and *when* that sleep is taken. Key metabolic processes take place between the hours of 10 p.m. and midnight, and critical hormones are released at this time that regulate many biological functions. So the maxim 'An hour before midnight is worth two after' appears to have more than a grain of truth. The secretion of the sleep-inducing hormone melatonin starts between 9:30 and 10:30 p.m., so it is important to go to bed as close to this time as possible. Melatonin secretion is also light sensitive, so sleeping in a dark room will maximize your availability.

But what happens when you can't sleep? Or when your sleep pattern is sporadic and disrupted? Or when you sleep, but still wake exhausted and fuzzy headed?

Over the years I have helped many clients successfully restore deep and healing sleep patterns. The disrupting factors are many and varied, but the main offenders include: an excess intake of caffeine, sugar or alcohol; electromagnetic pollution, including mobile phone, broadcasting and communication masts, alarm clock radios and geopathic stress; programming of the mind with violent or disruptive television before bed, thus putting the body into fight or flight mode and prompting the release of adrenaline; a build-up of toxins within the body, including heavy metals; nutritional deficiencies, specifically the mineral selenium and the vitamin B group; external noise levels; and significant mental and emotional stress.

We are all familiar with the sleepless nights when we toss and turn before a big day – whether taking a driving test, having an important interview or even getting married! But do not underestimate the power of more long-term, deeply held worries and subconscious anxieties in disrupting your sleep pattern.

If you, or anyone you know or love is struggling to get a good night's rest, dowsing can help you identify the factors disrupting healthy sleep patterns – often factors you or they may not consciously be aware of. So why not give it a try?

Suggestions for Questions

'Taking everything into consideration, how many hours of sleep per night do I require for my best health and well-being?'

'What is the optimal time for me to go to bed?'

'What is the optimal time for me to go to sleep?'

'How many factors are there in my disrupted sleep pattern? More than one? More than two...?'

'Is diet a factor? Is alcohol a factor? Is emotional or mental stress a factor? Is my partner's snoring a factor? Would I benefit from moving to another bedroom? On a scale of one to ten, how much would I benefit? More than one? More than two...?'

'Would the quality of my sleep benefit from opening a window/warmer bedclothes/a more supportive bed/a change of diet/increased hydration/a nutritional supplement?'

'Is my sleep pattern in any way disrupted by my current medical treatment or pharmaceutical drugs?'

'Is there an underlying factor for which I would benefit from seeking professional health advice?'

Exercise

Most of us are (often guiltily!) aware of the need for adequate and regular exercise in the quest for optimal health. Including exercise in your weekly routine is one of the most important and fundamental health improvements you can make. Exercise is known to strengthen immune function, improve the delivery of oxygen throughout the body, regulate key hormonal activity, improve the efficiency of the lymphatic system and prevent the build-up of toxins in the body, stimulate the release of endorphins (the body's natural 'feel good' chemicals), burn fat and build muscles, lower blood pressure, increase energy levels, help maintain flexibility, balance and strength – the long list of benefits is certainly not in dispute.

The simple fact is that exercise is a necessary non-negotiable factor in achieving optimal health and well-being. However, if you are already a fitness fan, there are also risks associated with too much exercise. It is possible to overdo it to the point where it becomes a destructive stressor on the body.

So how can dowsing help? By assisting you in establishing an exercise programme to match your body's individual and unique needs for your gender, age, body type and state of health, and by determining what types of exercise and what balance and combination of different exercises would most support and improve your health from aerobic exercise, core muscle exercise and strength training. As your body develops tolerance and resistance to certain exercises in your regimen, dowsing can also help modify, develop and fine-tune your routine. It may be that you are blessed with the services of a personal trainer to do this and benefiting from their expertise. But most of us are trying to do this alone.

In cases of injury, deteriorating health or recovery from disease, dowsing can really assist by identifying exactly what is and what is not in your best interests. For me, it was invaluable in establishing a strategy for my recovery from a back injury. I worked closely with a talented (and open-minded) Pilates instructor, Clare Lennard, to tailor-make an exercise routine for the steady restoration of the health of my back to optimal levels within the safest time frame. Her expertise and my dowsing proved to be a winning combination. She says:

> *Elizabeth came to see me to practise Pilates. Her back was in a very fragile state and I was in a quandary: on the one hand she desperately needed Pilates in order to strengthen certain key muscle groups whose weakness was partly the cause of her bad back, but on the other hand the wrong sort of exercise would have made the condition worse and been extremely painful. Working together, with my knowledge of Pilates and Elizabeth's dowsing, we were able to identify exactly the right programme of exercises for her to follow for her ultimate recovery.*

If you are thinking your exercise regime could use a bit of a boost, or even a total overhaul, why not consider dowsing on some of the following to fine-tune your approach?

Suggestions for Questions

> *'To meet my current needs, how many times per week would I benefit from engaging in aerobic exercise? More than once a week? More than twice...?'*

> *'What would be the optimal length of time for each session – more than 20 minutes? More than 30...?'*

> *'How many times per week would I benefit from core muscle exercise?'*

> *'Taking everything into consideration, what would be*

the optimal aerobic exercise to meet my body's needs – walking? Running? Swimming? Cycling...?'

'Taking into account my current health condition, would it be in my best interests to exercise today? This week...?'

'Taking everything into consideration, would it be in my best interests to avoid all forms of exercise at this current time?'

Diet and Nutrition

If you thought the water debate complex, you ain't seen nothing yet!

Diet and nutrition have become a 21st-century battleground – due in no small part to irresponsible reporting by the press, the vested interests of the processed food and pharmaceutical industries, and governments with minimal nutritional expertise. For many people, daily newspapers or the superficial soundbites of television news are their sole sources of information on this subject. When serious research projects with a basis in sound science are reported in a provocative and manipulative manner rather than in a constructive and informed way, it is no wonder that the public becomes confused – and eventually cynical.

The barrage of information, virtually *every day,* telling us what is good or bad for us has resulted in a public suffering from information fatigue to the point where people now believe officialdom is crying wolf and then are left to wonder what is left to eat that is at best not harmful and at worst not going to send them to an early grave. In fact on the day that I wrote this very page, an article appeared in the press highlighting a new eating disorder: *orthorexia nervosa.* Apparently this serious psychological condition is characterized by an obsession with healthy eating!

It would have been funny had it not been juxtaposed by another food article with the provocative headline 'Don't Give Children Ham Sandwiches, Say Cancer Experts'. The outcry from parents was predictable and loud, but the very sad fact is that although the odd ham sandwich is not going to give *anyone* cancer, this article *is* based on sound research. For more than 30 years the food industry has been aware of the presence of carcinogenic nitrosamines in processed meat and fish, resulting from the addition of nitrites for preservative and cosmetic purposes. But still they continue to use nitrites. Nitrosamines have been shown to produce tumours in 'a wide range of organs in a wide range of test animals'. And it is the cumulative presence of these carcinogens in our bodies over many years, from childhood onwards, that the researchers were attempting to highlight.

This style of attention-grabbing headline solely aimed at increasing newspaper sales trivializes serious research and fails the parents who are genuinely striving to improve the health of their children. But the fact remains that good nutrition is one of the *primary means of disease prevention*, so let us look at some constructive truths...

Nutrients from food are the vital components that form the building blocks of our bodies. *You are what you eat.* And although the composition and role of food is a highly complex subject requiring many years of study, we can help ourselves by:

1. Beginning to learn about our body's individual requirements.
2. Determining the quality and freshness of our food.
3. Identifying harmful and potentially carcinogenic toxins concealed within it.
4. Optimizing our nutritional supplementation.

Dowsing can help with all four.

If you want to experience the benefits that optimal diet and nutrition can bring – a strong immune system, increased energy and a reduced risk of chronic disease – pick up your dowsing rods.

The first step is to find and eat unprocessed, fresh and organic produce. It actually doesn't have to be *certified* organic – you will find plenty of small local producers at farmers' markets who cannot afford the expense of official organic certification but who will tell you if they avoid the use of chemical fertilizers and pesticides. The surreptitious use of your arm as a pendulum will soon confirm if this is so! Conversely, there have been occasions when I have dowsed on food labelled as organic in supermarkets and found it to contain sufficient levels of agrochemical toxins to be detrimental to health.

The second step is to maintain optimal levels of food groups and nutrients in order to meets your body's specific needs – dictated by age, lifestyle and any pre-existing health condition.

We can use dowsing to determine if we are eating too little or too much protein to meet our needs, or whether we have the correct balance of proteins from meat, fish and vegetables. We can determine the levels of healthy (mono-saturated) fats we need and whether our intake of carbohydrates is, or is not, in our best interests. We can discover if our diets include sufficient fibre for optimal functioning and whether our intake of essential fatty acids (omega 3, 6 and 9) is in the correct ratio. We can ask if we are eating sufficient portions of fruit and vegetables (current guidelines suggest seven portions a day). And we can ask even more specific questions:

'On an average basis, am I eating too many processed or refined foods for my best health and well-being?'

'Would I benefit from more wholegrains?'

'Does my diet contain sufficient raw foods for my best wellness?'

'Would it be in my best interests to eliminate processed meats from my diet?'

The sky is the limit!

If this has piqued your interest, purchase a book on nutrition like *The New Optimum Nutrition Bible* by Patrick Holford or *Fats That Heal, Fats That Kill* by Udo Erasmus. Learning more about the components will enable you to fine-tune your questioning and ferret out your best foods.

Minerals, Vitamins and Supplements

In an ideal world, we would obtain all our nutrients from the food that we eat. But sadly we don't live in an ideal world… Our food is grown in overworked soil, depleted of its mineral content. Fruit is harvested before it is ready, shipped thousands of miles and artificially ripened with ethylene gas. And being picked early compromises the level of nutrients – the estimated 10,000 different nutrients found in plant foods do not fully form until the sun-ripening process begins.

Fruits and vegetables are also contaminated with levels of pesticides, herbicides and chemical fertilizers that are often toxic and carcinogenic to our bodies. Regulatory bodies insist that the levels of individual chemicals are 'safe' – but where are the tests that prove that the various agrochemicals are *safe in combination*? Produce picked prematurely sits around in a warehouse (often for months and in some cases years) or supermarket shelf, further depleting vitamin content and life force. An orange picked freshly from an organically grown tree can contain up to 200 milligrams of vitamin C. By the time it reaches your fruit bowl, this can be as low as zero. Add to this the fact that many of the plant foods that we eat are deficient in vital enzymes and life force because they have been processed, irradiated or microwaved.

All these factors contribute to the alarming reality that over the past 50 years the levels of key minerals within fruits and vegetables in the UK have *declined by up to 70 per cent.*

Dr Robert Verkerk, BSc, MSc, DIC, PhD, is an internationally acclaimed scientist in the field of sustainability as it relates to the environment, agriculture and health. For many years this remarkable man has worked tirelessly to protect our free choice in the field of natural health – in the face of increasing regulation from government bodies. Dr Verkerk believes that as a consequence of the way we grow, harvest, transport, store and process our food, the majority of the population of the UK is suffering the worst nutritional deprivation in its history. He also believes that most people are unaware that restoring or optimizing their health is within their control. Nutritional supplements are not a luxury or unnecessary fad, they are a way of providing the vital key minerals and vitamins missing from our fruit and vegetables.

But what sorts of nutrients, and in what quantity? Dr Verkerk is emphatic that the whole issue of what dosage and nutrient form is best is currently one of the hottest topics in nutritional science. Health authorities around the world want us to accept one level of each nutrient that is safe for the vast majority of the population: in the UK, we have the Recommended Daily Allowances (RDAs). But did you know the RDAs were invented by government bodies during World War II to ensure that soldiers did not succumb to deficiency diseases such as scurvy (due to a deficiency of vitamin C), rickets (vitamin D) and beriberi (vitamin B1, thiamine)?

The amounts currently recommended, says Dr Verkerk, bear no relationship to the clinical nutritional research that demonstrates the levels of nutrients required for the optimal functioning of the human body. Nor do RDAs have any bearing on the safety of nutrients – something that was recognized in scientific literature decades ago. Since the instigation of RDAs, there have been many studies recommending considerably higher levels which have never been adopted by governments. We have to ask, why not? In fact, Dr Verkerk goes further and states, 'To use RDAs as a means of establishing the best levels to drive particular functions in the body is *simply madness.*'

So, in order to fulfil our nutritional needs for the optimal functioning of the human body, it would be fairly safe to assume that supplementing our diets would seem more than sensible. We just need to establish the 'best' levels.

Don't we?

For anyone relying on their daily newspaper for information, apparently not. Even the most cursory search in the press reveals the following headlines: 'Vitamin Pills Are "Useless"', 'Taking Vitamins "Fails to Lower Risk of Getting Cancer"', 'Vitamins Can Cause Harm and May Even Shorten Your Life', 'B Vitamins "No Help to Heart Patients"', 'Vitamins "May Do More Harm Than Good"' and 'Vitamins Can Increase Risk of Heart Disease'!

Even more confused?

There are several main reasons why studies on nutrition perform poorly in formal studies and trials:

- They are commissioned and driven by the vested interests of those who sponsor, initiate or run the tests and stand to gain the most from particular findings.
- The minerals and vitamins used in the tests are usually synthetic, manufactured chemicals rather than plant or food source nutrients, and often contain only parts of the natural complex. These synthetic forms are inferior, can be toxic and can actually block the very biological process that they are meant to perform in the body.
- The studies are nearly always carried out using synthetic nutrients in *isolation* or in very limited combinations. Nutrients work synergistically and, as in nature, fruits and vegetables contain broad and complex ranges of components that work in combination.
- No tests are carried out prior to the trials to establish whether the participants have adequate absorption or bio-availability rates of the nutrients being tested. Findings often state that a vitamin 'was shown to have no beneficial effect on patients with chronic illnesses'. But one of the key causative factors behind all chronic illness is invariably a low absorption of nutrients. This happens when the passage of nutrients and waste products through the cell membrane is compromised, due to the presence of drugs or toxins or electromagnetic fields disrupting intercellular communication. In this case, piling in high doses of nutrients is not going to be of any benefit! The underlying malabsorption needs to be addressed first.

What *is* clear is that when purchasing nutrients you definitely get what you pay for. Synthetic nutrients are generally used in the cheaper products that are sold by high street chains of drug stores and health shops. As a guideline, Dr Verkerk also suggests that, unless there is a specific vitamin or mineral deficiency to be addressed, the best supplement to take is a good quality *food form* (as opposed to synthetic) multivitamin and mineral product, which has optimal bioavailability to the body – perhaps a liquid supplement or powder that can be mixed with water.

However, please bear in mind that no amount of nutritional supplementation can ever compensate for a poor diet. It is important to understand that supplements should be exactly that – *supplements* to a healthy diet.

Regardless of all of the tests, conflicting recommendations, advice and guidelines, you now have a means to determine exactly what *you* would benefit from in terms of optimal nutrition and a healthy, balanced diet. As long as you formulate clear, informed questions, following the guidelines given in Part II, there are no limits to understanding your own body's needs.

Suggestions for Questions

'Is my present diet/supplementation meeting all of my body's current needs?'

'Am I deficient in any major vitamin?' If yes, work through a list.

'Am I deficient in any major mineral?' If yes, work through a list.

'Would I benefit from increasing my intake of vitamin A? Vitamin C...?'

'Is my body's absorption rate of any major vitamin/ mineral compromised?'

'Taking into account both diet and supplementation,

am I exceeding the dosage of any nutrient to the point where it is harmful to my health?'

'How many days a week would I benefit in taking this supplement? In what dosage? For how long?'

'When would it be in my interests to reassess my nutrient needs?'

'Would my overall health and well-being benefit from a consultation with a professional nutritional consultant?'

Toxic Load

In the last 100 years, the way in which we live has changed beyond all recognition. Instead of inhabiting a healthy world, we are now challenged to *remain* healthy in a *chemical world*. A brief glance at the WWF website reveals disquieting statistics:

- Between 1930 and 2000 global production of man-made chemicals increased from one million to 400 million tonnes each year.
- Seventy-six persistent, bio-accumulative and toxic industrial chemicals were present in the blood of those tested in a European survey.
- There is particular concern about three types of chemicals in use today: very persistent and very bioaccumulative chemicals that break down slowly or not at all and accumulate in the bodies of wildlife and people; endocrine-disrupting chemicals (EDCs), which interfere with the hormone systems of animals and people; and chemicals that cause cancer or reproductive problems or damage DNA.
- Tests carried out by WWF UK showed that all of the 155 people tested had a cocktail of potentially harmful chemicals in their body, including evidence of DDT and PCBs, two dangerous chemicals banned decades ago.

These toxic chemicals find their way into our water supply and our foodstuffs. They can be found in the air we breathe, in our home and workplace, as preservatives, fillers and carriers in pharmaceutical products, in products to clean and maintain our homes, and in the personal care and beauty products we put in and on our bodies.

In the course of my work, I have observed some of the detrimental effects that significant levels of chemical toxins can have on the human metabolism. Apart from disrupting the endocrine system, the presence of toxins can disrupt the integral membrane protein function of the cells, thereby severely compromising the body's absorption rate of nutrients from food and supplementation and laying the foundation for chronic metabolic disease. Furthermore, the bioavailability of some minerals (notably magnesium and selenium) is depleted in the very process of eliminating toxins from the body. In the absence of a toxic load, these minerals would be freed up to carry out vital maintenance, growth and repair functions. Experience with clients has shown that as soon as toxins are eliminated, this is exactly what happens.

I have countless client case histories where the debilitating effects of chemical toxins have been central to the collapse of their health and well-being. Two memorable ones spring to mind:

The client with 'terminal' leukaemia who requested I determine the causative factors behind her condition in April 2004. Her doctor had given her just a few weeks to live. Dowsing identified the main factor as raised levels of agrochemicals in her body, the sources being both airborne and in her water supply. She then revealed that she lived in an area of Australia where crop-spraying planes regularly operated. Formal laboratory testing determined that her body was 'saturated with Roundup', the world's biggest-selling weedkiller. After a supervised detoxification process, the laboratory reported that her blood platelets had normalized for the first time. Six years later, in 2010, she was still very much alive.

The woman suffering for many years with chronic fatigue syndrome (CFS). Although there were several causative factors (typical of this condition), dowsing determined the breakdown of her immune function began at the age of eight. At that time she had spent a year helping her father clear chest-high weeds from the grounds of their home using DDT and weedkillers that are now banned. Dowsing then pinpointed a subsequent factor that compounded the development of CFS. This occurred when she moved into an old cottage which needed fumigation for an infestation of insects. The combined effect of these chemicals with those of the lingering weedkillers led to a severe and systematic breakdown of her health. Today, after years of treatment, she is much improved, but lives a compromised life.

There is no doubt that minimizing your body's toxic exposure and load is a key factor in optimizing your health, well-being and longevity. But how can we reduce our exposure and risks? As total avoidance is a near impossibility, our aim should be to minimize our exposure as far as possible.

Guidelines from health professionals suggest that we:

- Minimize exposure to airborne pollutants, including artificial air-fresheners, dry-cleaning fumes, pesticides, herbicides, paints, glues and varnishes and heavily scented domestic cleaning and washing products.
- Use personal care and beauty products made from natural ingredients, avoiding those with petroleum derivatives and synthetic fragrances, and use organic where possible.
- Use a water filter to reduce levels of chemical contaminants, keep plastics, including cling film, out of direct contact with

food and never use cookware made of aluminium or with non-stick coatings.

- Avoid swimming, bathing or showering in chlorinated water.
- Avoid vaccination if possible and, if it becomes absolutely unavoidable, subsequently consult a natural practitioner specializing in detoxification to clear all potential chemical toxins, neurotoxins and carcinogens from the body.
- Maximize our protection against environmental toxins by maintaining a strong immune system through healthy eating and additional supplementation.

Whenever you are in doubt, have suspicions or are simply not sure whom to believe, pick up your dowsing rods. For me, dowsing is absolutely essential in determining a healthy lifestyle, especially in the choice of personal care, skin care and beauty products. These are the key questions to use:

'With the amount and frequency that I use/am exposed to this product/substance, is it on any level toxic for my body?'

'Is it on any level carcinogenic for my body?'

If you get a *yes* to either of these questions, then it is important to calibrate how much to enable you to make an informed choice on how to proceed. So:

'On a scale of one to ten, how toxic?'

'On a scale of one to ten, how carcinogenic?'

Dowsing has, for example, allowed me to safely continue using chemical hair products. It has enabled me to identify the presence of aluminium in my face powder – not listed in the ingredients but hidden under the ingredient talc (powdered magnesium silicate, which is itself a known carcinogen). It made it possible for me to eliminate all carcinogenic suspects from my bathroom, including products that contain parabens (endocrine-disrupting chemicals; dowsing suggests four or more in combination results in carcinogenic potential), mineral oils, paraffin and petroleum derivatives (disrupting to endocrine function and skin biology), sodium laurel or laureth sulfate (which combined with other chemicals can become nitrosamines), propylene glycol (a skin irritant that is linked to kidney and liver problems) and deodorants that contain harmful aluminium compounds.

Speaking of underarm comfort, there are some key facts to understand about deodorants and antiperspirants: deodorants mask odour by using a mixture of antibacterial ingredients and perfumes; antiperspirants *stop* perspiration, usually by the use of aluminium compounds, which are thought to block pores and prevent sweat from leaking out of the armpits. Using a deodorant should be perfectly adequate to address the issue of hygiene. If you suffer from regular excessive sweating, the answer is not to block the vital elimination points for waste products to leave your body. This is akin to blocking off your exhaust pipe because it starts emitting excessive white smoke and fumes! The solution is to *determine and correct the underlying cause* of excessive sweating, which may be symptomatic of a critical metabolic imbalance.

Whichever product you feel you need to use, always go for a cream, roll-on or stick, rather than a pressurized aerosol can. Aerosols contain propellants, typically propane, butane and isobutene (damaging to the environment and thought to be neurotoxic) that 'propel' the contents from the can and produce easily inhaled clouds of chemicals. Every time you use an aerosol, whether it is as a hairspray, disinfectant, cleaning product or insecticide, you inhale high concentrations of its chemical contents.

There's more: dowsing suggests that the presence of aluminium compounds in the body is a causative factor (combined with other factors) in 90 per cent of diagnosed breast cancer cases in the UK. The aluminium compounds in diagnosed breast cancer cases originate from deodorants and antiperspirants (60 per cent), pharmaceutical products and vaccines (30 per cent) and a variety of other sources (10 per cent).

For at least ten years, reports have appeared in the press linking aluminium and breast cancer. Philippa Darbre, PhD, from the University of Reading, maintains that a strong link exists between the use of deodorants or antiperspirants and breast cancer, and that the aluminium-based active ingredient used in these products mimics oestrogen in the body. She said:

> *Lifetime exposure to oestrogen is the risk factor that is tied most strongly to breast cancer. If the aluminium salts in antiperspirants enter the body and mimic oestrogen it stands to reason that constant exposure over many years may pose a risk.*

The response from the industry has perhaps been predictable. 'Consumers should be absolutely reassured that antiperspirants are completely safe,' said Dr Christopher Flower, director-general of the Cosmetic, Toiletry and Perfumery Association. Dr Jodie Moffat, health information officer at Cancer Research UK, said there was 'no conclusive evidence linking deodorants with cancer'.

Are you reading what I'm reading? 'No evidence' alert!

Dr Jane Flemming, a family doctor with a special interest in women's health, suggested switching to deodorant (from antiperspirant) only if you were at higher than average risk of breast cancer and felt genuinely concerned. 'This link has not yet been proven,' she said. 'At this point women need to use their own good judgement over this issue.'

With this level of dissent, how on Earth is the average man or woman in the street able to *use good judgement*? The following abridged entry for aluminium (aluminium compounds) from *Silent Killers* by P. M. Taubert might help:

> *Large amounts are found in the brains of Alzheimer's victims, and recent research has proven a positive link*

with this disease... When used with deodorants there is a link with breast cancer. Spray deodorants that contain aluminium are particularly hazardous, as they are readily absorbed into the brain via the nasal passages. Aluminium products are listed as either known suspected or suspected carcinogens (Cornell Carcinogen Database). [Aluminium] is suspected of being a neurotoxic hazard, and there is growing evidence of its role in hyperactivity. Aluminium binds to and damages DNA, concentrates in the brain, and accumulates in the stomach, thyroid, liver [and] bones (disrupting bone formation) and increasing the risk of osteoporosis.

The armpit is one of the most absorbent areas of the body. Women who shave are more susceptible, as any break or discontinuity in the skin surface can allow easier penetration. A doctor once said to me, 'You might as well inject aluminium directly into the lymph nodes.' But, whether male or female, why would you ever want to put aluminium under your armpits or up your nose, let alone on a daily basis?

Do you now feel in a position to make a decision from *good judgement* – or are you more confused than ever?

Reassuringly, you are privileged to have access to a source of truth that is neither swayed by vested interests nor befuddled by the need for a degree in chemical sciences. Pick up your dowsing rods and, with no preconceived ideas of the answers, put yourself firmly back in the driving seat of your health.

Suggestions for Questions

'Is my body currently carrying a toxic load that is detrimental to my optimal health and well-being?'

'Does my body currently have toxic levels of aluminium compounds?'

'Would I benefit from a supervised detox of these toxins?'

'Are there any toxins currently in my body that are compromising the optimal functioning of my immune system?'

'Are there any toxins within my body compromising the absorption rate of any mineral or vitamin?'

'Are there any chemical toxins within my body that are a causative factor behind my current health condition?'

Mental and Emotional Stress

We have talked about what you put *into* your body and *onto* your body; now it's time to consider what's going on *within* your body.

If anyone has any doubts about the power of the mind in *driving* biological processes, I urge you to read the books of Dr David Hamilton, *It's the Thought That Counts* and *How Your Mind Can Heal Your Body*. These excellent books, grounded in sound science but with David's inimitable sense of fun, are empowering tools to help us take responsibility for our own wellness on mental, emotional and psychological levels in exactly the way I am suggesting. They also fill in the gaps as to how our body is a product of our *thinking* on a moment-to-moment basis.

Dr Bruce Lipton's comment, 'The subconscious mind is a programmable "hard drive" into which our life experiences are downloaded,' points to the potency of our everyday thinking. The power of your mind is unlimited and you can use it to your advantage by restoring and reinforcing optimal wellness – or to your disadvantage by undermining your health on every level.

Many years ago, I had the privilege of attending a course run by the remarkable healer Matthew Manning. I will always remember his stories of the power of words in positively – or negatively – influencing human health. If you continually program yourself with phrases such as 'This job's a pain in the neck' or

'That person's a pain in the bum', guess what? After a short while you get a problem with your neck or a pain in the lower back. And when it gets to the stage of 'This job will be the death of me' or 'This commute is killing me', you know it's time to make some changes!

Your *mind-field* is extremely receptive to the nature of your conscious thinking. When you program it over a sustained period of time, it takes direction from your thinking. So, if we live our lives in a permanent state of fear, anger, bitterness, resentment, grievance, despair, despondency, jealousy, shame or guilt, our physical body responds accordingly. The biochemistry of our body changes; the immune system becomes compromised; the hormone system goes into a state of imbalance; the body becomes acidic, allowing unwanted bacteria, fungi and viruses to flourish; the digestive system malfunctions, leading to the incomplete digestion of foods and the build-up of waste products; and tension held in the body results in the musculature holding the skeleton in a rigid and unyielding way, causing strain and stiffness and constricting nerves and blood vessels. Never underestimate the role of mental, emotional and psychological factors in ill-health: toxins of the mind manifest as toxins of the body.

But you do not have to allow those toxins to take hold. The joy of Dr Hamilton's books is that they provide many useful tools to directly address and turn around specific health conditions. But what happens if our thinking and programming are on much more subtle levels and we have no awareness on a conscious level of what we are manifesting?

We have seen that, at ground-state level, all matter is information-carrying energy. Thoughts and beliefs *are the same*: vibrating, resonating energy. And their resonance reflects the level at which they were created. Critically, *the resonance of repetitive thoughts and long-held beliefs remains in the mind-field in and around our bodies*. This resonance interacts with other mind-fields around it, reacting to and attracting similar resonant energies.

These thoughts might be currently held worries of our own making or conditioned beliefs held since childhood, perhaps passed on from parents, family or friends. They accumulate in our mind-fields, positively or negatively affecting the potential of everything we do. When they are negative thoughts and beliefs, it is the resulting negative energy field that spiritual teacher and author Eckhart Tolle refers to as the 'pain-body'.

Unless we address, release and transcend this pain-body, not only do we face the prospect of a limiting and unfulfilled existence, but there is the strong likelihood that we will perpetuate the pain from generation to generation. We have a responsibility not only to ourselves but also to those around us to identify and let go of all inappropriate behaviour in order to allow ourselves, and others, to live fulfilled and happy lives.

But how do we become aware of our deeply held negative beliefs and conditioning and the impact that they have on our life? Most people are pretty poor at self-analysis and unless you have an insightful partner, family member or friend to point out a few home truths about the way you are living your life, these can evolve to become deeply ingrained driving forces in our life.

It becomes even more damaging when self-delusion steps in. Although unlikely to admit it, we often keep ourselves in a state of ill-health because it is to our advantage – because we benefit from *secondary gain*. Forms of secondary gain include being able to opt out of our responsibilities, avoiding work, being the centre of attention, having the upper hand in a co-dependent relationship, punishing or having control over others. These feelings and emotions can be extremely powerful – even on some occasions driving ill-health on to the point of death.

A client came to me with cancer. We identified the causative factors and, with the means to access the best allopathic and holistic treatment in the world, she addressed them all. Except one. Her husband's phi-landering was a constant source of pain and embar-rassment to her, but whilst she had cancer, he gave her his full attention and ceased all extra-marital activi-ties. When she went into remission, the affairs began again. The return of her cancer meant that she was in control of the one thing that caused her the most pain. The yo-yo nature of her cancer continued until she died. To this day, I don't believe that she meant to kill herself, only to stay in control and to be the centre of her husband's affections.

Looking back through my client files, it is rare that an emotional or mental factor does not play a part in a metabolic imbalance or illness. It might be a long-term worry, the overwhelming burden of a dense pain-body or a sudden and intense emotional shock that becomes the proverbial last straw, tipping the equilibrium from a coping strategy to disease – a betrayal, a deception, a bereavement, unemployment, financial loss or the loss of familiar surroundings such as a home, neighbourhood or country. With one client it was the collapse of the endowment mortgage market. The fact that he was nearing retirement age and his final lump sum was woefully short of paying off his mortgage, meaning he would have to continue working for the rest of his life, was enough to trigger his cancer.

Dowsing gives us access to information in the *mind-field* we are consciously unaware of and insight into suppressed mental processes. With this key information we can begin to instigate change and help restore balance in our body. Either alone, or with the benefit of guidance and support from practitioners and therapists, we can then take steps to effect a shift of consciousness and bring about profound and long-term change. In these cases, I am able to calibrate the level of the client's pain-body, dowse on the optimal practitioner or therapist for their well-being and monitor progress in their mental, emotional, physical and energetic bodies.

If you decide to use your dowsing to access hidden or underlying factors you may be unaware of on a conscious level, it is vitally important to revisit the dowsing guidelines: detach from the analytical mind; focus on the question, not the answer; stand aside and let the response unfold; and let go of any preconceived ideas or beliefs. Perhaps the most challenging of all is the fact that you cannot have any vested interest in the answer. It is not the *answer that suits you* that you are looking for, rather the answer that reveals the *truth*. This will ultimately give you the key to make profound change.

Suggestions for Questions

'Am I holding myself in any mental or emotional state that is detrimental to my health and well-being?'

'Is there a negative mental/emotional factor behind my current health condition? Is this in connection with my family? My relationship with my partner? My work or career? My long-term goals? My spiritual development?'

'Have I released, on every level, all grief ... anger ... hatred ... in connection with...?'

'Am I holding on to any long-term resentment? For how long – more than a month? More than a year...?'

'On a scale of one to ten, how happy am I with my current employment? Career path? Prospects of promotion?'

'How much longer would it benefit me to remain in my current employment from a financial perspective? From a career development perspective? From the perspective of personal fulfilment?'

This brief look at a few of the key factors underpinning optimal health and well-being gives some indication of the vast potential of the application of dowsing. Don't restrict yourself to the suggestions within these pages; instead let them inspire you to widen your scope of dowsing application.

As long as you remember the importance of asking clear, concise and informed questions, you have the means to take responsibility for your health and well-being and ultimately to enhance and enrich your life.

Before moving on, please consider the following: in the past century or so we have seen an astronomical rise in chemical production and use, we are suffering the worst nutritional deprivation in our history and, as we will see in the next chapter, we have changed our own electromagnetic background more than any other aspect of the environment. Is there any connection between these three combined factors and the rise in cancer diagnosis from one in every 600 people in 1900 to one in every two to three people today?

Dowsing suggests *yes*.

On a scale of one to ten? *Ten out of ten.*

So pick up your dowsing rods and give yourself the best opportunity of living a happy and healthy future.

CHAPTER THIRTEEN

ENVIRONMENTAL ENERGIES

*Certain scientists, some perhaps acting in a program of
deliberate disinformation, keep telling the public that we still
don't know whether electropollution is a threat to human
health. That's simply not true. Certainly we need to know
more, but a multitude of risks have been well documented.*

Robert O. Becker, MD, and Gary Selden, *The Body Electric*

*Intent in the human species is not fixed or locked into a rigid
network of energy and information. It has infinite flexibility.
As long as you do not violate the other laws of nature,
through your intent you can literally command the laws of
nature to fulfil your dreams and desires. The only caution is
that you use your intent for the benefit of mankind.*

Deepak Chopra, MD, *The Seven Spiritual Laws of Success*

In generations to come, historians will look back with disbelief
at the period spanning the 20th and 21st centuries as a colos-
sal social experiment. A social experiment that saw the blatant
commercial interests of the telecommunications industry and the
financial interests of governments put above the interests of the
health of humankind and the health of the planet.

The history of the electromagnetic smog that engulfs our planet is not yet long enough to have fully established the scale of devastation or the long-term effects. But in their meticulously researched work *The Body Electric*, Robert Becker, MD, and Gary Selden come to some sobering conclusions:

- The human species has changed its electromagnetic background more than any other aspect of the environment ... the density of radio waves around us is now 100 million to 200 million times the natural level reaching us from the sun.
- ELF electromagnetic fields vibrating at about 30 to 100 Hertz, even if they're weaker than the Earth's field, interfere with the cues that keep our biological cycles properly timed; chronic stress and impaired disease resistance result.
- The available evidence strongly suggests that regulation of cellular growth processes is impaired by electropollution, increasing cancer rates and producing serious reproductive problems.

Electricity in general and telecommunications in particular are so central to our lives it is perhaps understandable that we conveniently ignore the dangers and are confused by the mixed messages of governments and industries with vested interests who conceal, suppress and downplay potentially harmful effects. Every day we hear that there is *no evidence* that mobile phones/mobile phone masts/wireless technology/microwave ovens/video display terminals/fluorescent light tubes and so on are harmful to our health.

But research from scientific establishments in countless countries around the globe on the dangers of the increasing background of electromagnetic pollution persistently contradicts these claims. The sheer wealth of evidence from studies made by reputable bodies makes it impossible to even attempt a brief overview here – it would be an injustice to the tenacity, resolve, dedication and hard work of those whose mission is to uncover the truth. But to take the example of mobile phones, the level of denial, in the face of all the health warnings, by the manufacturers (and end users) is staggering. We can only conclude that both profit margins and convenience of lifestyle still far outweigh concerns for health.

When I was a child, one of the highlights of returning to school at the end of the summer holidays was being treated to a new pair of shoes. It was a highlight because shoe shops in the 1950s were equipped with small X-ray machines for the public to X-ray their feet – and therefore avoid the dangers of tightly fitting shoes.

Whilst our parents were occupied, we were allowed to play unimpeded on the machines. They were equipped with viewing eye holes. We gazed with fascination through the skin of our feet at our naked bones, oblivious to any dangerous exposure to radiation. In fact, we were assured by the authorities that the machines were totally safe – far more damaging to the feet was the wearing of ill-fitting shoes!

Are these the same authorities that assured us that asbestos, mercury amalgams and lead were safe? That Thalidomide and Vioxx were safe? That cigarette smoking was safe? The tobacco advertisements of the 1950s now appear shockingly absurd: doctors in clinics relaxing between patients, still dressed in their white coats and with stethoscopes around their necks, drawing heavily on a cigarette and proclaiming it, 'Just what the doctor ordered.'

Mobile Phones and Wireless Technology

Some experts are drawing parallels between cigarette smoking and the use of mobile phones. Michael Kelsh, principal scientist and epidemiologist for Exponent, a scientific consulting firm, says on the Mercola website, 'It was 15, 20 years after people began smoking that we saw concerns associated with it. Down the road, the same could happen with phones.'

World-renowned health authority Dr Joseph Mercola reports:

In February 2008, Dr Gautam Khurana, a Mayo Clinic-trained neurosurgeon with an advanced neurosurgery fellowship in cerebral vascular and tumour microsurgery, issued a paper entitled 'Mobile Phones and Brain Tumours'. This was after 14 months of independent research, reviewing more than 100 sources of recent medical and scientific literature.

Dr Khurana says: 'In the context of the fact that widespread mobile phone usage commenced in the mid-1980s (earliest in northern Europe), with the first 10 years of widespread usage ending in the mid-1990s, and the fact that solid tumours may take several years to trigger and form, it seems plausible to expect that if no appropriate changes are made by industry and consumers alike, in the next five to 10 years the aforementioned concerning associations will be likely to be definitely proven in the medical literature.'

He went on to say:

Given the calculated 'incubation time' and the commencement of mobile telephony's mass deployment in Sweden, it is no surprise that Swedish researchers were among the first to report a positive association between cell phone use and brain tumour risk. Taken together the data ... compellingly suggest that the link between mobile phones and brain tumours should no longer be regarded as a myth.

In fact Dr Mercola confirms that Australia has seen an increase in paediatric brain cancer of 21 per cent in just one decade – and this is consistent with studies showing a 40 per cent brain tumour increase across the board in Europe and the UK over the last 20 years. In August 2009 he reported that brain cancer has now surpassed leukaemia as the number one cancer killer in children.

You would think that would be enough to convince anyone, but on 25 August 2009 even more evidence emerged: a new report was released by the International EMF Collaborative entitled *Cellphones and Brain Tumours: 15 Reasons for Concern, Science, Spin and the Truth Behind Interphone.* A host of leading scientists and physicians worldwide endorsed this new report, which disputed the findings of an earlier Telecom-funded Interphone study and came to three main conclusions: *there is* a risk of brain tumours from mobile phone use, telecom-funded studies underestimate the risk and children have larger risks than adults.

So surely that is the final definitive word? Oh no…

In the very same week that the above report was released, a *Daily Mail* article revealed that the draft for the Department of Health's new mobile phone advisory leaflet removed the previous safety advice and made clear that no extra precautions need be taken by children. The new draft said: 'There is currently no scientific or biological evidence that radio waves cause cancer.'

Major 'no evidence' alert!

We can only hope that with the release of more studies the tide will turn with regard to the truth. I believe it has started: in the last few years the public has become less trusting and more unwilling to accept the blanket pronouncements of governments and industries. The internet has allowed the world to share information on unprecedented levels – the truth is accessible if we take responsibility, force ourselves out of a state of indifference and make the effort to look for it.

In what is seen as a significant step forward, in April 2009 members of the European Parliament voted to adopt the Reis Report, which called for more reliable information to be made available about the effects of exposure to electromagnetic fields. It also suggested changes to the law in response to the various reports of adverse effects on health to wireless technology such as mobile phones, phone masts, TETRA, wi-fi, Wimax and wireless communication systems.

In the meantime, while there will always be those who wait for conclusive evidence, you as dowsers *can stay one step ahead.*

Dowsing has been an invaluable tool in identifying the most potent risks and enabling me to ensure my home and environment are the safest they can possibly be. Would I have wireless internet connection installed in my home? No. Do I avoid places that have blanket coverage of wi-fi? Yes, wherever possible. Do I use a mobile phone? Yes, but only when it is unavoidable – and I use one that has a protective device installed to reduce harmful emissions. Do I live in an area that has mobile phone masts in close vicinity? No, but I have done. Did I ensure that my home was totally safe from EMFs? Yes. Do I wear a device to protect myself at all times in areas of high-level exposure, for example cars, planes, trains and tubes? Yes. Do I personally have any scientific proof for my beliefs and conclusions? No.

But I do have a wealth of empirical evidence.

Don't wait for a definitive study with conclusive evidence that mobile phones or wireless technology are safe – *it may never come.* Put your complacency aside and get dowsing.

Suggestions for Questions

'Is my mobile phone usage detrimental to my health and well-being?'

'Would I benefit from utilizing a mobile phone protective device?'

'How beneficial would device X be for reducing the harmful effects of my mobile phone?'

'What is the maximum length of time per day it is safe for me to use my mobile phone?'

'On a scale of one to ten, how safe is it to carry my mobile phone on my person when it is switched on?'

'On a scale of one to ten, how detrimental is it to carry my mobile phone on my person when it is switched on?'

'On a scale of one to ten, how detrimental is the current level of wi-fi emissions in my home? In my office?'

'Would my health benefit from switching from wireless internet connection to hard wired? On a scale of one to ten, how much?'

Geopathic Stress

Although the term 'geopathic stress' is used to cover many different manifestations of energy-field imbalance, general agreement exists regarding the *causes* of it. These include natural geological faults, man-made deep-pile excavations, mining and construction, fast-flowing underground water or underground water under pressure, some types of mineral deposits, noxious sites such as dumps and landfills and localized areas of human unrest such as battlefields or sacrificial sites. The term 'geopathic stress' is also used to refer to underground water when it conducts geopathic frequencies from the Earth (sometimes ominously referred to as 'black lines') or conducts radiation from man-made sources such as overhead or underground power lines.

To add to this, when man-made sources of electromagnetic fields such as high-voltage cables and transport systems are placed underground, rather than the residual field dissipating into the air, the natural magnetic grid of the Earth appears to conduct the radiation along its lines, rendering them disruptive to the human system. This grid can also be disrupted by water pumping under pressure from deep boreholes and sewage systems. And to make things even more complicated, geopathic stress does not manifest simply as lines – it can be zones, or pockets, or even vortices.

So, no matter what the shape of it, the potential dangers of electro-stress come not only from man-made electromagnetic pollution but also from sources that originate from changes or imbalances in the natural field of the Earth and that are referred to as 'geopathic stress'. But what exactly is it?

Ten years ago I wrote:

> *The earth, like all living things, has an energy field. This energy is partly magnetic in composition and partly a force not fully understood by mankind. It radiates from the earth in a system of grid lines. When in balance the energy is necessary, and restorative, to optimal health. However, when the natural field is distorted or disrupted, the field becomes harmful to our health. This is geopathic stress.*

I still stand by this definition. Ten years on, however, and with many more hundreds of client case studies behind me, I strongly believe we would be foolish to think that we fully grasp all the implications of geopathic stress. The interchange of magnetic, electromagnetic and other forms of energy between the Earth, the ionosphere, the solar system and the rest of the universe is complex beyond understanding. Dr Robert Becker says:

> *Far from a static simple magnetic field like that around a uniform bar of magnetised iron, the earth's field has turned out to have many components, each full of quirks... The potential interactions among all these electromagnetic phenomena and life are almost infinitely complex.*

What we can state without fear of contradiction is that geopathic stress doesn't go down well with the scientific community, mostly because it is all but impossible to measure with scientific instrumentation. Remember Dr Georg Walach, the geophysics professor in Chapter 2, who asserted whatever couldn't be measured didn't exist?

These energies can be measured by dowsing, however. Ever since German aristocrat Gustav Freiherr von Pohl undertook his dowsing surveys in the villages of Vilsbiburg in 1929 and Grafenau in 1930, clearly correlating areas of Earth radiation with the homes of those who had died of cancer, geopathic stress has been a hot topic. This was reinforced by over 11,000 individual studies of geopathic stress by Austrian teacher and researcher Käthe Bachler, who specialized in assessing its detrimental effects on schoolchildren.

One thing I am very clear about is that it is easier to observe the effects of geopathic stress than to define and label, with absolute certainty, exactly what it is. What makes it so intriguing is the astonishing improvement experienced in health and well-being once geopathic stress is removed, or the subject is removed from the source of the geopathic stress. Before you shout, 'Placebo effect!', please be aware this has been observed in young children, animals and sceptics alike.

Unfortunately these startling – and often immediate – turnarounds in health have in themselves generated a problem. Certain dowsers get carried away with geopathic stress, claiming it to be *the only common factor* in most cases of serious and long-term illness and attributing to it every disease and sickness known to humankind. These incautious claims tend to alienate the scientific and medical communities. There is some truth in them, but it is not the whole truth; as we have already seen, other health factors can be equally, if not more, pervasive.

So, how does geopathic stress manifest? The magnetic field of the Earth – or magnetosphere – stems from the circulating electric currents in the Earth's molten metallic core. It is believed that at the surface of the Earth, this field radiates out in a system of grid lines. Many research studies have confirmed that the behaviour of birds and animals is aligned with or prompted by the magnetic grid: the flight patterns of pigeons, the navigation of monarch butterflies, sea turtles and lobsters, the dances of bees, even the orientation of bacteria. And, of course, the biological responses of human beings.

When the Earth's energy field is in balance, we need this vital resonance or frequency for optimal health and functioning. It is believed that it facilitates many systems of the body, particularly the endocrine system, which is cued by pulsing from the Earth's field.

Scientific studies have also shown that the same bio-systems can be disrupted by change, imbalance or absence of this resonance. But it is important to understand that these reactions are not solely in response to the magnetic or electromagnetic component of the field. Our relationship with our planet is not limited purely to the physical prompts of our bio-systems. We are also fundamentally and intricately part of the planet's consciousness.

Geopathic stress *lines* are not to be confused with *ley lines*. There is a general consensus of opinion in the dowsing community that ley lines are lines of energy that link significant spiritual sites in geographical alignment and are in existence as a result of positive human intent. Perhaps the best known is the St Michael Line that runs from Cornwall to East Anglia and links Glastonbury, Avebury and Bury St Edmunds.

A difference of opinion exists, however, about the type of patterning of the Earth's natural grid and its terminology. At this point, while our knowledge of the grid is still incomplete, I believe it is enough to know there is a grid and that, as a living energetic dimension of the Earth, it is in a constant state of fluctuation and evolution. Imagine something like all the lines of latitude and longitude but much closer together – roughly every couple of metres or so. Or imagine a giant fishing net stretched across the whole Earth: in some places the grid will be perpendicular rectangles, in other places it will be stretched into rhomboid (diamond) shapes, in others it will be distorted beyond recognition, in yet other places there will be large holes or breaks. In some places the grid actually moves backwards and forwards periodically through a 24-hour period.

So what does geopathic stress (in any of its forms) feel like? Short term, it brings about an uneasy feeling, a lightness or fuzziness of the head, a feeling of disconnection. After an hour or two, disorientation, irritability, inability to concentrate or aggression can set in. Long-term exposure can bring about relentless exhaustion, a feeling that you cannot access the thoughts in your head, short-term memory loss, restless sleep or insomnia, migraines, leg pains and severe depression. And it has been found to be a causative factor in illnesses where the immune system is compromised, bringing about recurrent colds, viral, bacterial or fungal infections and heightened allergic responses.

In fact, geopathic stress and electro-stress can aggravate any existing condition or weakness and prevent the ability to recover from sickness or respond to treatment. During a normal day it is likely that we are often exposed for short periods to areas of geopathic stress. Our bodies are well equipped to deal with this and make a quick recovery. But long-term and relentless exposure, such as sleeping or having our desks or favourite chair in an area of geopathic stress, can bring about serious health repercussions.

But how – and why – can the effects of geopathic stress be so wide-ranging?

Like many dowsers, in the beginning I thought I had found the Holy Grail of health. The response and recovery of clients was nothing short of miraculous once the geopathic stress was cleared. But as case histories accumulated, it seemed that not everyone experienced a miracle. Some clients did indeed feel an immediate and rapid improvement, others thought they did but weren't sure and yet others reported that they actually felt worse. The vast range of responses puzzled me. Was it in their perception? Was it something in the deactivation process? Or was there something else going on?

In order to make some sense of it all, I began taking a series of health readings of the clients' condition prior to addressing the geopathic stress. I then monitored the readings by dowsing on a weekly basis, at a distance, after the deactivation had been completed, for a period of two to three months. This enabled me to do two things: observe any improvements, changes or downturns in health, and ensure that any adjustments I had made to the environment were permanent and total solutions and were in the *best interests of the health of the client*.

The readings, at first, were simple ones. Taken as a percentage, they were assessments of the overall general health, the strength of immune function and the general nutrient absorption rate. The optimal level was the level a client would be able to achieve in full and complete health. After the environment of their home had been restored to a safe and healthy place to be, the readings would start to respond. The client would invariably confirm the findings during a follow-up telephone conversation when they advised me of the improvements in their health and well-being.

I began to observe patterns in rate and evenness of the responses. What became abundantly clear was if the client's health readings did not respond to levels of between 70 and 80 per cent, there were *other causative factors* involved in their ill-health. This, at last, explained the variability in the clients' perception of their improvement. Geopathic stress was just one of many potential causative factors in a metabolic imbalance.

What about those clients who said they felt worse? They were absolutely right in their perception: when you suddenly deprive the body of anything 'toxic', such as alcohol or drugs, it will go through a rebalancing process as it regains its optimal equilibrium, sometimes referred to as 'withdrawal symptoms'. Geopathic stress is the same. During this period, frequent headaches, exceptional tiredness, depression or 'pins and needles' in the limbs can be experienced, and the symptoms of existing health conditions are often temporarily amplified. This rebalancing period can last for several weeks, depending on the severity of the geopathic stress and the length of exposure.

Over time my readings evolved to be more detailed. Reading *The Biology of Belief* by Dr Bruce Lipton enabled me to add the *integral membrane protein* function (IMP), which indicates the efficiency of the movement of nutrients, waste products and other environmental *information* through the cell membrane. This is a very powerful indicator of the state of health and one that responds immediately and positively to the clearance of disruptive electromagnetic fields (EMFs).

But what were the other indicators? I determined, through dowsing, that there were 13 main biological functions that could be disrupted by the presence of detrimental EMFs, whether these were from a man-made source or geopathic stress. But I had neither the physiological nor the biochemical knowledge to identify them and needed someone who had expertise in this field to complement my dowsing skills. The perfect candidate came forward in Dr David Hamilton, who has not only qualifications in biological and medicinal chemistry but also a PhD in organic chemistry. He was, thankfully, enthusiastic, with an open mind as to what we might find. This is the result of our combined skills:

Thirteen Biological Processes Detrimentally Affected by EMFs

1. Absorption of nutrients
2. Melatonin release from the pineal gland
3. HPA (hypothalamus/pituitary/adrenal) axis
4. Blood pH
5. Gene expression, specifically ZIF-268, which governs memory storage in the brain
6. DNA synthesis
7. Mitochondria function
8. Digestive function – low oxygenation encouraging bacterial/fungal/parasitic growth
9. Haemoglobin synthesis
10. Autonomic nervous system – sympathetic and parasympathetic nerves/heart rhythms
11. Nerve synapse communication
12. Receptor binding and specificity on cell membranes
13. Immunological memory

Hundreds of my case studies suggest that one of the most significantly consistent effects of EMFs on the human system is the resulting inability to absorb nutrients. *This is the one recurring key factor and the link between the vast array of reported symptoms.* Every client whose body is detrimentally affected by electromagnetic disturbance has a compromised nutrient absorption rate. And these discrepancies are not minor. The health readings consistently indicated absorption rates as low as 15–25 per cent out of optimal levels of 75–85 per cent. Health practitioners rarely assess nutritional absorption rates and patients can be lulled into a false sense of security by thinking, 'I'm taking vitamins and minerals so a nutritional deficiency can't be the problem.'

However, once the source of electro- or geopathic stress is deactivated or removed, the nutrient absorption rate returns rapidly (within weeks) to optimal levels. The simple fact is that anyone whose health is affected by EMFs is likely to be nutritionally deficient – with all the associated knock-on effects. Long-term exposure, with sufficient disruption to the body's intercellular communication, immune function and nutritional levels, can result in serious illness. My files show EMFs to be a regular causative or contributory factor in chronic fatigue syndrome (CFS), MS, cancer, immunological disorders, insomnia, depression and allergies.

When geopathic stress is deactivated or rebalanced by a practitioner, it is critically important that the solution is a total and permanent one. Several years ago I was approached by a woman with chronic fatigue syndrome. She asked me to identify the causative factors behind her condition and then added, 'I know it's not geopathic stress, as a consultant visited my home two years ago and corrected it.' As a precaution, and before I accepted the job, I checked her home – and found it to be extremely affected by geopathic stress. On visiting, I found it so badly affected that it was difficult to concentrate in order to carry out the work. Not only had the previous practitioner not deactivated the geopathic stress, but the measures they had taken had actually made it very much worse. The client had been lulled into a false sense of security, believing her home to be safe place, and as a result suffered two years of unnecessary ill-health and distress.

'How do I know it will be permanent?' is a question invariably asked by clients. I know through experience and because I put checks in place. In the majority of cases it is permanent, but, as we are dealing with energies and a living, breathing Earth, things do evolve and change. This is why all my clients know I am available to them should they need further help – and a quick check of their health readings will confirm this. But this brings us to one anomalous element of geopathic stress that needs to be mentioned: occasionally there is a rare case where geopathic stress returns again ... and again ... and again. These instances invariably require the client to address something within themselves, because their internal state of incoherence is manifesting incoherence in their environment. They may be chronically stressed, for example, or holding themselves in a state of fear. It is at this point that they begin to understand how our thoughts, feelings and emotions interact with and affect our environment. We will look at this further in Chapter 15.

Dowsing skills can be used to determine whether your home or place of work is a safe and healthy place to be. But although it is easy enough to identify the *presence* of geopathic stress, as it manifests in so many different ways, the clearing, deactivating and rebalancing of the environment can be complex. So you have a choice:

- *You can purchase a protective or deactivation device for the entire home.* If you go this route it is important to determine how effective the device is at addressing, removing or neutralizing the detrimental effects. These devices and their effectiveness vary enormously and they may not address all manifestations of geopathic energies to an adequate level. With dowsing you can ask for *the level of effectiveness as a percentage of the device addressing all harmful geopathic and electro-stress in your home.*

- *You can employ a consultant to deactivate, clear and rebalance your home.* But ensure that they have an established track record or are on the professional register of the British Society of Dowsers. And beware of those consultants who advise you that your only option is to move house – get a second opinion! In many years of doing this work, I have not yet come across a situation that could not be rectified. Also be wary of solutions that just involve moving a bed or chair or desk. In my experience, depending on the strength of the geopathic emissions and also individual sensitivity, householders or occupants can be affected for up to a six-yard radius. I believe the only completely reliable option is to make the whole home a safe and healthy place to be.

- *You can remedy the problem yourself.* However, because of the serious health implications involved, I would strongly advise that you first attend a training course with an established and knowledgeable geopathic stress practitioner, undertake some supervised practice and gain some experience. Your health is too important not to! There are various courses that you can take through the British Society of Dowsers and I myself run weekend workshops in dowsing, health and environmental energies.

So, back to the definition of geopathic stress. The safe, easily digested answer is that 'geopathic stress is an imbalance in the Earth's electromagnetic field that is consequently harmful to health'. This definition has to be incomplete, however, as we do know that certain species of plants, animals, insects, fungi and bacteria *thrive and flourish* in a geopathic frequency, so it is not detrimental to *all* forms of life. Perhaps geopathic stress simply points towards an inharmonious alignment between the consciousness of a person and the consciousness of their environment.

Suggestions for Questions

'Is my home/place of work detrimentally affected by geopathic stress in any form?'

'On a scale of one to ten, how detrimental is the geopathic stress/electro-stress in my home/place of work?'

'On a scale of one to ten, how much would I benefit from purchasing a protective device? Employing a consultant? Attending a course on geopathic stress?'

'Is there a device that would completely address the geopathic stress in my home?'

'To what percentage would device X alleviate the harmful effects of geopathic stress? Of electro-stress?'

'Is my current mental or emotional state in any way a contributory factor in an imbalance in my environment? On a scale of one to ten, how much?'

Chapter Fourteen

EVERYDAY DOWSING

*Every known fact in natural science was divined by the
presentiment of somebody, before it was actually verified.*
Ralph Waldo Emerson, *Nature*

*When a smile touches our hearts, when the forest stills us to
peace, when music moves us to rapture, when we really love,
or laugh, or dance with joy, we are one with the angels.*
Dorothy Maclean, from *To Hear the Angels Sing*

Time to have some fun!

Dowsing is not just for the serious stuff like promoting
optimal health and detecting underground water leaks. You can
also use it to enhance your well-being by enlisting the support of
the universe in negotiating a smooth path through the everyday
challenges of life. The intelligent consciousness that we are all
part of is not only benevolent but also has a joyous – and spirited
– sense of humour. It is also more than happy to contribute to the
harmony of your everyday living by giving some gentle guidance.

And it is all there for the asking.

Dowsing has been an invaluable tool in my life, adding to
the quality and joy of living, even in the most mundane minutia

of everyday existence. More often than not, it is in fact the little things that make our world go round, from boiled eggs to bookcases, gardening to power cuts.

I was that person in Ikea, surreptitiously arm dowsing in the bookcase department! I had been given the task of decorating and furnishing our new home from a distance of 1,500 miles. Having only seen it three times, and with just a few photographs to go on, it was proving a challenge. We had decided to cover a large wall with a long row of bookcases, hence Ikea. But what colour? Black and white both seemed too stark, red and green were out of the question and the various fake woods were not appealing. 'Dowse on it,' my husband suggested. So I calibrated each colour on a scale of one to ten for how appropriate it would be to achieve the effect we wanted. Four out of ten, three, two … not looking promising. Until I reached green, which calibrated at ten out of ten. 'Green?' I shouted, a little too loudly for my husband's comfort, as the milling Saturday shoppers assumed I was yelling at him rather than the universe. 'Green? Are you sure?' Thinking my dowsing was in error, I rechecked. Ten out of ten again.

It wasn't until several months later, when the green bookcases were in place, and looking gloriously appropriate and quite striking, that I realized how perfect the answer had been.

And then there's cooking the perfect soft-boiled egg. According to the experts, it seems you have to take into account the size and freshness of the egg, the water temperature, the height above sea level of the kitchen and personal taste in order to arrive at the ultimate hen's delight. Not anymore. With a few simple dowsing questions you're ready for toast: 'What is the optimal cooking time for this egg to meet my requirements of a perfect soft-boiled egg? More than two minutes? More than…?'

We live in an area where frequent power cuts are accepted as normal. Several times we have returned home to an ominous pool of water on the kitchen floor and the contents of the freezer in various states of defrosting. Rather than suffer the waste of having to jettison the whole lot, dowsing has enabled me to identify the food that can be saved to be eaten, the food that can be saved by cooking and the food that is past the point of safe human consumption.

And talking about cooking, how many times have you put something in the oven, or on the hob, only to realize some time later that you forgot to start the timer? Or perhaps you simply cannot work out whether that chicken or cake is fully cooked? Just dowse to determine the *period of time remaining for its optimal cooking*.

Living with a professional dowser can be inhibiting (I am told!), which is why the smallest triumphs can sometimes be the most satisfying. On one occasion, whilst in the process of building some pretty impressive cabinetry, my husband needed to purchase some angle brackets. On arrival at the hardware store, located some distance away and on the point of closing, he realized he had forgotten his shopping list with the specific size brackets needed for a restricted space. Heart initially sinking at the vast array on display, he resorted to some discreet dowsing to find the correct size for his needs. Sadly, I was not at home to witness the small smile of triumph when his brackets turned out to be a perfect fit.

The garden we inherited with our home was a young one, put together by the sterling efforts of the previous owners. Although some parts were growing well, there were many shrubs, trees and smaller plants that were lacklustre and struggling. As a young woman, one of the most profound influences on my life was *To Hear the Angels Sing*, Dorothy Maclean's magical account of her experiences as a co-founder of the Findhorn community in Scotland and its extraordinary garden. That garden was 'planted on sand in conditions that offered scant encouragement for the growth of anything other than hardy Scottish bushes and grasses requiring little moisture or nourishment'. Using her ability to communicate with the living creative principles within nature – what we might call the 'consciousness of the land and plant kingdom' – she was able to access specific instructions and spiritual assistance for the creation and development of the garden. She writes, 'The resulting garden, which came to include even tropical varieties of plants, was so astonishing in its growth and vitality that visiting soil experts and horticulturists were unable to find any explanation for it within known methods of organic husbandry.' The garden went on to achieve worldwide renown.

I had always wanted to put her enthralling findings into practice and now I had the chance. Working our way around our new garden my husband and I calibrated, on a scale of one to ten, the health and well-being of each and every ailing plant, shrub and tree. We then asked, *'How many factors need to be addressed in order to restore this plant to optimal happiness and well-being?'* With a finite list of factors making the process easier, and our combined gardening knowledge (in my case, scant!), we then started with the first factor, asking: *'Is this factor in connection with hydration? Too much water? Too little water? Is this factor in connection with nutrition? Would it benefit from a mineral solution? From fertilizer? From effective micro-organisms? Would the plant benefit from less sun? More sun? Full shade?'*

If the factor was in connection with location of the plant, I would then ask my dowsing rods to indicate the optimal location. We followed the rods dutifully. They would twist and turn and finally come to a stop, crossing in an X to indicate the optimal place. Sometimes the new location did not make sense, but over time the logic was often revealed to us, as the plants flourished and grew. And grow they did! The results were startling. We were able to restore a magnolia tree that was on the point of dying. We nursed many bushes with fungus and disease back to health, totally organically, by identifying which factors would strengthen their immune function, thereby enabling them to shake off the disease themselves without recourse to toxic chemicals. Before buying any new plants, we were able to establish if they would thrive and flourish in the garden or if they were incompatible with the soil type, the location, the prevailing winds or the energy of the land. Being able to communicate with the consciousness of the plants and the land removed any element of guesswork. Dowsing never let us down and gardening became a joyous two-way process of communing with nature.

It wasn't just in the garden that dowsing proved its worth. When our trusty plumber had exhausted his very long list of ideas after our gas boiler broke down, it was invaluable in determining what needed to be done to restore it to full working order. When faced with the prospect of a major overhaul of my car, dowsing established exactly which bits were necessary and which bits were purely wishful thinking on behalf of the repair garage! And when we purchased our new home, dowsing determined exactly which dates for exchange and completion of the contracts were to the best benefit of all parties concerned. We were rewarded not only with a totally smooth administrative process but also unseasonably warm and dry weather on the day of the move.

Above all, dowsing allows us – perhaps even encourages us – to live in the state of perfect synchronization that can be found in all of life. When faced with the vast array of choices we have in the Western world, it is often difficult to let go of judgement, resistance and life-long conditioning in order to make decisions that *feel right* to our intuition. The spin and misleading advertising that accompany so much of modern-day living only add to our uncertainty and vacillation. So, before choosing a restaurant, hotel or new place to visit, we will invariably calibrate it first. These resulting locations, occasions and visits have without fail proved to be a joy, and more often than not have brought with them additional and totally unexpected gifts. One day, without prior knowledge, but simply on the prompting of dowsing, we ended up visiting a town on the very day of its annual festival – a rich and joyous occasion of celebration. As the day unfolded, we were blessed to find ourselves in exactly the right place, at the right time, to have the privilege of meeting exceptional people, full of joy and laughter. By using this process of selection, we often end up staying at places where surprising events and special souls add to the richness of the experience and to the life journeys of all concerned.

'Life was never meant to be a struggle,' says author and teacher Stuart Wilde, and he's right – it wasn't! But it is so much easier to *go with the flow* when you know you have made choices that are in your best possible interest. Your dowsing allows you to do this – and there is a whole extraordinary universe out there just waiting and wanting to help, if you can just get out of your own way and let it.

It is all there for the asking, so pick up your dowsing rods or pendulum and *just ask…*

CHAPTER FIFTEEN

SUBTLE ENERGIES

If we centre our consciousness in our spiritual selves and focus our intentionality through our hearts, we will diminish any possible attachments to the psychic domain.

Professor William A. Tiller, PhD, Stanford University,

Science and Human Transformation

The doors of the many mansions of the mind open both ways. They can let you enter other states of consciousness – or they can allow something or someone to enter yours. You should open these doors with care and caution – but, first, you must know how to close them. And, above all, you must know which doors should be left unopened.

Michael Bentine, *Doors of the Mind*

Writing about subtle energies is always going to be controversial. The risk in bringing attention to this subject lies in potentially alienating those for whom it is outside their personal experience or belief system – just one step too far. But I have observed too much, and been told too much, to omit acknowledging these energies in a book that examines the world of communicating energy. The simple fact is: they exist.

My professional dowsing career involves identifying *any* form of energy that is detrimental to the health and well-being of the human condition, and in the course of my work I have encountered many things that defy explanation in terms of current mainstream science. Some of my observations have come about as a result of my direct experience, the rest as a result of the experiences of my clients and colleagues – sound and rationally minded men and women, often educated to academic level, who are certainly not prone to flights of fantasy and whose accounts I have no reason to doubt. More often than not, they conclude their stories with 'I would never have believed it if I hadn't seen it with my own eyes.' However, this is neither the time nor place to elaborate in any detail, as I have consciously rooted this book in sound contemporary science. So why even mention subtle energies here?

For two reasons: awareness and self-protection.

If you are going to sensitize yourselves to a world of energy in dimensions that cannot be experienced with the five senses (which is what you are doing when you are dowsing), you need to be aware – at the very least – that all manner of subtle energies exist. This does not mean that you have to engage with them, but acknowledging their existence is strategically important. Michael Bentine, a man with his feet firmly on the ground after a career in military intelligence and years of experience in paranormal research, was always adamant that you should never 'open a door' unless you had the knowledge and wherewithal to close it.

And as Dr David Hawkins, a man who expertly straddles the realms of both science and consciousness, summarizes so accurately:

> *There are many energies in this universe that would not like to see you advance spiritually. And they are very adept at it – extremely clever – cleverer than you are. They've been at it a long time...*

So what comes under my definition of subtle energies? Let's start gently…

At the age of three, I had some very special friends, one in particular. He was so special that no one else could see him and so my parents referred to him as my 'invisible friend'. He was, of course, invisible to everyone else, so he was rationalized away as the product of a lonely child's imagination and it was concluded that I would grow out of it. In fact, I said goodbye to him at the age of five, when we moved house, but I never did grow out of it! Years later I realized that the friends I had been playing with were spirit children.

At the age of 14 I was blessed to bump into my first metaphysical teachers. They carefully and gently opened my eyes to the world of subtle energies and guided me through it. This was done with a great deal of responsibility for my welfare and a no-nonsense approach. They were and, at the time of writing, 40 years on, still are an influential and guiding light in my life. With care and sensitivity they showed me tangible manifestations of the subtle realm; awakened my awareness of the discarnate energies around us all and cultivated within me the ultimate gift – that of an enquiring, reasoning and open mind. My visits to their home over the years were, without fail, heady and exhilarating events – never knowing what would materialize, who would turn up, what they would show me or how my thought processes, ideas and beliefs would be gently challenged. We would always start with a glorious home-cooked meal and then invariably talk late into the night. I would hold these visits like magical gems, hugged tightly and secretly to my chest, while I negotiated the more earthly journey of school, exams, college and career.

It was on one of these occasions, when I was in my early twenties, that I was handed a piece of rock with the instruction, 'Tell me about this rock and where it is from.' My incredulous protests were ignored and I was told to focus on the muscle in my left wrist and relate what I could see in my mind. I can recall my answer with clarity even today:

I can't see anything. Nothing. Just blackness ... well,
not quite blackness ... more of a blueness ... well, blue,

like water. And there's some blackness ... well, black cliffs actually, and the sea below, and small flowers on the cliffs...

As the rock was taken away from me, I was told I had described exactly the place it had been taken from, where their boat was moored near a small Cornish harbour. We continued with our supper, which gave me time to recover from my surprise. I didn't know at the time that what I was doing had a name: psychometry, divining facts from inanimate objects by reading their 'memory'.

Twenty minutes later I was handed a second rock, with the same instructions. At this point I really did think they had lost their marbles: how on Earth was it possible to tell the difference between two *rocks*, for heaven's sake? My protests were once again ignored, so I closed my eyes and focused on the muscle:

Umm ... I can't see anything... Oh! I see stakes in the ground... No, not quite stakes, more like bars. Oh, it's a prison ... but not a normal prison ... it's a prison to keep people out, not keep people in... I don't understand... It's a type of prison. Oh, and there are bodies, death, many bodies...

The rock was swiftly removed from my hands.

'Do you *know* where this rock is from?' I was asked.

'Well, of course I don't – I thought that was the whole idea…'

The rock was from the walls of the 2,000-year-old mountaintop fortress of Masada in the Judean desert. At the time I had never heard of Masada, so the impact was quite lost on me. It was only years later when I saw the film with Peter O'Toole and Anthony Quayle that the implications of psychometry really hit home: Masada was a Jewish stronghold in the Zealots' revolt against the Romans. After a siege of nearly two years, in AD 74 the Romans breached the fortress by laboriously building a huge ramp all the way up to the top – only to find all the defenders already dead. Rather than facing Roman slaughter or slavery, nearly 1,000 Jewish men, woman and children had chosen mass suicide.

But how was I able to discern the information I did from a *rock*? Remember Neale Donald Walsch in Chapter 4:

> *Built into all things is an energy that transmits its signal throughout the universe. Every person, animal, plant, rock ... sends out energy like a radio transmitter...*

The organized field at the *ground state* of the rocks retained the memory of where they had been. And what is relevant here is that *everything*, whether it is matter or non-matter, retains a memory in its field. Even our homes. Dr Valerie Hunt says:

> *Thoughts, then, are structured vibration – some fleeting and others that are recorded and become permanent. ...Some thoughts are so strong that they colour the entire environment in which they occurred. ... Stated more simply, there are thought fields in the home, the office, and in organizations and groups, by virtue of the thought vibrations of those who created these institutions and those who live there.*

In my early days of being a geopathic stress consultant, I visited a beautiful cottage in the south-east of England. It was, in fact, three cottages converted into one large house, with a striking architectural interior of exposed beams. The owner had been severely ill and wanted to rule out her home as a contributory factor. There were a couple of minor anomalies, but nothing that was contributing to her ill-health. After the work was completed, we shared a cup of tea in her kitchen and I remember telling her that something still didn't feel quite right – that I kept sensing an overwhelming sadness and despair. She turned to me quickly and, with a tired look on her face, pointed to a beam and explained that was where the son of the previous owner had hanged himself.

Several years later I was surveying a house for environmental energies in the Bournemouth area. It was extremely badly affected by man-made electromagnetic pollution and geopathic stress. I had nearly finished the rectification when the owner came to see how I was getting on. 'Almost done,' I told her, 'just the dining room to sort out.' I remember saying that I couldn't understand why a dining room would be so badly affected by what felt like anger, bitterness and total desperation. She told me that the previous owner, an elderly man, had been diagnosed with cancer. He had lived on his own so, in the last few weeks of his life, the dining room had been converted into a bedroom, as it was on the ground floor. He had died alone in that room.

On another occasion I carried out a pre-purchase survey on a totally empty, unfurnished house a client wished to buy. Both on an environmental and subtle level it had a clean bill of health, except for one room – the master bedroom. It felt like a warring battleground, with a palpable atmosphere of anger, resentment, taunts and a barrowload of grievances. When I reported back to the client, she laughed: the couple that had lived there were known to her – and had been going through a long drawn-out, extremely acrimonious divorce.

These are just three of hundreds of cases of embedded memories, where previous thoughts and actions still affect our physical environment. Most of us have experienced visiting what we perceive to be a 'happy house', occupied by those with a positive attitude, a sense of fulfilment or joy. Conversely, we avoid visiting 'unhappy homes' where anger and frustration prevail or where distressing or tragic events have occurred. Two extreme examples easily imaginable are an uplifting and inspiring place of worship and the unspeakable atmosphere of a concentration camp. However, these memories, negative or positive, don't just embed themselves in the fabric of a building but can be present in personal effects and artefacts and in the land itself as a result of battles, skirmishes and burial grounds.

All of these illustrations are examples of subtle energies and clearly demonstrate that *our thoughts and actions influence and create the fabric of our physical reality.*

So, if you are going to dowse your home, your office or your personal effects for the presence of detrimental energies, bear in mind that what you find may not be obvious or tangible manifestations of EMFs or geopathic stress. But do take on board that these subtle energies can still affect your well-being.

If you're still with me, I'm delighted, because there's a bit more…

Our environment can also be affected by the influence of *thought forms* or *streams of energy* from discarnate beings, otherwise referred to as 'ghosts' or 'entities'. Often we assume that these influences are always negative; however, many places are protected by energies that might be considered benevolent guardians or protective spirits. On the other hand, I have visited countless locations where the unhappy, restless and sometimes aggressive residual energy of previous occupants has made life very uncomfortable for the current residents.

Using dowsing as a communication tool, I have conversed with the energies of those who once inhabited earthly bodies and occasionally, when it was deemed necessary, talked with their consciousness at soul level. And although some of the history and circumstances would be enough to make anyone's hair stand on end, I should say at this point that I have never, ever been threatened, felt harmed or vulnerable, or in any danger at any time. Most of these situations have unearthed lonely, unhappy, fearful and disorientated thought forms who have simply lost their way from A to B – whatever your concept of what or where A and B might be. I have also encountered evil so pure it was chilling, but I chose not to engage with it. Again, on this subject Dr Valerie Hunt agrees:

> *Never in my many years as a mystic have I seen or expe-rienced a demonic entity or vibration that in any form threatened me. True, I have felt some chaotic fields, morphogenic ones in places, and anti-coherent ones around people in my travels into so-called 'haunted houses', and in Haiti and Africa where black magic and*

voodoo are performed... But I have never been attacked or bombarded, or even upset by what is called a dia-bolical entity or a negative energy. I have found these to be merely an organised energy or thought form. If one decodes these thought forms, and for some reason has similar thoughts, one's field resonates and one is affected. If one doesn't resonate, one can perceive the thoughts without effect.

I wish I could say the same for some of my clients who, to borrow from Mr Bentine, have opened doors they really shouldn't have. As a result they have become involved in dodgy activities such as séances and ouija boards or have become sucked into unenlightened covert groups whose sole focus is the basest expression of energy they can find and muster. All of these can be defined as subtle energies, albeit in many different manifestations.

It is vitally important to remember that your own personal intention and attention will become *attuned* to similarly resonating fields of intent. If your intent stems from powerful emotions of the ego – greed, fear, revenge, need or self-aggrandizement – you will, by the same token, align yourself with and attract corresponding fields of energy. But should you find yourself in a situation you cannot handle, *please seek professional advice from someone with a proven track record.* In the meantime, if this is a subject that interests you, I suggest you read *Dancing with the Devil* by David Ashworth, or any of the books written by Michael Bentine.

If your intention is the highest possible expression of consciousness – love, compassion and joy – then that in itself will be your best protection.

PART V
DOWSING FOR LIFE

CHAPTER SIXTEEN

HINTS, TIPS, TRUTHS AND MYTHS

Men occasionally stumble over the truth, but most of them pick themselves up and hurry off as if nothing ever happened.
Sir Winston Churchill

Truth is divinity expressed in a form comprehensible by man.
David Hawkins, PhD, *The Highest Level of Enlightenment*

I have long thought that one of the secrets to living a successful life is learning to recognize opportunities when you stumble over them – and having the courage to seize them before they pass by.

Life is a series of choices – choices often veiled from our immediate recognition, or choices we disregard because our logical mind, our fears, the fears of our family and friends, our inhibitions or – more tragically – our childhood conditioning get in the way of our inbuilt natural antennae. When our gut instinct is to make a positive move towards someone or something, we are often our own worst enemies, holding ourselves back from seizing the moment and its opportunities – opportunities that are just waiting to be recognized, grabbed, nurtured and fulfilled, opportunities that ultimately allow us to realize our dreams.

Balance

Used in *the right way*, dowsing can help us negotiate the plethora of choices and identify what might or what might not be in our best interests. It can provide invaluable guidance, shining light onto seemingly impossible dilemmas. It can help us hone our decision-making abilities and sharpen our ability to spot opportunities from the many choices that come our way. It can also help us differentiate between genuine openings and false leads, thereby helping us to shape and determine the quality and path of our life.

How? In two important and compatible ways. First, we can use dowsing to ask direct questions about the options we have available to us – which might be in our best interests to pursue and which we should quietly leave behind. Second, the more you use dowsing, the more your confidence will grow from having your initial intuitive response, hunches and gut feelings confirmed on an ongoing and consistent basis by its more tangible process. The more your confidence grows, the more you will learn to trust that still, small voice within. And the more you learn to trust it, the more audible and resonant that small voice will become.

But which way is *the right way*?

Is it really in our best interests to use dowsing to make everyday decisions? Are we not in danger of over-using it, thus inhibiting and hampering the development of our natural reasoning, discernment and common sense?

Many self-appointed spiritual teachers counsel against using dowsing too often and for all modes of life. However, life is about balance, and dowsing is no different. Remember you are not abdicating responsibility to some outside source or authority when you dowse. You are simply, and naturally, accessing a field of infinite intelligence that is, at one and the same time, within you and to which you are connected. And in this way you will only be enhancing your intuitive faculties by constant application and confirmation.

Even so, I believe the best advice is to exercise judgement and discretion as to how, and how often, you apply your dowsing ability. Do not become a slave to it, not making a move before you have consulted your dowsing tool. In essence, it is important to succeed by your own efforts in life – but it is also perfectly in order to apply the dowsing faculty to complement these efforts. In his book *Science and Human Transformation*, Professor William Tiller describes dowsing as a device similar to 'training wheels' and includes it on the list of aids that help us to fulfil our journey of evolution of consciousness. He says:

> When our own body's structural organisation at physical and subtle levels has reached the point where it has attained a high level of geometrical, radiation type, radiation frequency, and radiation amplitude discrimination for both receiving and sending, then these particular training wheels are no longer needed and they can be dispensed with. Until that graduation day, they are useful in that they enhance our present capabilities. Of course, it is also important to remember that one can become chained to a crutch by failing to exercise without it.

The *process* of being a dowser is an ongoing process of self-development. In time, you will reach a point when you will just *know* when it is appropriate to use your dowsing faculty and when it is unnecessary.

A dowsing student of mine once expressed surprise that we were 'allowed' to dowse on personal information for ourselves. As we have already seen, of course we are allowed. But if you are not sure if it is appropriate to dowse on a question, just ask! *'May I have access to this information?' 'May I have permission to dowse on this subject?' 'Is it in my best interests to dowse on this topic?'* Your dowsing tool will soon let you know whether it is an appropriate question or subject to ask about: you might receive an answer, or your dowsing tools might stubbornly refuse to move in any direction and no amount of questioning or rephrasing of the questions will coax them into action.

But remember, as Father Jean Jurion discovered many years ago, dowsing works best when there is an explicit *need*. For example, you wouldn't dowse when you woke up every morning on what to wear that day. However, you might consider dowsing on the choice of a specific outfit for an important interview by asking if it would create a favourable impression on a prospective employer.

Similarly, once you have used dowsing to identify the basics of a healthy and nutritious diet, you wouldn't, under normal circumstances, then dowse on every morsel of food that passed your lips. You might, however, use dowsing to determine whether the few sad leftovers in the fridge had deteriorated to the point of being detrimental to your health, or whether the sell-by or use-by date on an item did actually mean that it was no longer fit for human consumption. Or, after a stomach upset, you might use dowsing to determine which foods, if any, would promote the optimal restoration of your health.

I even use dowsing to calibrate films before viewing, either on a scale of one to ten for the entertainment or educational value, or on Dr David Hawkins' scale for the level of consciousness and truth. This has invariably saved me time, money and unwanted exposure to the low level of energies that deplete and dull our senses, suppress our immune systems and deaden our spiritual sensitivity.

And, as Dr Hawkins points out, just the act of being in the presence of higher-energy consciousness has a profound effect on *our* energy and level of consciousness. The more we expose ourselves to and align ourselves with the higher levels of consciousness of beauty, truth and unconditional love, the more we will raise our own energetic vibrational rate. The reverse is just as true.

So, if you use your dowsing responsibly and with discernment, you will not only optimize your opportunities of honing your intuitive skills, but also of enhancing the quality of your life. More profoundly, dowsing's wonderful gift of insight into the truth of any situation, experience or reality gives us a unique opportunity to choose the consciousness with which we surround ourselves and, in turn, to evolve through ever-higher levels of consciousness and awareness.

Dowsing for the Future

The question of whether it is possible to dowse for the future has always been controversial. In my own experience the answer would be yes, you can – but before I get jumped on by those who believe that the future cannot be predicted by any means, I will firmly qualify this with a couple of caveats.

The only way to dowse reliably for future events is by determining possibilities, probabilities, potentialities and trends. Although I personally suspect that there are some events that are predestined in our lives, especially when we have spiritual assignments to fulfil, most of the future is set not in stone but as a series of choices and potentialities. In our world, free will is paramount and the outcome of any future happening will always be affected by the choices and decisions of those involved in the given scenario. If those choices and decisions have not yet been made, the outcome will not yet be definitive.

So, if you decide to dowse on the future, my advice would be, *be realistic*. Your questions would be most sensibly phrased along the lines of '*Taking everything into consideration, on a scale of one to ten, what is the likelihood that…?*' This way of posing the question will be far more likely to give helpful guidance that can be used in a constructive manner. And check whether your answer is the *possibility* of something coming about or the *probability*. A probability is more definite than a possibility. A further way of asking would be to determine the *potential* of something happening, given all causal factors involved.

The second caveat regards timing. Albert Einstein once said, 'Time is not at all what it seems. It does not flow in only one direction, and the future exists simultaneously with the past.' Our interpretation of time is subjective and incomplete: mounting scientific evidence suggests that it is far removed from the neatly ordered linear progression that we perceive it to be. As all time is relative, pinning down timing is notoriously difficult. So when dowsing, you need to make allowances for this perceived human measurement of reality and phrase your questions accordingly. It is far better to ask for a time-scale, rather than specific dates, giving yourself plenty of leeway and wide margins and regularly reaffirming your answers right up until the event.

In my own experience, dowsing for the future has always brought about helpful guidance. In early 2008, I was told through dowsing that the pound sterling to euro exchange rate was going to reach parity in the near future. At that time, the pound was strong, with an average value of €1.45, so this information appeared to be, quite frankly, ridiculous. I rechecked my answers. Still a definite *yes*, but when unable to pin down the timing I assumed this was due to too many variables in the global economy. Ten short months later, and to the shock of the majority of people, the pound and euro did indeed achieve parity for the first time since the single European currency was launched.

More recently, I was due to fly to the Middle East on a business trip. Unfortunately the trip was cancelled, but having already booked the non-refundable tickets, I had the choice of whether to still use them by taking a short holiday to the same location instead. I decided to dowse for guidance. The answer was an unequivocal *no*. Naturally, it was very disappointing, but I have learned to trust the information and follow it.

On 2 February 2009, the morning I was due to fly, London woke up to sudden heavy snowfall, Heathrow airport was under several inches and all long-haul flights were grounded. In excess of 800 flights were cancelled, resulting in severe disruption for three days, with passengers queuing for up to ten hours and sleeping on the airport terminal floor. Not a good way to start a short holiday! I was grateful, to say the least.

But keep in mind that often it is not in our best interests to be party to future information; the bigger picture is often obscured to protect us. There have been instances where I have been asked by one partner, in the absence of the other, about the state or the future potential of the relationship. This, in anyone's estimation, is a delicate path to tread. Which leads us to privacy and permission…

Privacy and Permission

It frequently comes as a great comfort, to clients and students alike, to hear that when dowsing on personal issues, we are usually denied access to any information that might be deemed an unwanted or unnecessary intrusion, or an unwarranted invasion of privacy. In fact, I would go further and state that I believe there to be a Universal Data Protection scheme in place!

Working with a client at her home one day several years ago, I successfully determined the causative factors behind her compromised health and those behind the poor health of her young daughter and baby who, at the time of the consultation, were being cared for at a neighbour's house. She was delighted. So delighted, in fact, that she asked if I would identify the causative factors behind her husband's long-standing psoriasis. He too was absent, at work for the day. I told her I would ask to see if it would be possible. The answer, from dowsing, was a very definite *no*.

As I had been able to access the critical information for her children, both of whom were absent, my client was surprised and disappointed. Why, therefore, could I not do the same for her husband? I explained that accessing this information could be seen as an invasion of his privacy and I would need his permission to do this.

Later, at home, out of curiosity I dowsed on the main reasons for not being able to access the information to help her husband. It was revealed that one of the main causative factors behind his psoriasis was a significant psychological issue from his childhood, which he had not shared with his wife. Revealing this information to any person other than the husband himself would have constituted an unwarranted invasion of privacy and thus at the time I was not allowed access. The information, and his unwillingness or inability to share it with his wife, could potentially have changed the dynamics of their relationship and could possibly have been damaging to their marriage. Whether, in the long-term, this change would or would not have been ultimately beneficial is immaterial – it was simply not in my remit, nor had I been given the authority to initiate this process.

This is just one example of many cases where access to information has been denied. The most important thing we can take from this is that when our dowsing does not reveal the information we request, *we must not automatically assume that this is some failure on our part.* There is usually a very good reason why, which we must learn to trust and accept. I, for one, am happy to leave the decisions of where or when it is appropriate to help to the vastly superior infinite intelligence of the universe!

In my own practice, specifically in the health field, denial of access to necessary information may denote that, in that particular instance, I cannot interfere with an individual's recovery, current health treatment, life path, karma or personal growth. Alternatively, it may be that even though *they* have approached *me* for a consultation, ultimately the information I give them, or perhaps the *process* of obtaining that information – when it comes to the crunch – would be outside their belief system. They would therefore reject it as having no value.

An awareness of the dowsing process and all its implications regarding the fundamental interconnectedness of the universe is not only a journey of evolution in consciousness for the dowser concerned, it will also be part of the journey of the client or subject. And although for some, witnessing the dowsing process can be a revelatory and positive life-changing experience, for others it can be just the reverse. There are those who are simply not ready to be open to extra-sensorial processes and dowsing may result in an uncomfortable full-on challenge to deeply held core belief systems. Any process of personal enlightenment or expansion of awareness cannot be engendered or forced, but only allowed to unfold in a timely manner.

Above all, I have learned to never, *ever* step in and help where it has not been requested. It is perfectly in order to make others aware of your dowsing abilities and field of speciality and expertise, but a request for help should always be initiated by the other party. This will help avoid potentially frustrating and embarrassing situations further down the line. And for your own clarity of mind it is wise to give well-grounded thought to your motivation, intent and aims before starting out dowsing, whether on a personal basis or in a professional capacity.

Truth

Dr David R. Hawkins states, 'Truth is whatever is subjectively convincing at one's current level of perception.'

When asked about the reality of eternal truth in his book *The Eye of the I*, he responds by saying, 'Begin by accepting the very important statement that *all truth is subjective*. Do not waste lifetimes looking for an objective truth because no such thing exists. Even if it did, it could not be found except by the purely subjective experience of it. All knowledge and wisdom are subjective. Nothing can be said to exist unless it is subjectively experienced.'

For dowsers and seekers of truth alike, both these statements could be disconcerting. But what is important for us as dowsers to understand is that all truth is subjective, so it can only be *relevant* truth when it is properly in context.

We can only experience truth within the limited context of our sphere of knowledge, understanding and awareness. And as greater and more expansive spheres of knowledge will always exist, all truth, therefore, is relative. On how many occasions have we believed something fervently and deeply, only for an extra fact or piece of knowledge to emerge that radically changes the context of our understanding and leads us to conclude, 'Oh well, that throws a completely different light on things…'

Whilst refining our questioning technique, we saw the importance of having an awareness of the bigger picture and also differentiating between opinions and facts. Undeniably, simple facts exist. It is not a *subjective* truth that the current monarch of Great Britain is Her Majesty Queen Elizabeth II. This fact is easily verifiable. And bigger facts are verifiable too. Or are they? Author, spiritual teacher and visionary Eckhart Tolle gives us this pertinent example from his book *A New Earth*:

> *As an illustration of relative and absolute truth, consider the sunrise and sunset. When we say the sun rises in the morning and sets in the evening, that is true, but only relatively. In absolute terms it is false. Only from the limited perspective of the observer on or near the planet's surface does the sun rise and set. If you were far out in space, you would see that the sun neither rises nor sets, but that it shines continuously.*

Several years ago, the renowned English specialist paint manufacturer Farrow & Ball brought out a colour chart containing solely white paints named 'off whites'. At a quick glance, the chart initially appeared to be another fashion fad – white is the new black! Rather than coming close to resembling shades of white, the colour samples looked more like varying shades of grey, taupe, pale pink, blue and beige *in relation to the background of the pure white chart*.

And herein lies the key. The colours had been inspired by the 'whites' found in historic houses, whites tempered and aged with the patina of time, which had been developed for conservation and restoration projects. The colour swatch named 'off white', which appeared in the chart to be a shade of pale grey, actually came across as bright white *in the context* of most period country houses where old colours survive. Another colour, 'Hardwick white', the greyest of all the Farrow & Ball whites, was named as a result of being used throughout the National Trust property Hardwick Hall. No one looking at it on a colour chart would ever think of it as white, but in large areas and relative to the dark tapestries of Hardwick, it looked very different. In fact it looked white. Farrow & Ball concluded: 'Whiteness is always a matter of degree, and can only be judged by the colours surrounding it.'

Truth is the same.

As in the salt anecdote in Chapter 8, we see that the only way of posing the question to obtain a relevant and meaningful answer is to put it in the context of the current circumstances and occasion. *Similarly, the only way to determine the accurate truth of any condition, situation, event, concept or reality is by placing it in relationship to the background of its context.*

So, if dowsing has a limitation, it is as a consequence of the fact that we can only ask questions from the standpoint of our individual level of awareness and our resulting ability to place the questions that we ask in context.

But if all truth is relative, and is only relevant as truth when it is in context, how, as dowsers, can we pursue absolute Truth?

The more that I work with truth, the more I understand that Truth is not a purely fact-based concept but a state of awareness – and therefore a way of being. It cannot be acquired, searched for or procured. It cannot be found *out there*, only within. Truth is found in the consciousness within all of us. So it is found within you. It manifests as a consequence of what you have become and the principles with which you align yourself. And the simple stark fact is, the higher your level of consciousness, the higher your alignment will be with the state of Truth or Divinity and, as a result, the more accurate your dowsing will be.

Access to Truth will always be a reflection of where we are in our state of awareness.

And any growth in our awareness, by definition, requires a change of consciousness. We should not view this with discouragement or impatience, but embrace it as a gift to help us understand where we are in the process and, in turn, embrace the opportunity to grow. We each have the option to *choose* to align ourselves with the highest principles, to strive to fulfil the highest possible vision of ourselves and to endeavour to be kind, loving and compassionate to all forms of life, *including our own*.

And as we grow in consciousness and awareness, we are 'given' access to higher levels of universal consciousness – or perhaps, more accurately, as a consequence of this growth we are able to align with these higher levels. Having access to information is a very powerful tool – a tool that begs to be used with discretion, diplomacy, good judgement, wisdom, compassion and, most critically, the best interests of the recipient at heart. Never attempt to use this tool from a position of ego, with a self-congratulatory pat on the back or with the self-delusion that you have a unique and exclusive power. Instead, develop a healthy respect and gratitude for the source with which you are able to connect.

Ultimately, if you have a truly open mind and come from a position of humility, you can't go far wrong.

How Accurate Is Dowsing?

The *process* of dowsing has the potential to be 100 per cent accurate. As a consequence of its very existence, the complete knowingness of the all-encompassing, infinite field of the universe can never be wrong. If anything, as we have seen, it is the dowser's *interface* with that field that will compromise the accuracy. So a far more pertinent question would be: *How accurate are dowsers?*

As in any profession where a unique combination of skills is required to consistently achieve outstanding results – acting, music, writing, football, teaching, athletics, cooking – there are few *really good* professional dowsers. This reflects the number of elements to be mastered in professional dowsing: focus of intention and attention, emotional detachment, clear questioning, a physically, emotionally and mentally balanced body, unquestioning belief in the process, an in-depth knowledge of the field of expertise, a high level of consciousness or awareness and the complete absence of ego. And, in addition, years of sometimes exhausting, occasionally embarrassing, often exhilarating, but always hard-won practical experience! This is all something to aspire to, but the giants of dowsing, such as George Applegate and Abbé Alexis Bouly, are testimony to the fact that it *can* be done.

Achieving accuracy in personal dowsing is much more immediate and accessible. You don't have to study a field of speciality to achieve good results – your field of speciality is you! Simply believe that you can do it, formulate accurate questions, build your confidence with practice, keep an open mind – and enjoy the process.

All Dowsers Find Something Different...

This oft-repeated phrase is sometimes used by dowers in their own defence – and sometimes seized on by sceptics as a criticism. It is a rather irritating generalization, nonetheless it is frequently true, and true for several reasons.

The inconsistent or diverse findings by those dowsing on the same project or subject often result from the fact that they are a) asking different questions or b) asking questions from a different perspective.

There is an ancient fable that perfectly illustrates this predicament. Similar versions of the tale exist in several religions, including Jainism, Buddhism and Hinduism, and although the story varies slightly from version to version, the underlying message is the same. Six blind men are gathered together and are asked to examine an elephant to determine what it looks like. Each of them touches the elephant's body and describes it. One blind man touches its leg and declares it to be a pillar, one feels its tail and says it is a rope, one feels its trunk and pronounces it to be a tree branch, one touches its tusk and says it is a spear, one feels its ear and declares it to be a hand fan, and the last one feels its back and believes it to be a throne. They then share their conclusions, believing they have touched the whole of the elephant, and find they are all in disagreement. A wise man then explains to them that they are in fact all correct and the reason that they have come to different conclusions is that they all touched a different part. In actuality, of course, the elephant has all the features identified.

Dowsing is often the same. Depending on training, context, belief systems and spheres of experience, dowsers will invariably ask questions corresponding to these parameters – all possibly relevant, but all from an individual perspective. Hence, like the blind men, all dowsers can find something different. If there were an occasion where a group of dowsers asked an identical ten questions, however, then there would be a higher probability of their reaching the same conclusions. I say probability, rather than certainty, as each individual dowser would still *interpret* the answers obtained within the limitations of their own level of understanding.

A second reason why all dowsers find something different is because in many fields of dowsing application there is no universally agreed pre-established terminology. Water divining has been in existence long enough to have formulated a common terminology, but in the fields of Earth energies, environmental energies, bio-field energies and subtle energies, the nomenclature is still in its infancy. There is little or no recognized agreement and it is down to individual understanding and interpretation. One woman's positive energy line is another woman's ley line; one man's discarnate entity is another man's ghost!

Not only are we working with a movable feast in terms of vocabulary and classification, but in the dowsing process we are also attempting to *translate* the language of the intangible world of energy and consciousness and portray it in a meaningful and constructive context in the world of matter. Although there are undoubtedly areas of correlation, a cautious approach is prudent, as these energies often have scant proof of existence (especially from mainstream science) and can be elusive in their definition, especially within the context of the bigger picture. As with geopathic stress, it is perhaps easier to observe the *effects* of an imbalance of energy rather than it is to define and label, with absolute unerring certainty, the source of the imbalance.

Once a terminology to portray the realms of consciousness and subtle energies has been categorized and established on a formal basis, I suspect the margin of error for dowsers finding something different will decrease.

In the meantime, 'all dowsers find something different' highlights the challenge that potential clients can face when attempting to source and hire a dowser. In order to obtain optimal results, *for both dowser and client*, it is crucial that there exists mutual trust and confidence.

For anyone thinking of instructing a dowser, my best advice is to take guidance from a professional dowsing body or follow up on personal recommendations from friends, neighbours or colleagues. Having selected a potential dowser, familiarize yourself with their track record, take the time to read their testimonials and ask to speak to one or two of their recent clients. Ensure that they use a methodology with which you are comfortable, whether it be working on site or at a distance. And ask them about any specific approach or slant they have in their specialist field. Don't be afraid to ask probing questions, even ones you feel might sound naïve. Any experienced dowser will answer them with patience until you are fully satisfied. And most dowsers are more than delighted to talk about their favourite subject!

Source

In the early days of my teaching, whilst giving an environmental energies seminar in Ireland, I began with a practical demonstration of information dowsing, asking questions and obtaining answers from my dowsing rods. I had been in full flow for at least 45 minutes when towards the back of the room I spotted a hand in the air. There was a pregnant pause and then, in a lilting Irish accent, a woman struggled, 'But ... but ... but,' pointing to the rods, 'who are you talking to?'

My flow came to an abrupt halt. It could have been funny, but it wasn't – because with one simple question she had hit on the fundamental key to the whole dowsing process.

As we have seen, when we are dowsing, the source of our information is the universal information field, or the A-field of Dr Ervin Laszlo. But sometimes it is not quite that simple, because the field is made up of many dimensions and levels of complexity far beyond our understanding.

In a simplistic model, the extending of our consciousness to access this information field is similar to our being a radio transmitter and receiver. On a radio, we tune into a specific bandwidth and station. We pick up a particular signal and we are able to access the information being broadcast. Generally, we expect the signal to be clear and easily audible. Sometimes, however, radio stations are very close together and you can hear two stations broadcasting simultaneously. And sometimes pirate broadcasters or ham radio operators cut in and interfere with reception, disrupting legal radio transmissions. Occasionally, the signal is faint and hard to hear, full of crackle and interference or alarming whoops and whistles. Certainly, whilst listening on a car radio, irritating mobile phone and communication mast blips will frequently drown out a broadcast. On the rare occasion, a police frequency will even cut in, the transmitted message startling in its blast.

Tuning in to pick up a dowsing signal can be exactly the same. Occasionally your *line of communication* will be disrupted by unwanted outside interference – otherwise known as gremlins in the works!

If in the process of dowsing you are obtaining answers that just don't make sense or don't *feel* quite right, or if your intuition is prodding you with an uneasy niggling feeling, always, *always* go with your intuition. Either put down your dowsing tool, walk away and take a break for an hour, or if – and only if – you feel comfortable, pursue a line of questioning to identify the reason why:

'Is there interference with my dowsing?'

'Is this interference benevolent?'

'Is this interference malevolent?'

'Is it in my best interests to cease dowsing?'

'For how long – more than an hour? Two hours...?'

The only caution with this line of questioning is that the very interference you are enquiring about will have the potential to distort these answers as well.

An alternative way to identify the reliability of your dowsing answers is to calibrate the *source* of your information. In circumstances such as these, perhaps the most reliable way is to use Dr David R. Hawkins' *Map of Consciousness*, which is published in most of his books. If your source calibrates at less than 200, then you know you are dowsing below the level of truth and your answers will be undependable and inaccurate.

If there is no outside interference with your dowsing and you are satisfied that the source of your information is reliable, then identify whether the glitch is within yourself. Suggestions for questions include:

'Am I in the right frame of mind to dowse?'

'Are my intentions clear to dowse?'

'Am I too tired/unwell/stressed to dowse clearly and accurately?'

'Is my emotional state currently detrimental to the accuracy of my dowsing?'

'Am I affecting the accuracy of my dowsing with any unwanted mental or emotional input?'

'Is it in my best interests to cease dowsing for my own protection?'

Sometimes there is no obvious, logical or rational answer as to why our dowsing tools refuse to co-operate. For short periods, it may simply not be the *right time* to dowse.

On one occasion, upon commencing dowsing for the day, I found that all my rods would produce was nonsensical rambling. I ran through the list of obvious questions, checking as to why, and every answer was in the negative. Out of sheer frustration, I shouted, '*Well, is the universe on a coffee break then?*'

To my amusement, the answer was a very strong *yes*. Thankfully, half an hour later, it was back to work…

So, if you get stuck or are unsure how to go on, make a sensible decision on how to proceed. Ask for help from another trusted dowser or a trained, experienced energy worker.

Your best protection from unwanted interference is to always ensure that you yourself are in alignment with the highest level of Truth and not allow yourself to resonate in any way with lower-level fields of thought. Grounding yourself is also essential, of course – both to maintain an even and balanced flow of energy throughout the body's chakra system and to prevent a destabilizing short-circuit of energy throughout the upper chakras. Over time this can be exhausting to the physical body. But attempts to protect yourself with *barriers* should be treated with caution. Dr Valerie Hunt comments:

> *Some people, when they do this kind of work, wrap themselves in white light as a sort of protection. These ideas about 'black' and 'white' energy need to be clarified. Actually, energy is energy. We, on the other hand, judge the information by our worth and standards, so that the blackness and whiteness is our judgement; it has nothing to do with energy per se. For those reasons, I do not wrap myself in white light when I work. I am protected by the strength, clarity and spiritual vibrations of my field. I am therefore free to interact with whatever I choose and to radiate my coherent energy to the world and to all people.*

So your alignment with Truth should be your one and only intention – and this in turn will ultimately be your principal protection. Conversely, if your intent is to obtain information to cause harm to others or *any* form of life, by opening the door of negative intent you will become the magnet to all the dodgy energies out there in the universe.

If you are using your dowsing rods or pendulum as a communication tool to access specific guides, protectors or other persona and thought forms that exist in the various dimensions outside the physical plane, by all means go ahead and have a chat with them and ask for their opinions. But again, proceed with caution. You might get some fascinating insights from an ancient guru or Aunty Edna who died in 1910 – just don't blindly rely on them for the highest level of truth! It would be astute to calibrate them as a source of information first.

When you have been employing your dowsing skills for some time and your alignment with the conscious universe becomes more coherent, you may begin to notice certain changes. When posing a question, you may find that you suddenly *know* the answer before your dowsing tool responds. Please do not automatically assume that this is a result of your imagination, that you 'made it up' or pre-empted or influenced your dowsing tool to move in a particular direction. Your intuitive process is just becoming more coherent, so the moment a question takes form in your mind, an answer is there for you, with the physical process of the dowsing tool response taking a second or two longer.

How does this happen? Having asked a dowsing question, you stand aside as the observer to await the answer, thus *creating space* between thoughts. It is this space between thoughts that those who meditate aim for when they put aside the chattering conscious mind. Soon, with practice, whether you are meditating or dowsing, the spaces merge together and become a continuous flow of consciousness. You are now connecting with Source. It is at this point that you will no longer need your dowsing tool. It is at this point that you will just *know*.

You may even find that the dowsing response or the *knowingness* is accompanied by fleeting images, impressions or strong feelings. Key words may start to come into your mind, or you may 'hear' prompts or ideas, or even phrases or sentences. This is all simply a result of your stepping aside and allowing the flow of consciousness into your mind-field.

And if your dowsing tool starts to do something out of the ordinary, take heed! One of the defining moments of my dowsing career was when my dowsing rods gave their first independent *pro-active* demonstration. I was with a client and her husband in their charming 400-year-old Surrey cottage and deeply immersed in a health consultation. She had suffered for many years with chronic fatigue syndrome and they intuitively felt that there was something very wrong with the cottage. I was in the process of identifying at exactly what point the breakdown of her immune function had initially occurred, and in answer to the questions my 'L' rods were swinging to and from their usual *yes* and *no* positions, when abruptly they stopped and, as the three of us watched in totally fascinated silence, began a very specific and precise movement: one revolution to the left. Stop. One revolution to the right. Stop. One revolution to the left. Stop. One revolution to the right. Stop. After this had continued for a minute or two, I told my (thankfully very open-minded) clients that it appeared I was being given a message.

The moment I observed verbally that the movement of the rods was akin to the sweep of a radar screen, they rapidly responded with a very emphatic *yes*. In fact I quickly established that I was under active surveillance from a third party, perhaps akin to being on someone's radar screen – attention that I had certainly not solicited and definitely did not want. I choose not to disclose who the third party was, but I took appropriate measures for my own protection and to safeguard that of my clients, as their confidentiality and privacy were my primary concerns.

I was, however, extremely grateful for the alert I was given. This was just the first of many occasions when my rods have given me pro-active and invaluable feedback, sometimes for my benefit and sometimes for the benefit of my clients. Inventive and resourceful, they will swing and point to objects, locations, parts of the body – in fact to anything that might bring further knowledge or insight, or give clues to critical information I may not have identified in my questioning process. This often enthralling display has been witnessed by many and frequently inspires awe and delight as the rods dance with grace and joy, revealing, in a tangible way, our connection with an intelligent and benevolent cosmos.

Any pro-active feedback you receive will be a sign of an evolving awareness, an affirmation of your growing willingness to step aside, let go of ego and allow the process of transformation. This will lead to the experiencing of a profound interconnectedness with other human beings, with nature and with all life. Above all, never assume anything. Dowsing is an adventure where something new can be learned every day and a totally open heart and mind will give you your greatest opportunity to learn, grow and evolve.

The remaining factor to ensuring the successful application of your dowsing skills is identifying your niche. This aspect of the overall adventure merits a chapter all of its own.

Chapter Seventeen

FINDING YOUR NICHE

There is an inconceivably vast and complex network out there that makes our primitive Internet look Neanderthal. Each one of us is already linked in, and while for a time we lost the delicate art of tuning in to the whispering energies of the universe, dowsing has re-opened a door to our evolutionary birthright.

Hamish Miller, dowser, author, *The Definitive Wee Book on Dowsing*

The wonderful order of the world, which we scientists investigate, is a sign that there is a divine mind behind that order.

Professor Sir John Polkinghorne, Cambridge particle physicist, in an interview with Jonathan Margolis

Finding himself short of work in the early days of his professional water-dowsing career, Peter Taylor decided to advertise in his local paper. This generated just one response – not for water, but for Peter to dowse on the opening and closing of the Financial Times Stock Exchange 100 index, the FTSE 100.

Knowing nothing about it but always keen to have a go, he threw caution to the wind and dowsed on what the FTSE 100 would open at the next morning. The following day he was proved to be absolutely correct – his dowsing was spot on. He was astonished and his male caller was excited. This procedure continued, morning and evening, for one week. On every occasion Peter's dowsing was correct. By this time, the man could hardly contain himself and offered Peter a contract of work to do this on a daily basis.

At that prospect, Peter admits to an inkling of doubt – it was not the noblest application of the craft for which he had trained for many years. His instincts were right. The very minute he commenced his paid contract, his dowsing failed. He was wrong each and every time he dowsed. The man lost £20,000. Worse was to come.

The next day, when picking up his dowsing rods, he found that they would not move. They simply froze. In fact, they didn't move again for *over 18 months*, despite Peter trying and retrying on a regular basis.

Similarly, I once spent a very embarrassing weekend attempting to use dowsing to help my husband find his lost spectacles. Despite a very definite *need*, my dowsing responses proved to be nonsensical, sending my husband scuttling backwards and forwards only to find no trace of the spectacles whatsoever. Eventually he found them by his own efforts.

An equally fruitless evening was once spent trying to find a lost photograph album. Not finding it in its normal place, I decided to use dowsing to speed up the process.

Or so I hoped.

With vivid memories of the spectacles débâcle, I asked permission and carefully formulated my questions. The rods quite clearly and firmly pointed to a bedroom closet, albeit a large, tightly packed affair. Dowsing, I narrowed down which shelf, and emptied it, box by box. Nothing. I rechecked my question and rechecked the shelf. Dowsing then indicated a different shelf. I cleared this one too. Nothing. Stoically I emptied the closet. Only at the last shelf was it obvious that the album was not there. I reconfirmed that the album was definitely in the bedroom and dowsed again for the location. The rods then pointed to a different closet…

I turned my flat upside down before I gave up. Only after I had sunk, exhausted and irritable, onto the sofa in the sitting room, did I see the elusive album reclining on a bookcase. I reluctantly acknowledged that dowsing for *lost objects* was not my forte.

So, as you might imagine, when a neighbour asked for assistance in finding her lost dog, I was hugely unwilling. 'Finding things really isn't my field,' I said nervously. But this delightful, madcap Old English Sheepdog had simply disappeared and such was her anguish that I eventually agreed to help. After all, surely on *this* occasion there was a very clear-cut need?

Dowsing, I asked if it was within the scope of my abilities, if I had permission and if it was in the best interests of all concerned. After three affirmatives, I dowsed that the dog had decided to have an impromptu adventure, during which it had become injured and trapped on rough terrain. And, more crucially, that it was dying, most likely of exposure, or was already dead.

After a break, I went back and rechecked everything. The rods confirmed the previous information, but indicated that the dog was indeed now dead.

'I'm sorry – it isn't looking good,' I stuttered as I phoned my neighbour, feeling hugely sad for her.

Days later she rang, hysterical. 'Oh no,' I thought, 'they've found the poor dog's body.'

'*He's back! He just bounded through the door, grubby and matted, but healthy and happy.*'

Failure to find spectacles is one thing. This was in a completely different league.

With gratitude, I realized there wasn't an ounce of reproach in her voice. She was just ecstatically happy to have her dog back. I, on the other hand, was now experiencing the anguish. Examining my motives, I concluded that I clearly hadn't taken on this job from ego – my initial unwillingness testified to that. My intent had come from a desire to help someone in distress and my motivation had been compassion. My methods had been pretty watertight – methodical and painstaking in their detail. And hadn't dowsing confirmed it was in the best interests of all parties concerned? I could not fathom what had gone so horribly wrong.

There had to be an explanation. If someone has the ability and training to dowse, surely that means they *have* the ability? Full stop. Period. And that the ability can be applied to any field of dowsing? No – herein lies the lesson. Ever since, the memory of this débâcle has kept me firmly on the path of my specialist practice of health and well-being, where I continue to enjoy considerable success.

In Peter's case, being a strongly religious man, perhaps he was convinced that he had transgressed his personal belief system in some way by using his gift in a dubious money-making application rather than for the benefit of mankind. Consequently, his guilt may have been stronger than his belief in his ability to dowse. Only when he forgave himself at some fundamental level did his ability return. Happily, today he is one of the UK's top water dowsers, which has turned out to be his own particular niche. I have been privileged to see him working and witnessed his dowsing 'V' rod, firmly gripped in his strong and weathered hands, complete a full revolution, distorting and bending the heavy-duty plastic in response to hidden underground water.

While it is critical to determine your own niche over time, the fallout from these sorts of failures can be huge, undermining your confidence in your ability to do *any* type of dowsing, including the field in which you are normally proficient. I mulled over my and Peter's failures for some time. There was clearly more to them than met the eye: it was almost as if we had each been set up to fail. I had quite definitely been told it was in my best interests to proceed and Peter had spent a trial week obtaining accurate results, yet in the crunch, neither of us could come up with the goods. What were we to infer from these discouraging results?

Besides turning his hand to forging dowsing rods, Hamish Miller was also a veteran dowser, world authority on Earth energies and the author of several DVDs and books. His *Definitive*

Wee Book on Dowsing is utterly delightful in its down-to-earth humour and striking in its humility and enlightened approach – which is why I turned to Hamish for his guidance on this conundrum.

Without hesitation he explained:

> *Dowsers are as much specialists as surgeons. You don't have a brain surgeon doing your feet! I've been dowsing Earth energies for 26 years and recently I wanted to find water, so I actually got a water dowser in. I recognize that dowsers specialize in very specific things and I don't think that any dowser can claim to do all sorts of dowsing – I think it is quite wrong. Or they can, but they can't do it that well. Your specialist practice makes you a much, much better dowser at that particular thing.*
>
> *You see, dowsing for me is not just about finding things, it's about moving us through into the next series of senses, and I think there is a great deal of management guidance about this. You are a particular specialist, because you can find things that I can't. And I think that once the management begin to realize that you are into finding that order of thing, they gently guide you back to what you should be doing. An awful lot of dowsers think they can dowse for anything, and I believe they can to a certain degree. But to become a really competent dowser I think you have to specialize.*

Hamish explained that the term 'management guidance' is his personal expression for universal guidance from a higher level. When we have some sort of spiritual assignment to fulfil, or when we have a role in helping improve the human lot, he believes that we are gently guided onto a particular path in order to do this. In other words, he was suggesting that not only was it in my best interests not to find the missing dog *but it was also in my best interests to fail*, and fail spectacularly.

With regard to the money dowsing, whilst it is more than acceptable to charge an equitable fee for dowsing services, reflecting the value of the work, using dowsing to *directly* make money or for speculation is another matter. There are those who say categorically that it cannot be done. If you do choose to go down this road, be prepared for it not to turn out as you expected. Certainly in Peter's case he confirmed the episode taught him not to stray outside the scope of water and oil, pronouncing it 'the strangest experience I have ever had in my life'.

Ultimately, there will be an element of trial and error in finding your niche, so enjoy the process of discovery. There will be fields of dowsing that you are naturally drawn to, fields that hold no interest for you and fields that fire your passion or compassion. My best suggestion is that you join a dowsing group and explore all avenues. The British Society of Dowsers is the largest group of its kind in Great Britain, publishes a dowsing journal, supports local groups and meetings around the country and has formed special interest groups, including water dowsing, archaeology, health and Earth energies. When you are starting out, there is nothing like sharing time with like-minded people – and nothing like watching the magic of the dowsing rods at work to fire your enthusiasm and imagination.

Attending dowsing courses, workshops and lectures may also be beneficial. Here you can learn from professionals and also find comfort in learning from other students. The British Society of Dowsers offers an educational programme with a core curriculum from beginner to advanced level. Depending upon how serious you are, you may even be lucky enough to find a professional dowser who will take you on as an apprentice.

Dowsing can also bring a new dimension to your existing profession, hobbies or special interests. But keep an open mind: the sky is the limit with dowsing and you might even pioneer a new field of dowsing application. Whichever route you choose, stay grounded, talk to as many dowsers (professional and amateur) as you can, trust your intuition, follow your passion, always have the courage to *have a* go, process everything through your own truth filter and never, ever let anyone undermine your confidence or convince you that there is only one way – their way – of doing things.

The final words of comfort come straight from Hamish:

> *Dowsers don't have the prerogative of being 100 per cent right. If a businessman gets six decisions right out of ten they're onto a winner – it means that they are only wrong four times out of ten. You have to get this into context. If you can get 90 per cent of your dowsing right, then you are doing extraordinarily well.*

Hamish Miller died in January 2010. A wiser and more humble dowser would be difficult to find.

Chapter Eighteen

IN PURSUIT OF TRUTH

I believe that the focused mind-field has the power to tap into everything going on in the world. Many of us intellectually accept this as true, but our experience does not confirm it, and our brain is so busy with the things of the day that we don't even test it.

Valerie Hunt, PhD, Professor Emeritus UCLA, *Infinite Mind*

Long experience has taught me this about the status of mankind with regard to matters requiring thought: the less people know and understand about them, the more positively they attempt to argue concerning them, while on the other hand to know and understand a multitude of things renders men cautious in passing judgement upon anything new.

Galileo Galilei, Italian astronomer and physicist, *The Assayer*

It is unfortunate that dowsing does not typically respond well to official testing or rise to meet the challenges of experimentation under controlled conditions. As this is one of the biggest and most condemning criticisms of it by mainstream science, in order to raise the credibility of the craft we need to carefully examine the reasons why.

Why is it *perfectly possible* to obtain accurate results in the field, on site, alone or with clients, in both personal and professional situations and when and where there is a genuine need, but frequently fail abjectly when tested under controlled conditions?

There are several significant contributory factors to dowsing's poor performance under scrutiny.

The first is loss of focus. When under stress it is a challenge to remain focused. Being tested in a television studio is the antithesis of a relaxed and calm setting; consequently, even the most focused individual can have their concentration undermined the moment a camera or film crew appears. From personal experience, and despite a previous career filming over 200 television commercials, I find it phenomenally challenging to dowse as television cameras scrutinize my every move. Not apparent to the conscious mind, this scrutiny can intrude very deeply into the subconscious mind, throwing the concentration off and putting the physical body on alert – and dowsing requires the flow of energy through a relaxed and happy body.

There is also the pressure of being *tested*, having to perform and fear of failure. Remember school examinations – the sinking feeling when you first set eyes on the examination paper and the cold panic as your mind went blank? Add to this the emotional need to prove something you believe in, and cool, calm emotional detachment is nigh impossible. All these factors are enough to unsettle the relaxed and happy physical, mental and emotional self that is absolutely essential to dowsing.

The negative impact of disrupted focus on dowsing is verified in a film on YouTube featuring Clive Thompson, ex-President of the British Society of Dowsers, rising to the challenge of proving that dowsing does indeed work. His challenger is the American stage magician and professional debunker James Randi. For years Mr Randi has made a living from the exposure of alleged charlatans, frauds and tricksters. His targets have ranged from spoon benders to the proponents of homoeopathy. He purportedly unmasks those who try to pull the wool over the eyes of the public – a master of trickery exposing the tricksters! He has put up one million dollars for anyone who can show 'under proper observing conditions, evidence of any paranormal, supernatural or occult power or event'. According to him, dowsing fits into this category: it is dismissed in his online newsletter as 'a medieval notion, a crackpot idea, and a phenomenon that has zero evidence to support it'.

But in a paper entitled 'Science versus Showmanship: A History of the Randi Hoax' published in the *Journal of the American Society of Psychical Research* in 1995, psychologist and parapsychologist Michael E. Thalbourne writes:

> ...the magician had (and still has) a reputation among parapsychologists as an unduly vociferous and occa-sionally irrational skeptic possessed of an unfortunate tendency to distort the truth so as to obtain favour-able publicity for himself and his crusade against psi. In short, Randi is a showman rather than an unpreju-diced critic.

To learn why Clive Thompson would valiantly, even recklessly, go head to head with James Randi, I spoke to him at his home in Wales where, at the age of 85, this talented traditional water dowser is still putting down wells with drillers two or three times a week – men who hire him directly and would testify to a near 100 per cent success rate.

Why, I asked, did he even *think* about pitching himself against Mr Randi?

It quickly became evident that the overriding catalyst was Mr Thompson's sense of righteous indignation at having dowsing dismissed as something that did not work when, after over half a century of dedication to the craft, he clearly knew it did. Secondly, he wanted to know why dowsers consistently failed when being tested by Mr Randi. Even after his experience, however, this is still not clear. What *is* evident is the extraordinary way that he was treated. Prior to filming he was kept waiting alone for over two hours in a tiny, cramped room. He was shown the studio set-up and returned to his room, and then, when he was invited back out to film, he found everything was set up in a completely different way. By that point, he told me, his mind was already full of doubt and he was thinking, *What the devil is going on?*

Surprised, confused and disorientated, with little information and no support, he felt unable to concentrate and, in his own words, 'not in a fit condition' to dowse.

Not surprisingly, his dowsing performance suffered. He located the object of the search, a piece of zinc ore, on the third attempt, leading James Randi to proclaim that this was no better than what would be expected by chance. Coincidentally, his last words to Mr Thompson before the experiment began were: 'We'd expect you to locate the zinc ore sample by your third or fourth attempt.' Was this a coincidence? Or is award-winning magician James Randi trained in using the power of suggestion?

With regard to the careless treatment of Mr Thompson, perhaps this is standard in a television studio? I spoke to an ABC Television producer in New York, who assured me that nothing could be further from the truth. She explained that everything possible is done to put the guests at ease: they are briefed thoroughly beforehand, given regular updates and kept waiting for a minimum time – all with the simple aim of getting the best out of them.

It would be very easy for a cynic to conclude that James Randi used deliberate psychological techniques in order to disorientate Mr Thompson and disrupt his sense of focus. But what is relevant here is how Mr Thompson felt after his experience. His answer was immediate and simple.

I felt I'd been tricked.

As we have said before, to be composed, relaxed and fully able to focus is absolutely fundamental to the dowsing process.

The second contributory factor in dowsing failing to respond to testing is ego. As we have seen, when we are dowsing we are connecting through consciousness to the information field or A-field. The moment the ego gets the upper hand, our alignment with consciousness is compromised, we enter a negative or low-consciousness state and our dowsing suffers accordingly. Those who try to prove the principle of dowsing through ego – as in 'I'm going to be the one to prove you wrong' – will invariably fail. You cannot apply the laws of truth under the jurisdiction of ego.

An illustration of this comes through the kinesiological assessment of the levels of consciousness in Dr David R. Hawkins' book *Power versus Force*. His scale of consciousness runs from one to 1,000. He states:

> *The scale of consciousness may be seen in one aspect as a scale of ego, with the level of 200 being the point where selfishness begins to turn to selflessness...*
>
> *Through kinesiology, we can demonstrate that if one is motivated by any of the energy fields below Courage (200), one goes weak. The notorious Achilles' heel that brings down not just athletes but the potentially great in all areas of human achievement is pride. Pride, calibrated at 175, not only makes the performer go weak, but it can't provide the motivational power of love, honour or dedication to a higher principle.*

So, proving that dowsing works from the motivation of personal ambition, rather than the desire to restore the honour or principle of dowsing, will not work! Although it was transparently evident that Clive Thompson's motives were entirely honourable and dedicated to a higher principle, his challenger was clearly the shrewder showman.

Which brings us to the third contributory factor detrimental to the testing of dowsing under controlled conditions: the potentially negative input from the instigators, organizers or witnesses. This is not to say that they consciously or deliberately influence the dowers, but their negative intent may do so without them realizing.

We know that scientific research has determined that the negative (or positive) intent of one person can significantly affect, at close proximity or at distance, both the autonomic and the central nervous systems of another. Author Dean Radin speaks of this research in his books *Entangled Minds* and *The Conscious Universe*, and Lynne McTaggart details experiments in her book *The Intention Experiment*. In his book *It's the Thought That Counts* Dr David Hamilton confirms that scientific experiments have shown that distant influencing or intent can also affect the growth of brain cells, the reduction of blood pressure and the rate of the bursting of hypertonic (salty) blood cells *even when the influencers and their targets are in different locations*. In the process of my work, both by direct observation and from the accounts of my clients, I have also been made aware of the momentous effect that the projection of positive and negative intent can have on the physical, mental and emotional well-being of another.

Whilst dowsing, we are functioning in the mode of a powerful and highly sensitive transceiver, transmitting and receiving information on an energetic level locally and at distance and negotiating a vastly complex matrix of energies. Dowsers have to have the grounding, training, experience and level of consciousness (or thick skin!) to minimize *unwanted or disruptive* outside influences and to maintain a finely tuned balance of their physical and energetic bodies, or *mind-field* as identified by Dr Valerie Hunt.

So in what form, and from what source, might this negative input come? In this extract from his book *Entangled Minds*, Dean Radin is referring to psi phenomena in general:

> In spite of the evidence, many remain skeptical. There is nothing wrong with this attitude; doubt is healthy. But extreme skepticism is another matter. This is not the place to examine the psychology of hyper-skepticism, but it's difficult to overlook the fact that fanatically skeptical groups seem to be motivated more by anger and cynicism rather than by a dispassionate search for the truth.

In other words, in the dowsing tests instigated, organized or administrated by sceptics, *we are not starting with a level playing field*. Many of those who set out to prove that dowsing does not work do not have the capacity to remain dispassionate. At the heart of their quests are often very powerful emotions – cynicism, ridicule, anger, hostility, derision and even fear. As a result, there is always the potential that their prevailing field of intent will be disruptive to the dowser's intention and attention.

A second notable clip on YouTube features a series of dowsing tests administered by Chris French, Professor of Psychology at Goldsmiths, University of London. The tests contributed to a television series entitled *The Enemies of Reason* released by evolutionary biologist Professor Richard Dawkins. In the clip, a group of volunteer dowsers is put through scientifically designed double-blind tests in order to identify the location of a single plastic bottle of water from five plastic bottles filled with sand. All the bottles are hidden underneath plastic bins. It constitutes a double-blind test, as neither the dowsers nor Professor French knows the location of the bottle of water.

As the dowsers systematically fail, their shock is palpable. The film once again shows that dowsing results from testing undertaken in artificial and controlled conditions are unlikely to exceed those at mean chance expectation.

In fact, when I spoke to Professor French at Goldsmiths he confirmed that the final results were *exactly chance level*. When I then asked him if the results reflected what he had expected to find under controlled conditions, he said, 'Absolutely.' In other words, not only did he not expect positive results but he had also made up his mind even *before the experiment had begun*.

I am not suggesting that Professor French's sceptical preemptive intent was the only factor in the failure of the dowsers to meet the challenge – if I did I would be culpable of the same state of denial or delusion that Professor Dawkins observes of the dowsers. But I do believe it to be a majorly significant factor: if trials are administered by sceptics and we are dealing with the transmission of energetic information, *how controlled can the conditions really be?*

Am I being unfair in labelling Professor French as a sceptic? I don't think so. He is the editor of *Skeptic Magazine*, 'the UK's only regular magazine to take a skeptical approach to paranormal issues'.

My conversation with Professor French turned out to be more valuable than I had ever imagined. By far the most revealing fact was his perception of the basics of dowsing: he believes that dowsing is nothing more than an example of the *ideomotor effect*, a known psychological phenomenon where a subject makes motions unconsciously, the body reacting reflexively to ideas without the person consciously deciding to take action or (usually) realizing that their actions are originating solely from within themselves. The ideomotor effect is often utilized in hypnosis and neuro-linguistic programming (NLP) to set up a feedback method with a client's unconscious mind. A system of physical signals such as finger signals or blinking is used to enable the unconscious mind to give answers.

And so Professor French believes that *a dowser unconsciously moves the dowsing tool themselves!*

When I heartily agreed and said that of course dowsers know that *their own* minute involuntary muscular reactions move their arms and wrists, resulting in the subsequent movement of the dowsing tool, I simply wasn't prepared for his rejoinder.

'Not the dowsers I've spoken to,' he said. 'They put it down to *some mysterious outside force.*'

Unfortunately, this misconception was confirmed by the film clip of Professor French's experiment. When asked by Professor Dawkins how he achieved his results, one of the dowsers replied, 'I think some *thing* is helping me to dowse.' A second dowser elucidated, 'I think the question, and I expect God to respond in a way I understand.' Sadly, his dowsing failed spectacularly. But for sheer entertainment value, when he was asked *why* by the arch-atheist professor, you have to marvel at his daring response: 'It's God having His laugh, isn't it?' And, pointing heavenwards with his dowsing rod, he concluded, 'He loves a joke...'

These sorts of examples give self-proclaimed sceptics like James Randi and Professor French plenty of ammunition to debunk dowsing. A lack of understanding of the mechanics of the craft even by some dowsers means that the sceptics can have a field day. They believe they are really onto something when the arms, hands and/or wrists of the dowser can quite clearly be seen to be moving, thus tipping and moving the dowsing rods in turn. Dowsers are saying that an outside force is moving the dowsing tool and the sceptics are falling over laughing, saying, 'But I can see your arms move!' This is pointed out, somewhat hilariously, in the film clip featuring Clive Thompson and James Randi. When Clive Thompson is dowsing live on camera, arrows are superimposed on the film, pointing to his arm with a caption saying, 'His own arm movements cause the rotation of the dowsing rod,' and, 'Notice the elbow and shoulder movement.'

This, to the sceptics, is evidence that dowsers are in denial and deluded, and as long as this fundamental misunderstanding of how dowsing works persists, dowsers will always be hapless fodder for exploitation. This is why it is so important for the dowsing community to achieve some coherence in its methodologies and for dowsers to research their subject.

My conversation with Professor French revealed further insights. He confirmed that no vetting procedure was carried out to establish the track record or competence of the dowsers involved in the experiment; rather, they had been recruited on a volunteer basis from adverts in the media, on the radio and online. On being questioned, he admitted he also had no idea if any of them were full-time professionals – but doubted they were.

When I asked him why he thought that dowsing did not perform well in tests under controlled conditions when dowsers were able to obtain extraordinarily accurate results in a professional working situation, his reply was a simple: 'But do they?' The examples I quoted were dismissed with ease. Of the track record of George Applegate (of whom he had never heard), he said that water dowsers pick up their clues from the landscape; of the scope and successes of the Russian dowsers working with the police and military authorities, he said they might *believe* they were being helpful, but in reality they were not; and of Russia's practice of setting dowsing examinations and awarding qualifications, which by definition would involve testing, he said that the examinations didn't necessarily have any value.

Rather than accepting the final word of Professor French, I decided to speak directly to the world-renowned Russian scientist Dr Konstantin Korotkov. This accomplished man is Professor of Computer Science and Biophysics at Saint Petersburg Federal University of Informational Technologies, Mechanics and Optics, Deputy Director of Saint Petersburg Federal Research Institute of Physical Culture and a member of the Federal Russian University Scientific Board on new medical technologies. He has led a research career for over 30 years, published some 200 papers, written seven books and given lectures, seminars and training sessions in 43 countries. He also holds 15 patents on biophysics inventions and has pioneered the Gas Discharge Visualization (GDV) technology, which is described as the first device in the world that measures the distribution of energy levels of biological objects and is used by doctors and practitioners worldwide.

He is also a dowser.

I asked Dr Korotkov how it was possible for educational establishments in Russia to train dowsers and award qualifications, as this, by definition, would involve testing under the controlled conditions that appeared to be their very downfall. He replied:

In Russia we are able to give people training. Dowsing, as any other human talent or human potential, should be trained, and then it may be tested under controlled conditions. So we have tests and testing for dowsers, and anyone can do it. In Russia dowsing is a very well established, respectable line. From our point of view, any special or psychic abilities may be trained and tested.

So why does dowsing consistently fail to exceed chance-expected average, particularly when tested by those with a sceptical viewpoint?

> *It is known from our instruments that any psychic ability immensely depends on the environment. So if people are in a friendly, supportive environment then they can achieve their best. If people are in a very negative environment, then they can even lose their potential. In our experiments we can prove dowsing many times but it has been shown that it strongly depends on the condition of the particular person: in one mood or condition a person can be very precise, in another mood, they may do nothing.*

I asked Dr Korotkov how he thought it might be possible to improve dowsing's reputation and the negative perspective of mainstream science. He replied:

> *It is not an instant process because we have a high level of scepticism in society – mostly scientific society – which is very difficult to overcome in a short time. In science we need repeatable experiments done in a very strict protocol, which is very time- and resource-consuming. And this is not an area of public interest!*

The Gas Discharge Visualization (GDV) technology pioneered by Dr Korotkov and his team is the result of 20 years of research. A special camera has the ability to capture living energy fields in direct real-time viewing. Not just human energy fields, but also the physical, emotional, mental and spiritual energy emanating from all living beings, plants, liquids and inanimate objects. More technologically advanced than Kirlian photography, the camera's operation is based on the stimulation of very weak photon and electron emissions. It operates on the quantum level and can provide quantum-field information about a human or plant and their biological functions. The resulting image, captured instantly on a computer, can be analysed using software in a variety of ways.

Dr Korotkov indicated that the incredible implications for the diagnosis and treatment of physical, emotional, mental and spiritual conditions are only just being realized, and the applications in medicine, psychology, biophysics, genetics, forensic science, agriculture and ecology have only just begun. So I asked him if he had ever monitored the energy fields of a dowser whilst they were in the process of dowsing. He said:

> *We have done many tests with a particular profes-*
> *sional dowser and he can demonstrate very stable*
> *results – practically a 100 per cent correlation. He*
> *can change his own condition (consciousness) and we*
> *can measure this with the GDV machine. Professional*
> *dowsers go into an altered state of consciousness the*
> *very moment they start to dowse. And we can detect*
> *this specific condition in our camera. With this pro-*
> *fessional dowser we can detect it virtually every time*
> *we do the experiments.*
>
> *We have new equipment that allows us to measure*
> *the change of space and environmental conditions*
> *under the influence of strong emotion and the psychic*
> *process. When people are dowsing, they transform*
> *and alter their state of consciousness. Our new sen-*
> *sor is very sensitive. It shows that when people trans-*
> *form their consciousness,* particularly in the process
> of dowsing, *they also change the environment around*
> *their location.*

Dr Korotkov concluded our interview by extending an enticing invitation for me to visit Russia in order to be tested with their equipment, whilst dowsing, under laboratory conditions.

Because of its complex nature and the variables involved, proving the unquestionable benefits of dowsing is always going to be a challenge. However, tests and trials, large and small scale, undertaken with dowsers around the world have successfully demonstrated results *higher* than chance expectation.

Russian research apart, by far the largest dowsing project – and the most ambitious – appears to be the government-sponsored research undertaken in the 1980s by the German physicist Professor Hans-Dieter Betz. It spanned a period of ten years and involved over 2,000 drillings exploring innovative water-detection methods in arid regions. The research was initially carried out in Sri Lanka; due to its outstanding success it was then extended to nine further countries, including Egypt, Kenya, Namibia, Yemen and the Philippines.

Initiated by the German government via the German Association for Technical Cooperation (GTZ), the project teamed geological experts with experienced dowsers and a scientific group led by Professor Betz, which monitored and evaluated the results. The final reports were published in the peer-reviewed *Journal of Scientific Exploration* in 1995 and they make riveting reading.

The sheer enormity of the project renders report conclusions complex and multipart, but these excerpts, highlighting the indisputable facts that emerged, are an extremely positive testimony to dowsing:

- A few carefully selected dowsers are certainly able to detect faults, fissures and fractures with relative alacrity and surprising accuracy.
- So far, neither critical consideration of all possible objections nor attempts at reasoning have yielded a conventional explanation for the persistent success of the dowsing technique – an outcome which has been corroborated by a number of specifically designed control experiments and comparative tests.
- Provided that certain conditions are met, the results obtained show the dowsing technique to be a serious alternative for groundwater prospecting.

- The effectiveness of locating ground water in certain hydro-geological situations could be raised significantly if conventionally organized operating teams were to make additional use of appropriately tested and selected dowsers in order to pinpoint drilling spots.
- The techniques of conventional hydrologists yielded results of between 30 and 50 per cent; where dowsers were included in the process, the success rate shot up to between 80 and 96 per cent.

On one occasion, Professor Betz placed a particularly proficient dowser, Hans Schröter, in direct competition with a hydro-geologist and his collaborating expert team. Their brief was to pinpoint drilling spots yielding more than 100 litres of water per minute in the same geographical area. The conventional team took several weeks to pinpoint 14 drilling spots by using modern hydro-geological methods, geo-electrical procedures, maps and aerial photographs. The dowser took a few days and pinpointed seven drilling spots. The drilling of all 21 positions began. In all cases the same drilling team used the same drilling technique and the same criteria.

Hans Schröter won hands down. Six out of his seven drilling points exceeded the target, in comparison with only three out of the 14 determined by the conventional technique. Altogether, with a success rate of 86 per cent, the dowser significantly surpassed the 21 per cent result obtained with the conventional method.

Professor Betz summed up:

> There are two things that I am certain of after ten years of field research. A combination of dowsing and modern hydro-geophysical techniques can be both more successful and far less expensive than we had thought. And we need to run a lot more tests, because we have established that dowsing works, but have no idea how or why.

A second project, known as the Munich Project, ran for two years. One double-blind experiment, which was carried out in the laboratory rather than in the field, took place on two floors of a barn. Dowsers were asked to walk a ten-metre course on the top floor and, by using dowsing techniques, identify the location of specially constructed water pipes concealed on the ground floor below. Professor Betz reports that the success rate for this contrived laboratory experiment was disappointingly low:

> The experiences gained from the Munich Project have repeatedly revealed that certain artificial test situations, such as the attempts to locate pipes or other (small) objects, do not yield notable success rates and, therefore, must be rejected as general qualifying tests for dowsers. In particular, one should strictly refute 'tests' that are allegedly designed to prove the principal existence or non-existence of the dowsing phenomenon... Certain biased 'skeptics' often produce some turmoil by publicizing experiments in which naïve and self-appointed dowsers have to pass all sorts of unrealistic tests, such as the location of hidden coins or other small objects – tests that, for a long time, have been well-known to lead to failure, especially when high success rates have been aimed at.

These observations of Professor Betz and the importance of training stressed by Dr Korotkov highlight a weakness in the 'research' instigated by those purporting to establish the validity of dowsing. However much the sceptics may argue that their attempts are sincere and unprejudiced, this has to be questionable if they do not use trained professional dowsers with established track records.

For anyone who is *genuinely* interested in examining the validity of dowsing, this process will only be equitable if the experiments are conducted in a benign environment, are administered by those with truly impartial and open minds, and are undertaken with professional dowsers who have established a level of competence. Any other way leaves dowsing still vulnerable to a distortion of the truth.

Speaking of truth, there is one more factor to consider. If the dowsing process is fundamentally an alignment with Truth, and Truth is by its very essence self-existent and All That Is, by definition how can it be possible to *test* it…?

Nonetheless, with Dr Korotkov's protocol more than meeting the above criteria, in order to help demonstrate the validity of dowsing, I for one will be packing my bags and booking a flight to Russia…

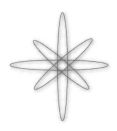

CHAPTER NINETEEN

UNQUESTIONABLE BENEFITS

How strange is the lot of us mortals! Each of us is here for
a brief sojourn; for what purpose he knows not, though he
sometimes thinks he senses it. But without deeper reflection
one knows from daily life that one exists for other people –
first of all for those upon whose smiles and well-being our
own happiness is wholly dependent, and then for the many,
unknown to us, to whose destinies we are bound by the ties of
sympathy.
Albert Einstein

In a gentle way you can shake the world.
Mahatma Gandhi

In his address to the British Society of Dowsers in 1993, Professor Alexander Dubrov touched on something of great significance. In accordance with Professor Hans-Dieter Betz, he explained that it was on the occasions when dowsers and professionals in their chosen fields combined their skills that the most accurate and effective results were achieved.

The key to maximizing successful results in dowsing is either pooling your abilities with skilled professionals (in any field) or, as Hamish Miller briskly pointed out, by being a specialist in your own chosen field. Water dowser George Applegate's staggering track record of a less than 1 per cent failure rate across more than 2,500 borehole sites identified and explored is due in no small part to the fact that he is a qualified geologist and engineer. He explained, 'Before I go on site I study geological maps, and I won't put a borehole down unless I'm satisfied that the geology will support the water and the quality of the water is going to be reasonably good.'

My own dowsing abilities are applied in the fields of health and environmental energies. Specifically, I work as a *causative diagnostician*, identifying the *causative, contributory* and *trigger* factors behind a previously diagnosed disorder or a set of symptoms that has no label. These are often cases where, for example, a doctor is unable to determine the root cause of a condition or is simply under pressure with limited time to do the detective work to identify it. As a result, the symptoms are treated with pharmaceutical products, but the underlying cause(s) often remains unaddressed.

My transition from the spectrum of environmental and subtle energies to the specifics of causative diagnosis was driven by demand from clients. It evolved gradually, but the day I visited a lovely young woman in a leafy London square was the catalyst. Her charming flat was at the top of a large stucco-fronted Georgian house. After ten years in residence she loved it overall, but despite redecoration and every attempt to lighten the atmosphere and energy, she *loathed* the bedroom, only going there when it was absolutely necessary. Intelligent and with an intuitive awareness, it frustrated her that she couldn't put her finger on *why*.

Dowsing immediately revealed a strong line of electro-magnetic pollution running through the middle of her bedroom – and her bed. This was swiftly dealt with, along with several other energetic anomalies, and her home restored to a safe and healthy place. Afterwards, over coffee, we chatted about other health concerns. Suddenly she asked me, 'So, did the electromagnetic pollution cause my cancer then?'

This was the first mention of any previous cancer and in truth I hadn't a clue. But my keenness to help and an overwhelming curiosity to know the truth drove me forward. Formulating careful questions I dowsed that, no, the electromagnetic pollution had not been the *cause* of her cancer. But it had been a *contributory factor*.

Her starkly simple comeback was about to shake my world – and change the course of my career.

'So what *did* cause my cancer then?'

Spurred on by her faith in my abilities, I carefully worked through a mental list of substances and conditions that I knew to be carcinogenic. Every dowsing response was negative until I reached the group of chemicals that are found in hair dyes. Immediately the dowsing rods reacted with force. Glancing up at the client, I took in her long, glossy, *naturally* dark hair. My logical mind kicked in: this simply couldn't be correct.

Eventually, and very reluctantly, I said, 'Umm, I'm getting that it's something to do with the chemicals involved in hair dying. Have you ever dyed your hair?'

Her hand covered her mouth in shock. She told me that she had dyed her hair for four years, only stopping after the onset of the cancer. The main causative factor in her cancer was a group of carcinogenic chemicals in hair dye. Further analysis by dowsing suggested that, along with the electromagnetic pollution, chemical toxins and aluminium compounds from her deodorant were also a contributory factor. The *trigger factor* had been sustained emotional stress from a difficult close relationship.

In the weeks after our meeting she told me that simply witnessing the dowsing process had been deeply moving, reminding her of something that she instinctively knew: the existence of an omniscient and benevolent field of intelligence. The information dowsing provided had changed her life. Understanding the different underlying causative factors involved enabled her to move forward with confidence, knowing which lifestyle factors had to be addressed and changed. Rather than battling with an unknown enemy, she felt back in control. With the fear of the unknown removed, she was able to develop positive expectations for the future. This, perhaps, was the most profound step because *fear in itself* can become an extremely potent driving factor in ill-health and disease.

The health disorders with which clients approach me for a consultation vary enormously, but inevitably they are those disorders and symptoms that repetitively dog the headlines of our daily newspapers: cancer, ME (chronic fatigue syndrome), IBS (irritable bowel syndrome), allergies and sensitivities, insomnia or exhaustion, digestive disorders, skin conditions (urticaria), immune system disorders – asthma, eczema, rheumatoid arthritis – or sets of symptoms that don't fit comfortably under any orthodox label. The conditions are usually those where the search for 'a cure' continues, despite the fact that they are invariably of a *chronic metabolic nature* and where the means to restore health has been known to holistic practitioners for many years. And they rarely have one causative factor but a potent combination of several, resulting in the crucial tipping of the equilibrium of health.

It is important to stress that I am not *diagnosing* disease or conditions – in most countries this remains illegal without recognizable medical qualifications – but *determining the causative factors behind them.* With the information I provide, the client has the means to address the imbalances in the environment of the body, thus facilitating the body's innate healing.

In his book *Quantum Healing*, Dr Deepak Chopra states: 'Recent surveys taken in England and America have shown that as many as 80 per cent of patients feel that their underlying complaint, their reason for going to the doctor, was not satisfactorily resolved when they left his office.' Once the root causative factors are known, treatment ceases to be a lottery and becomes a carefully tailored plan that is in *the client's best interests.* Furthermore, having access to this key information empowers the client: they no longer feel they are battling with an unknown enemy in their body, but instead can recognize it for the wake-up call that it is and move forward, confident they can help address and prevent the likelihood of the condition returning.

And, in agreement with Professor Dubrov, I believe the best results are obtained when dowser and practitioner work together. I work with, and in support of, qualified health practitioners, whether they are from allopathic or holistic sectors. Doctors and therapists most often refer clients to me when they have exhausted their skills, options or lines of enquiry, or suspect that what they are dealing with is outside their field of experience. Electro-stress, geopathic stress and other subtle energies would fall within this category.

Once I have identified the underlying causative and contributory factors, I then individually prepare a 'checklist' of everything that needs to be addressed. At this point, the referrals frequently go the other way, as I determine the optimal resources – whether they be a doctor, practitioner, course of treatment, process or product – for my client, giving them the best possible opportunity of a return to balanced health. Quite simply, it would be impossible to achieve the resulting turnarounds in health that I do without the skills, patience and open minds of the practitioners, in a broad cross-section of disciplines, to whom I refer my clients. These experienced and highly skilled professionals subsequently address the causative factors that dowsing has identified.

To illustrate the powerful benefits of dowsing in identifying underlying causative factors, I have chosen two case studies from the many hundreds of consultations I have undertaken over the years. In each case, the application of dowsing improved the client's well-being and quality of life. Many of the details are extremely personal, so out of respect for my clients' privacy, I have chosen to keep their names confidential.

Client A

Client A contacted me after being diagnosed with haemochro-matosis, with symptoms manifesting as chronic fatigue. Medical opinion states that haemochromatosis is an inherited or genetic disorder of iron metabolism that causes the body to absorb and store an excess amount of iron. If left untreated, it can result in the progressive accumulation of iron in the liver, pancreas, heart, joints and pituitary gland, leading to potentially serious complications. The objectives of treatment are to remove excess iron from the body and prevent organ damage.

Orthodox medicine's approach in this case consisted of therapeutic phlebotomy (bloodletting) every week until the iron levels returned to the normal range. My client's blood ferritin levels were in the range of 1,100 to 1,200. His consultant wanted to see them below 100. The hospital also told my client that haemochromatosis was a genetic disorder, that there was no cure, only management, and that periodic phlebotomy to control the iron levels would be necessary *for the rest of his life*.

The consultation took place by telephone. Dowsing immediately pinpointed that the client's immune function was currently a low 24 per cent and his body's alkaline/acid ratio was completely out of balance, so I worked on identifying the causative and contributory factors behind this. High levels of metals, including mercuric compounds from pharmaceutical and dietary sources, sustained emotional and mental stress and an extraordinary and puzzlingly high level of unknown chemicals were identified. When I asked if he knew of any chemicals he might have been exposed to, he reluctantly admitted that he was undertaking an extensive hair restoration programme involving oral preparations and a chemical treatment for the scalp. In addition, he had been topically applying a well-known hair restoration product on and off for 20 years.

Dowsing then identified a checklist of items, which included a detox procedure to clear metals and toxic chemicals from the body, a natural product to promote the alkaline levels in the body, a full nutritional programme and a referral to a holistic practitioner to clear all remaining toxic substances and restore the health of the liver.

The client continued the phlebotomy programme for one year. The ferritin levels slowly began to decrease. During year two, when the holistic practitioner was still continuing to restore the damage done by the toxic chemicals, he had only three further phlebotomies, in the February, May and September. Before each of them a blood test was taken. These samples showed that *before* any phlebotomy was done, his ferritin readings had maintained levels below 100, even over a period of five months, in one case dropping to 79. The nurse expressed surprise that the levels were so low, saying that she would have expected them to rise between treatments. Over the next few months, the readings maintained a level of 79.

The hospital remains pleased – but surprised – by Client A's progress. His last ferritin level reading was 68 *without any treatment,* so it would seem that no more phlebotomies are necessary and he told me, 'The hospital staff don't want me back in a hurry!' In addition, apart from observations by family and friends that he looks well, he holds down two jobs, leads a full and healthy life and his immune function has been restored to a very respectable 77 per cent – a quantum jump of over 50 per cent.

Client B

Client B saw me in my London office. Her opening line, 'I know the location, the opening times and the length of queue of every public lavatory inside the M25,' would have been funny had it not barely masked her quiet desperation. As a married woman with three children she was struggling to maintain her life due to the frequent need for lavatory visits, in her words 'just to pass blood'. Daily life had lost all semblance of normality as everything had to be planned around these visits. During the worst times, they peaked at *15 a day.*

Her symptoms had begun in 2001. The initial diagnosis had been inconclusive, the gastroenterologist considering haemorrhoids or ulcerative colitis. He had settled for haemorrhoids. Over the next six years, Client B had been on a rollercoaster ride of symptoms, diagnoses, treatment and varying periods of remission. Several courses of steroids had produced 'horrendous and disgusting' side-effects, but the condition had not responded. Finally she had turned to acupuncture and, for the first time, enjoyed a sustained period of remission. But in November 2006 the symptoms had returned and this time had not responded to acupuncture. She had resorted to a 'massive dose' of steroids in February 2007, which had helped, but by the time she came to see me six months later, the symptoms had returned. According to the medical opinion that she had received, she had ulcerative colitis and it was a genetic condition. But Client B was tired of measures that simply treated the symptoms, only for them to return. She was now ready to explore the underlying causes.

Dowsing, I took all the relevant health readings and then worked to identify the main causative factors behind the ulcerative colitis. There were four:

1. Raised levels of toxins (metals) within the body. These included mercuric compounds from pharmaceutical products and vaccines, and aluminium from personal care and beauty products, pharmaceuticals and vaccines.
2. Two parasites in the body, one of which was dormant, one semi-active.
3. Significant nutritional deficiencies, particularly of potassium and selenium, resulting from compromised absorption rates due to toxins within the body.
4. Mental and emotional stress from personal issues.

I put together an extensive checklist to restore the balance of the body. (Not being a qualified medical practitioner, I am not legally permitted to claim that I can do more than *restore balance* – and I am certainly not allowed to suggest that I 'cure' in any way.) The checklist included the detoxing of heavy metals, a referral to a holistic practitioner to eliminate the parasites from the body (plus the viruses and fungal imbalance that dowsing also identi-fied), a full nutritional programme and measures to address the mental and emotional stress.

Undoubtedly, the credit in this case lies with the extra-ordinarily skilled holistic practitioner who took on the case and with Client B herself, who threw herself into the programme with determination and trust. From this point onwards, my role was mainly limited to the monitoring of health readings to ensure she responded positively to the checklist suggestions. These I monitored first on a weekly basis, then subsequently on a monthly basis, by information dowsing at distance. They can be seen in Appendix II.

We communicated occasionally by email. Six months later, in February 2008, only partway through the treatment plan, she informed the practitioner she had 'no signs of the ulcerative colitis at all' and was enjoying 'the best health I have had for well over a year'. However, given her history, I was keen to monitor her readings for a full year.

After 13 months, with the treatment plan completed and the health readings looking particularly positive, I telephoned her for a consultation catch-up. While health readings might appear to be outstanding, the only thing that really counts is how the client perceives themselves to be. Client B told me, 'I am totally, utterly symptom-free. It is extraordinary – even the little things that were wrong are now better. And it is not just the difference you have made to my life, but also the difference you have made to the quality of life of my whole family.' She explained that she no longer needed to plan her day around the constant anticipation of the unexpected, but was able to live life normally, free of the fear that had affected her for so long.

In both examples I suggest that if the causative factors had been identified at the time of diagnosis, treatment plans could have been instigated conducive to minimizing further and unnecessary damage to the body and distress to the clients and their families.

Far-reaching Benefits

The unquestionable benefits of health dowsing are not limited to these types of examples. Sometimes the information given is more far-reaching and perhaps from a more intangible realm, but with no less value for the human condition. These instances are often beyond the technological sophistication of advanced medical testing.

It was 9:30 in the evening when I walked past my office door and heard the telephone. I would never normally answer at that time, especially not when I have just enjoyed a large and very fragrant bowl of pasta and am partway through a second glass of wine. Why I picked up the phone I don't know – perhaps it was that fateful *something*.

The young woman's voice was calm and measured as she introduced herself. She gave no hint of any unfolding drama, and while I sensed she had a big story to tell, I was not prepared for what came next: a few days earlier her brother had stepped under a London tube train. He was still alive and there were no amputations, but there was severe damage to his head and he was in a coma. The medical team looking after him wasn't hopeful and switching off his life-support system was a very real consideration.

The woman told me her brother was an internationally known and respected figure – a hugely well-liked, kind and gentle person. He had, however, experienced enormous challenges with personal and family issues and more recently had found simply coping with life extremely difficult. As a result, he had been taking a cocktail of at least seven pharmaceutical drugs for depression and anxiety. The day of the incident he had attended an appointment with a psychiatrist and then afterwards, in a very out of character move, had been for a drink before making his way to the tube station.

After his admission to the hospital's intensive care unit, no one really knew what to do or which way to turn. But his sister felt that if they were going to be able to improve his chances of survival, time was of the essence: she needed answers to her questions and she needed them now. Was it deliberate? Could her brother hear what she and the family were saying, despite being in a coma? What was the best plan of action? How could they optimize his chances? Most vitally, *was he going to survive?*

My mind suddenly focused with a sharp clarity and the dowsing rods swung into action. Accessing several levels of consciousness at the same time, including his mind-field, his personal Akashic record, his guides and protectors and, with their express permission, his soul level, I began to ask questions.

No, it wasn't a deliberate suicide attempt. His actions had come about as a result of the balance of his mind being disturbed. Yes – absolutely yes – he could hear all that they were saying to him and he knew of their love and support. Was he going to survive? *He hadn't decided yet…*

Through dowsing it was explained that, although he was in a coma, his consciousness was still very much active. At this level he was examining his options and, exercising free will, was in the process of deciding whether to resume his life in the world, with its very real challenges, or whether to move on. That this would be *his* decision, and his decision alone, made at soul level, was made abundantly clear. If he decided to opt out and move on, this would bring its own set of challenges and the prospect of facing and resolving similar life experiences again at some point in the future. Deciding to stay would need superhuman courage and tenacity. But it was crucially important that everyone involved understood that he would make the decision that was right for him and his personal journey.

His sister asked me if there was anything that they could do to support him in the decision-making process. The answer was yes and, through dowsing, I was given a very specific set of instructions. These included bringing his young children to the hospital to 'talk' to him and, very explicitly, that any words of comfort and encouragement must not be general assurances of love and care, but clearly defined practical support. Dowsing then suggested what this might be.

As I replaced the receiver I took a few moments to recover whilst pondering on the extraordinariness of life. I couldn't help wondering what course this man would take.

A few days later, the woman telephoned again. I was surprised to hear from her so quickly; perhaps there were more questions? In her measured and calm voice she told me she had just returned from a meeting at the hospital with her brother's medical team. The consultant had told her that, in their business, they didn't use the word 'miraculous' lightly, but there had been a miracle.

Her brother had made his decision.

He had regained consciousness. He was lucid, but his conscious mind remembered nothing of the incident. The long road back to rehabilitation had begun.

Solving Mysteries

Where health dowsing really comes into its own is in solving mysteries, specifically those to which Father Jean Jurion referred, those he thought *practically impossible to solve* because doctors had given up on them. Sets of symptoms that have no orthodox 'label'; a seemingly unrelated array of complaints that don't match any medical diagnosis; mysterious manifestations such as sudden hair loss, unexplained skin outbreaks; unsolved allergies and intolerances, sustained exhaustion, insomnia, headaches... The list is endless.

How invaluable would it be to the patient – and doctor – to reveal quickly, incisively and inexpensively the root cause of these mysteries? Including dowsing in the diagnostic process would mean that solving these cases would no longer be a shot in the dark. Solutions that are fast and inexpensive would be pinpointed, bringing relief to the patient and preventing further distress and damage to the body, avoiding the dispensing and prohibitive costs of unnecessary pharmaceutical products, reducing expenditure for overstretched health authorities and freeing up medical staff and resources for the administration of more urgent and major medical cases – a win–win situation. Surely these are compelling enough reasons to wholeheartedly embrace the inclusion of dowsing? The doctors win, the patients win and the government health budgets win!

Out of hundreds of my own cases, a few memorable ones spring to mind: the client with a swollen and gaseous stomach every time she drank her favourite tea – the cause being the chemicals used in the paper teabag manufacturing process. The client with sporadic insomnia – brought on when she ate wheat products containing pesticides. The client with an inflamed neck rash and distended face and eyes – resulting from chemicals in the manufacture of his jumper. The client with an inexplicable and painful inflammation over her whole body, making taking showers and baths excruciating. Exhaustive allergy tests and exploration over months by both medical teams and Rentokil staff (to rule out the possibility of an infestation of fleas, lice or parasites) revealed nothing. Dowsing solved this *in one session* by identifying an extreme reaction to the high levels of chlorine in London tap water.

With allergies, not only can dowsing quickly and exactly identify the culprit factors, but it can also determine whether the reaction is a genuine allergy or an intolerance or sensitivity. A client writes:

> *A blood test identified over 25 problem foods that I was told I would have to avoid for the rest of my life. Elizabeth was able to not only identify to which foods I was intolerant, sensitive or actually allergic, but also to distinguish whether it was the food itself I was reacting to or the pesticides, herbicides and toxins within it. I am delighted to have logic brought to the weird list of foods and also a timeline to enable me to reintroduce them and get back to a normal life! Within four months, I have lost a stone of excess weight and brought my liver function tests and cholesterol back to normal.*

And there is obviously an overwhelming need for this type of *causative* diagnosis. Consider this case, where the set of symptoms could only be classified by medical tests as 'chronic stomach spasms'. The testimonial comes from my client's husband, who was initially doubtful of the dowsing process, especially as it had taken place via a telephone consultation:

> *My view on my wife's recovery is one of amazement – from being at an all-time low, the transformation*

was miraculous. She was hospitalized with extremely severe nausea, vomiting and chronic stomach spasms; she suffered lack of energy and concentration, a general feeling of apathy and being very down. All sorts of tests were carried out, to no avail. She saw a gastro‑ enterologist and had a colonoscopy, ultrasound, CT scan and blood tests. She visited a kinesiologist, clinical nutritionist, homoeopath and acupuncturist. She had a barium meal, X-rays, and blood samples taken for parasites – all of which had been done previously and returned as 'normal'. There were times when I thought no one could continue to endure the stress and physical pain she was having to. I don't think that doctors and friends knew just what she was having to endure. Fortunately, thanks to Elizabeth, she is back to her old self, and I'm sure that the hellish three years are a thing of the past.

Returning her 'back to her old self' included minimizing exposure to damaging electromagnetic fields, detoxifying the body from toxic substances, including mercuric compounds and agrochemicals, addressing the severely compromised nutrient absorption rates of the body and restoring the optimal functioning of the immune system.

On one occasion I was referenced on a popular magazine's doctor's page as being proficient in identifying the causative factors behind urticaria, an umbrella term for a dermatological disorder (skin rash) that has a broad range of variants, which resulted in an astounding 15,000 hits on my website and hundreds of enquiries. Medical sources state that urticaria affects 15–20 per cent of the general population at some point in their lifetime and the aetiology (scientifically identified causes) of it is undetermined in at least *80–90 per cent of cases*.

The desperate emails I received only served to confirm the accuracy of these statistics: unhappy stories of antihistamine tablets; hydrocortisone and other steroid creams; 'heavy-duty' antibiotics; severe side-effects when drug doses had been doubled in an attempt to control the symptoms; money that could be ill-afforded spent on blood tests, skin tests and biopsies that still did not identify the root cause; dermatologists and other specialists who could not locate the origin of the problem; the subsequent itching controlling the life of the sufferer or persistently preventing sleep; and symptoms that were still very much present after two, five, ten or a staggering 30 years. Two sample emails detail the despair:

> *I have been suffering from chronic urticaria for the past two years. I have been to a dermatologist consultant, but there is no change. Every day I'm suffering – it seems it's part of my everyday life. I suggested to my consultant that we did some tests to know the cause of my allergy, but he just kept on changing my tablets every month. I said to him, how could he treat me if he didn't know the real cause? But he didn't listen, so I'm very depressed, to the extent that I don't go to my consultant anymore. Please help me as soon as possible...*

> *I have had chronic urticaria since I was 21 (I am now 51). It just appeared overnight. I cannot manage without antihistamines. The specialists have discharged me – they said they could not find what was causing it. Some days the itching is unbearable. If I did not take tablets I would be covered in rashes from scratching. It took 17 years for them to diagnose it. I was told it would just go one day, but I would have thought 30 years was long enough to wait. I am really fed up with the thought that it may continue for 30 more years...*

And each and every case of urticaria that I have worked with has had one thing in common: a significantly compromised immune system. Once the underlying causes were addressed and the immune system restored to optimal levels, the urticaria significantly improved and, in the majority of cases where the client conscientiously addressed the items on the checklist, completely disappeared.

Some of these very basic but vital steps included modification of the diet; the elimination of any potential toxins from the body, including metals, agrochemicals, petrochemicals and pharmaceutical products; correcting any vitamin or mineral deficiencies; addressing exposure to detrimental environmental energies and electromagnetic fields; the changing of certain personal care, environmental and household products that might be causing or exacerbating the condition; and dealing with any suppressed or sustained negative mental and emotional states – in fact any factor that might disrupt the natural and balanced metabolism of the body

Symptoms and Causes

When determining the causative factors behind a condition or set of symptoms, dowsing has a further benefit. Swiftly and easily, it is possible to differentiate between a *symptom* and a *cause*. For example, a simple question can be asked to determine whether a fungal infection that is present in the body of a client who has a compromised immune function is a *cause* of the compromised immune function or a resulting *symptom* of the immune system being compromised. This information allows the practitioner to prioritize what, and in which order, the manifestations of the health condition (in this case a compromised immune function) should be treated. Valuable time is not then spent treating symptoms when it can be more efficiently and effectively be used to directly address the root causes.

Moreover, dowsing helps to prevent the misconception when there are two co-existing symptoms present, that one *caused* the other. Rather, they may be 'symptoms in common' rather than one being a *cause* and one an *effect*. An example of this might be the presence in the stomach of both gastric ulcers and the bacterium *Helicobacter pylori*. Orthodox medical opinion believes that because *Helicobacter pylori* is present at the same time as a gastric ulcer, the *H. pylori* bacteria *causes* gastric ulcers. Dowsing suggests that both the *H. pylori* bacteria and the gastric ulcer are symptoms, and the *root cause* is an imbalance in the environment of the stomach. The causes behind the imbalance in the stomach environment can then be determined by dowsing.

Dowsing can also distinguish between the *causative* factors, *contributory* factors and *trigger* factors behind any condition, thereby identifying the urgency or responsiveness to treatment. It is also possible to assign a percentage to each factor to indicate the extent of its detrimental effect. Clients have found this sort of structured information to be extremely helpful in the understanding of the imbalances in their health.

As long as the questioning process is concise, unambiguous and informed, there are no limits to the benefits of dowsing in supporting the restoration of optimal health and well-being. And the *informed* part of the questioning comes about by including the expertise, education and experience of doctors.

Doctors and Dowsers

To become a proficient and successful doctor takes years of training – and even more years of putting that training into practice to attain experience and a track record. To be a proficient professional dowser requires exactly the same. Because of the degree of training and experience required in both fields, it is therefore rare to find these two sets of skills in one person. However, I personally do know a medical doctor in private practice who is a highly competent dowser. He applies his combined skills to empower his patients by teaching them to dowse. Dr David Mason Brown, MB, ChB, writes:

> *I have to admit, like many sceptical medics, it took me eight years from when I first saw some medical dows-ing techniques demonstrated to when I actually started really learning and using it. That was when I was hav-ing great difficulty in judging doses of medication and*

nutrition, and also which individuals were intolerant to what. However, now that drug reactions, intolerances and medical mistakes are the fourth most common cause of death in the USA, it is essential for doctors to stop their guesstimates. [This was at the time of writing. A study in 2004 suggests that the American medical system – or iatrogenesis – is the leading cause of death and injury in the USA. See Notes and Resources.]

I have developed dowsing techniques to help in chronic fatigue syndrome/ME, but dowsing can also be used to see if a vaccine is safe for someone, to see whether they have an infection, and what type, to choose the best antibiotic, then its dosage and the duration of the treatment...

As a result of his tuition, Dr Mason Brown's patients are able to dowse, on a daily basis, to determine the nutritional supplements and detox products required to meet exactly their body's individual needs, on that day, in their particular and unique circumstances. This is invaluable, as any detox process undertaken by a person with severely compromised health (for example ME or chronic fatigue syndrome) requires precise and delicate management. What better manager than the primary state of the body – its organized field of intelligence!

Of course, there must be other doctor-dowsers discreetly applying their skills for the benefit of their patients. *But imagine the benefits if doctors and dowsers combined their skills.* Imagine the advantages available to doctors if they could know anything, the moment it is asked, about the individual requirements of their patients, transcending all misguided officialdom, vested interests, general fit-all guidelines, government incentive schemes, blanket recommendations and occasional guesswork. What would be placed firmly and unequivocally at the heart of this dynamic process would be the *patients' best interests*.

It goes without saying that any dowsers considered for a joint or shared venture would need to have a proven track record and to be able to meet, in the United Kingdom at least, the requirements of the British Society of Dowsers' professional register. And any venture would have to be closely monitored, with the information obtained by dowsing being confirmed by orthodox medical testing. But this presents an exciting opportunity to determine not only what is needed for the patient, but when, in what dose, for how long and whether individually or in combination with another factor. And whether there is the presence of some as yet unexpressed underlying serious condition.

The invaluable role that dowsing can play in the restoration of health and well-being has successfully been integrated into at least one branch of medical practice – that of Psionic Medicine. Founded in 1968 by Dr George Lawrence, a family doctor and qualified surgeon, its fundamental aim is encapsulated in its motto, *Tolle causum*, meaning 'Seek the cause' of the illness. Predominantly an energy-based approach it is, nevertheless, thoroughly based upon orthodox medicine, but also integrates homoeopathy and dowsing. And, crucially, it recognizes an organized *field* as the basic element in the living organism and enabled Dr Lawrence to develop a system of medicine that has proven to be highly successful over the last 40 years.

Three prerequisites are ordinarily considered to be necessary prior to training with the professional body, the Institute of Psionic Medicine: a medical, dental or veterinary qualification registerable in the UK, a working background knowledge of homoeopathy, and the ability to dowse. The British Society of Dowsers has undertaken to train interested doctors, dentists and veterinary surgeons prior to their introduction to the medical applications.

Professor Ervin Laszlo penned the foreword to the book *Psionic Medicine: The Study and Treatment of Causative Factors in Illness*. He writes, 'I have the privilege of first-hand knowledge of the efficacy of this form of medicine, having been under psionic medical care for nearly a decade.' He goes on to state, 'Recognising the primacy of *fields* in the maintenance and reestablishment of health is fundamental to contemporary medicine.' He also makes reference to the 'mind-boggling remote diagnostic feature' of dowsing 'functioning across any hitherto tested finite distances'. Not a problem, according to Professor Laszlo, as this is easily accounted for when we recognize that the field embedding and governing the cellular and multi-cellular organism is a *quantum field*, with a scope of biological coherence that transcends the scope of biochemical signal transmission. We have, of course, already examined this in detail.

I spoke to Dr Keith Souter, a long-standing member of the institute, and asked him to encapsulate the value of dowsing for him and his practice. He told me:

> In the field of homoeopathy it brings me a short-cut method of arriving at a diagnosis – it is almost like having the laboratory and the X-ray department in homoeopathy. Otherwise a homoeopathic consultation can be a lengthy process. We ask the field, and if you ask the right question then it will give you a very specific remedy. It also produces precision in terms of remedy selection.
>
> It is brilliant for diagnosis and also for treatment – it tells you not only which remedy, but which remedy to use at a particular point in time, and the potency. And with psionic medicine you are trying to seek the cause – you're going down to a deeper level and often removing things that are obstacles to cure. It gives you information about what is happening in the current situation and when the next analysis is needed. You have to be precise in your questioning of course...

Precise questioning is something that we certainly can't argue with!

An Integrated Future

So why don't more doctors work together with dowsers?

I believe there are three main reasons. First, medical practitioners are, by and large, unaware of the potential benefits of dowsing. Second, even if they were aware, it is likely that they would dismiss them, as dowsing wouldn't fit comfortably within their belief system. And the third and very powerful reason is the fear of damage to their professional status from peer pressure and official medical bodies, with the associated risks of litigation or suspension. One medical doctor confided that he would risk certain 'professional suicide' if his colleagues knew he was recommending the skills of a dowser, albeit with the undoubted benefits for his patients in mind. Consequently, this is why it is important that all dowsers contribute to ensuring the profile of dowsing is made more credible on every level. Hopefully this book and my established track record have gone some way towards addressing this.

A doctor who had once specialized in the field of cancer and was currently working in general practice asked me to identify the causative factors when, ironically, he himself was diagnosed with bladder cancer. The consultation took place at his home. Not long after we began, I was slightly alarmed to see a strange expression on his face. I immediately put down my rods and asked him if he was comfortable with the dowsing process. 'Yes,' he said, evasively. I persevered, expressing concern at his facial expression. He sighed, 'It's just I envy your freedom to do this. As a medical doctor, that is something that I don't have.'

But here's an exciting opportunity for all practitioners out there – Father Jean Jurion was right: *no law forbids doctors from working together with unorthodox healers.* This was confirmed in a conversation I had with Mr Michael Keegan, policy advisor with the Standards and Ethics Team of the General Medical Council (GMC). I was assured that as long as medical doctors implemented the GMC core guidance set out in *Good Medical Practice 2006* and in their publication *Consent: Patients and Doctors Making Decisions Together*, there was no prohibition in law.

The world is currently on a long journey towards integration of allopathic and holistic medicine. In that spirit, I believe it is time for dowsing in the field of health to be done in the open rather than in secret. Therefore, I gently throw down the gauntlet to all pioneering doctors, practitioners and seekers of truth to keep open minds and hearts and, in the best interests of their patients, consider the potential benefits of including dowsing as part of a fully integrated health programme.

Ultimately, perhaps we can bring dowsing out of the closet and into the open, finally acknowledging its invaluable and unquestionable benefits and gently starting to shake the world.

Chapter Twenty

VOYAGE OF DISCOVERY

Know you what it is to be a child?
It is to be something very different from the man of today. It
is to have a spirit yet streaming from the waters of baptism; it
is to believe in love, to believe in loveliness, to believe in belief;
it is to be so little that the elves can reach to whisper in your
ear; it is to turn pumpkins into coaches, and mice into horses,
lowness into loftiness, and nothing into every-thing...

Percy Bysshe Shelley, in the *Dublin Review*, July 1908

Beliefs, and the feelings that we have about them, are the
language that 'speaks' to the quantum stuff that makes our
reality.

Gregg Braden, *The Spontaneous Healing of Belief*

To fully understand dowsing, you must understand belief at its most profound level. Being the best dowser you can possibly be requires you to *believe* in belief. By doing so, you will enhance your dowsing skill to a level that will serve you well for a lifetime and that can be used in a myriad of ways. You just never know what you might need to find…

Like most people, I have always been fascinated by the enchanting qualities of dolphins. For some, they appear to be a catalyst for healing simply by their very presence. For others, they captivate the imagination and encapsulate the magical connection between man and the animal kingdom. So when I had an opportunity on my first visit to New Zealand to see dolphins swimming in the wild, I jumped at the chance.

The day was clear, with blue skies and a wonderful stillness, when the boat left the jetty of a small town in the Bay of Islands along New Zealand's northern coast. Twenty people, like me, full of anticipation. I was in a party with three friends. One of them, a New Zealander by the name of Lee Farrington, takes up the story:

> It was Elizabeth's first visit to New Zealand and so it came as a major disappointment to hear the skipper of our vessel inform us that there had been no sightings of dolphins for days. Apparently this was due to the presence of orca whales within the coastal waters and the need for the dolphins to protect their newly born babes by remaining well below the surface.
>
> 'Dolphin Encounter' trips are of four hours duration and soon we had been searching for some three-and-a-half hours with no luck. Not promising.
>
> Nothing from the other dolphin boats either. It was all so very disappointing. Our time was running out...

Orcas are predators of dolphins. And our boat seemed to be going round in ever-decreasing circles, more than once retracing her steps. Despite refreshments and copious amounts of wine inducing a jolly good humour, the frustration and resignation of our fellow passengers began to show. One of my party then said, 'Go on, dowse for the dolphins.' My retort, 'And what am I supposed to do with the information, even if I do find them?' met with an obvious, 'Tell the skipper!'

Yeah, right.

I was quietly horrified. Not from the perspective of the safety of the dolphins – I knew the universe would not reveal information that would endanger any form of life. But could I trust my dowsing? And could I remain sufficiently emotionally detached not to influence the outcome in any way with wishful thinking? I simply didn't want the responsibility (and embarrassment) of sending a boatful of passengers off in potentially the wrong direction. But after half an hour more fruitless searching, and more good-natured bullying, out of curiosity I relented.

My question was carefully worded, asking for the location of dolphins that would be happy to communicate with our boat without compromising their safety in any way. The answer was immediate.

'About three kilometres in that direction,' I told my friends. I drew the line, however, at telling the captain.

Nevertheless, sometime later he came tearing down the boat, looking slightly bewildered. He stopped abruptly at our group and said, 'Which one of you just came and told me where the dolphins were?'

One of our group sheepishly put up his hand. I glared at him.

'How do you know?' fired back the captain.

I was about to be outed.

A finger pointed in my direction. 'And how do *you* know?' he enquired, turning his full attention to me. Very quietly I muttered something about being a dowser. 'Great!' he said. 'Come up to the wheelhouse and give us directions.'

I was taken aback, to say the least, and only went because of my state of surprise.

Inside the wheelhouse the skipper introduced me to his second mate, who greeted me warmly and openly, but without ceremony. 'I'm a Maori and my uncle was a water dowser. Which way are the dolphins?'

Sitting in the wheelhouse, I asked the rods for the nearest location of dolphins who could safely make themselves known and communicate with the boat. My angle rods swung to my right and hung on the diagonal. The captain swung the boat in the direction of the rods and, as I watched in awe, simultaneously the boat moved and the rods gently straightened out until boat and rods were in alignment.

Lee continues:

> I had seen Elizabeth use her dowsing rods previously, but I was about to see something that even she would be astounded by. Elizabeth ascertained that there were four dolphins keen to make contact. They were 3.2 kilometres away and her dowsing rods indicated the exact direction. By now, our party had been invited onto the bridge with the skipper and he set his GPS unit to the exact spot determined. We proceeded in great haste. I admit to feeling a huge wave of apprehension at the prospect that it would all be in vain, as the remaining 20 plus people aboard wondered why we were suddenly heading, at such great speed, to what appeared to be 'nowhere'.
>
> When we finally reached the spot determined on the GPS unit, the captain slowed the vessel to a standstill. And we waited...

My belief in my dowsing was being put to the ultimate test. The skipper had asked me to sit on the roof of the wheelhouse. He came up and stood beside me, scanning the bay and the distant horizon. I looked up at his face, intent with concentration. Nothing. All was stillness. I looked down into the main part of the boat and 20 pairs of expectant eyes met mine.

No pressure then.

But my rods were frozen in the 'neutral' position, pointing straight ahead.

Still nothing. We waited in total silence.

Suddenly, the rods crossed and straightened out again. And crossed and straightened out *again*. With a start I realized the dolphins were swimming backwards and forwards at depth under the boat. Tired, hot and very uncomfortable, I focused.

Nothing.

Then, when it happened, it was breathtaking. In one heartbeat, the rods swung hard to my left and the captain shouted, 'Dolphins!'

I turned my head, looked down the length of my rods and four dolphins leaped in a perfect curve from the water.

Lee remembers:

Three adults and a beautiful baby dolphin began performing their gymnastics in front of us. If I had not experienced this sequence of events with my own eyes I would have found it very hard to believe. I was speechless.

Late in the day, running wildly over schedule, the boat made its way back home. To my delight, and the delight of all of the passengers, the dolphins accompanied us almost the whole way back. A magical escort. We returned at speed, but still they kept up with us, with extraordinary agility, often only inches from the boat and sometimes turning on their sides, appearing to look up at us. Close to our mooring, they finally left us. I was both exhilarated and relieved to see them returning safely to the depths.

On the journey back I talked to the skipper. Once a professional shark diver, he felt a natural affinity with dolphins. He explained how he frequently attempted to communicate with them, but was not absolutely sure if they understood him and what he was trying to do, or whether they reciprocated. He had many questions: Did the boats bother or frighten the dolphins? Did they mind the boats approaching them? How old did a dolphin calf have to be before its parents were comfortable with an approaching boat? Did the dolphins know and understand when he was communicating with them? I answered them all, and was able to confirm that, yes, not only did they know he was communicating with them, but they also understood what he was saying, his thoughts and his intent. He thanked me warmly and said he would always remember this special day.

Later, Lee told me that observing the sequence of events, steering to that location, watching the rods moving and witnessing the dolphins leaping changed his life. He wasn't the only one.

Whether institutionalized thinking doesn't want to, isn't allowed to, or simply cannot bring itself to acknowledge the validity and benefits of dowsing, the empirical evidence is beyond question for those with open hearts and minds.

For those who simply and clearly recognize that a world exists outside the limitations of our immediate understanding, dowsing is a tangible manifestation of our profound connection, on every level, to each other, to all forms of life and to the universe.

And my own understanding of belief intensifies daily.

EPILOGUE

As the twenty-first century dawns, astounding new visions of reality are stirring.

Dean Radin PhD, *The Conscious Universe*

When you have reached a certain stage of inner connectedness, you recognise the truth when you hear it.

Eckhart Tolle, *The Power of Now*

The ultimate paradox is, of course, that when you have truly mastered dowsing you will no longer need to dowse.

Dowsing is just a means to an end. Training wheels. A tool along the way. The tangible manifestation of your innate connection to the infinite field of consciousness, All That Is and All That Will Ever Be.

Then you will be at one with Source. With the Oneness. That of which you are and that which you are of. You will understand the interconnectedness of all things and you will *know* the truth.

So there you have it.
No more thoughts of being flaky or spooky.
No more skulking or hiding under cover of darkness.
Not only are you a custodian of a timeless, ancient art
You are also a pioneer on the frontiers of cutting edge science.
Go out and dowse with confidence, but without ego,
Dowse with conviction, but without presumption.
Dowse with joy and purity of intent.
And dowse in Truth.

Appendix I

DR HARRY OLDFIELD PILOT STUDY REPORT

Dear Ms Elizabeth Brown,

Report: Experiments conducted with Ms Elizabeth Brown

Date: 24 June 2008

Venue: e-Innovation Centre Telford Campus, University of Wolverhampton

Also present: Dr Oldfield, DHom (Med), FRMS, DSc, Piers Whitley, Evy King

These observations and experiments were done under controlled conditions, however not in Faraday Cage enclosures.

The apparatus used was the PIP system (Polycontrast Interference Photography), which looks at subtle changes of light values in and around the human energy field and the environment. Many articles have been published and studies conducted with my invention since 1987.

The first step was to get base control readings observed with Ms Brown. These showed very little change from the subject's base levels and the environment around her, even when holding the dowsing rods passively.

The second phase was to observe her in an activated state; she duly obliged. This showed energy connections on the ground to her feet and also some minor changes in the environment and the field around her.

One particular anomaly we observed was when she tuned into a distant client for dowsing analysis and a white light luminescence appeared to her left side, which could clearly be seen in the film footage. This showed a definite intensity in luminosity around her. There were no other light changes that would have accounted for this, as the lighting in the environment was constant and fully controlled (i.e. the light therefore must come from some other source).

A second anomaly that stands out was when she was connecting with a third-entity energy field in connection. Very interesting light phenomena, including increases in luminosity, appeared.

We finished the day with a pilot study on the way that Ms Brown was able to change environmental energy levels in the university experiment room.

I wish to state the pilot study done with Ms Brown has shown very interesting observable anomalies connected with her work. I feel that with further study, even more experimental evidence will accumulate, and although we conducted only a one-day pilot study observation, I believe it showed genuine energetic phenomena in and around Ms Brown.

Yours most sincerely and with deepest respect for your work,

Dr Harry Oldfield

CLIENT B HEALTH READINGS

Date	Health	Immune System	Nutrient Absorption Rate (AR) (opt. 87%)	Calcium AR	Potassium AR	Selenium AR	Physical Energy	Alkaline/Acid ratio (opt. 80/20)	Clearance of virus factor in physical	Clearance of parasites	IMP function	Recovery to optimal health
14 Aug 07	49%	38%	39%	31%	18%	12%	69%	50/50			54%	
21 Aug 07	49%	38%	39%	31%	18%	12%	69%	50/50			54%	
28 Aug 07	49%	38%	39%	31%	18%	12%	69%	50/50			54%	
4 Sept 07	49%	38%	51%	33%	18%	12%	69%	50/50			57%	6%
11 Sept 07	49%	38%	61%	42%	24%	38%	69%	50/50			65%	21%
18 Sept 07	49%	44%	68%	59%	34%	58%	69%	50/50			75%	29%
25 Sept 07	49%	50%	70%	70%	41%	70%	69%	50/50			80%	39%
2 Oct 07	49%	50%	70%	70%	43%	70%	69%	50/50			80%	41%
9 Oct 07	49%	50%	70%	70%	43%	70%	69%	50/50			80%	41%
16 Oct 07	49%	50%	70%	70%	43%	70%	69%	60/40			80%	41%
15 Nov 07	49%	54%	70%	70%	45%	70%	69%	60/40			80%	44%
15 Dec 07	51%	57%	70%	70%	50%	70%	69%	60/40		18%	80%	49%
15 Jan 08	53%	62%	80%	70%	57%	70%	69%	60/40	20%	40%	80%	58%
15 Feb 08	57%	69%	87%	79%	70%	87%	69%	60/40	35%	59%	80%	72%
15 Mar 08	63%	75%	87%	81%	75%	87%	69%	70/30	61%	90%	80%	80%
15 Apr 08	64%	77%	87%	81%	75%	87%	69%	70/30	67%	92%	80%	89%
15 May 08	69%	77%	87%	81%	75%	87%	69%	70/30	82%	100%	80%	94%
15 June 08	71%	77%	87%	81%	77%	87%	72%	70/30	99%	100%	80%	94%
15 Sept 08	73%	75%	87%	81%	78%	87%	72%	70/30	99%	100%	80%	94%

AR – absorption rate; IMP – integral membrane protein

NOTES AND RESOURCES

Chapter 2: The Changing Perception of Dowsing

All information not otherwise referenced about the history of dowsing was taken from Christopher Bird's *The Divining Hand* (E. P. Dutton, 1979).

More information about the work of David Ashworth can be found at www.davidashworth.com

Professor Alexander's full report can be viewed at www.whale.to/v/dubrov.html

For more information about remote viewer Major Paul H. Smith and the application of dowsing, see his website, rviewer.com/index.html, and DVD, *The Shotgun Wedding Between Dowsing and Remote Viewing*, IRVA, 2007.

George Applegate can be contacted through the British Society of Dowsers (*see below*) or through his website, www.george-applegate.co.uk/.

The British Society of Dowsers can be contacted through their website at www.britishdowsers.org or at The British Society of Dowsers, 4/5 Cygnet Centre, Worcester Road, Hanley Swan, Worcestershire, WR8 0EA. Telephone: 01684 576969.

The website for the American Society of Dowsers is www.dowsers.org

Chapter 5: The Dowsing Instrument

A whole range of dowsing tools are available from the British Society of Dowsers at www.britishdowsers.org

Extra-sensory statistics from Dean Radin, PhD, *Entangled Minds* (Simon and Schuster, 2006).

Chapter 6: In the Mood to Dowse

More information about the work of Dan Kahn can be found at www.meditationmastery.eu or at www.bi-aura.com

Chapter 8: Fine-tuning

The information about fluoride comes from the website of Dr Mercola: www.mercola.com/Article/links/fluoride_links.htm

More information about the Bi-Aura Foundation can be found at www.bi-aura.com

Chapter 10: The Phenomenal Mechanics

Information regarding Dr Jan Merta comes from wonderworkers.com/dowsinganUncannyArt.html and Christopher Bird, *The Divining Hand* (E. P. Dutton, 1979).

References attributed to Dr Bruce Lipton are from his book *The Biology of Belief* (Hay House, 2008).

For more information about the Institute of Noetic Sciences, see www.noetic.org

Statistics for studies into precognition are from Dean Radin, PhD, *Entangled Minds* (Simon and Schuster, 2006).

The information about Dr Zaboj V. Harvalik comes from Christopher Bird, *The Divining Hand* (E. P. Dutton, 1979).

More information about the work of Dr Jude Currivan can be found on her website, www.judecurrivan.com, or through the Hay House website at www.hayhouse.co.uk/Author/Jude-Currivan

The interview with Dr Valerie Hunt can be accessed at www.teleconferenceinfo.net/august08.html

The work of Mamdoh Badran can be viewed at www.badran.it

More information about Edgar Cayce can be found on the website of the Association for Research and Enlightenment at www.edgarcayce.org

Chapter 11: **The Evidence So Far**

More information about Dr Harry Oldfield and his work can be found at www.electrocrystal.com

For information about brainwaves see: 4mind4life.com/blog/2008/08/05/delta-brain-waves-slowest-most-confusing-brainwaves

More information about the Mind Mirror can be found at www.mindmirroreeg.com/w/equipment/mm3/unique.htm

The creative work of Phil Argyle can be viewed at www.wholebeing.org

Chapter 12: **Health**

For more information about toxins in water, see articles.mercola.com/sites/articles/archive/2009/02/07/tap-water-toxins-is-your-water-trying-to-kill-you.aspx#178117 and www.enn.com/top_stories/article/32699

Information about the Centre for Implosion Research (CIR) and water systems can be found at www.implosionresearch.com

For further information about nitrosamines and other carcinogens, see *The Politics of Cancer Revisited* by Samuel S. Epstein, MD (East Ridge Press, 1998).

Further information about Dr Robert Verkerk and the work of the Alliance for Natural Health can be found at www. anhcampaign.org

Information about environmental toxins can be found on the WWF website www.panda.org

For more about Matthew Manning and his clinic see www. matthewmanning.com

To learn more about the pain-body, read Eckhart Tolle's *The Power of Now* (Mobius, 2001).

Chapter 13: Environmental Energies

For further information about the International EMF Collaborative, the Interphone study and the latest research on electromagnetic radiation and its effects on health, see www. radiationresearch.org

For information on the author's workshops and seminars, see www.gentlepowers.com

Chapter 15: Subtle Energies

The passages attributed to Dr Valerie Hunt are from her book *Infinite Mind: Science of the Human Vibrations of Consciousness* (Malibu Publishing Co., 2000).

Chapter 16: Hints, Tips, Truths and Myths

Farrow & Ball can be contacted through www.farrow-ball.com

The passage attributed to Dr Valerie Hunt is from her book *Infinite Mind: Science of the Human Vibrations of Consciousness* (Malibu Publishing Co., 2000).

Chapter 17: Finding your Niche

Water dowser Peter Taylor can be contacted through the British Society of Dowsers (*see above, Chapter 2*).

Chapter 18: In Pursuit of Truth

For the full article, 'Science versus Showmanship: A History of the Randi Hoax', see www.aiprinc.org/para-C05_Thalbourne_1995.pdf

Water dowser Clive Thompson can be contacted through the British Society of Dowsers (*see above, Chapter 2*).

For more about the work of Dr Konstantin Korotkov and the GDV technology, see www.korotkov.org

For the research projects of Dr Hans-Dieter Betz, see:
www.scientificexploration.org/journal/jse_09_1_betz.pdf
www.scientificexploration.org/journal/jse_09_2_betz.pdf
twm.co.nz/dowsing_jse_com.html

Chapter 19: Unquestionable Benefits

For more information about iatrogenesis, see the report 'Death by Medicine' at www.credencegroup.co.uk/Eclub/Eclubsearchable2/230304/death%20by%20medicine.htm

Further information about Psionic medicine can be found at: www.psionicmedicine.org

General Medical Council (GMC) guidelines can be found at: www.gmc-uk.org/guidance/ethical_guidance/consent_guidance/contents.asp

FURTHER READING

Georgius Agricola, *De Re Metallica* (The Nature of Minerals), 1556, reissued Kessinger Publishing Co., 2003

George Applegate, *The Complete Book of Dowsing*, Element Books, 1997

David Ashworth, *Dancing with the Devil*, Crucible, 2001

Dr Fereydoon Batmanghelidj, *Your Body's Many Cries for Water*, Global Health Solutions, 1994

Robert O. Becker, MD, and Gary Selden, *The Body Electric*, William Morrow & Co., 1985

Michael Bentine, *Doors of the Mind*, HarperCollins, 1984

Christopher Bird, *The Divining Hand*, E. P. Dutton, 1979

Father Jean-Louis Bourdoux, *Notions Pratiques de Radiesthésie pour les Missionaires* (Practical Notions of Radiesthesia for Missionaries), Desforges, Paris, 1965

Gregg Braden, *The Divine Matrix*, Hay House, 2007

—, *Spontaneous Healing of Belief*, Hay House, 2008

Deepak Chopra, MD, *Quantum Healing*, Bantam Books, 1989

—, *The Seven Spiritual Laws of Success*, Bantam Books, 1996

Dawson Church, PhD, *The Genie in Your Genes*, Elite Books, 2007

Dr Wayne W. Dyer, *The Secrets of the Power of Intention* (CD), Hay House, 2004

Dr Masaru Emoto, *The Hidden Messages in Water*, Beyond Words Publishing, 2004

Udo Erasmus, *Fats That Heal, Fats That Kill,* Alive Books, 1993

Amit Goswami, PhD, *God Is Not Dead*, Hampton Roads, 2008

Dr David Hamilton, *It's the Thought That Counts*, Hay House, 2006

— *How Your Mind Can Heal Your Body*, Hay House, 2008

David R. Hawkins, PhD, *Power versus Force*, Hay House, 1995

— *The Eye of the I,* Veritas Publishing Company, 2001

— *The Highest Level of Enlightenment*, CD set, Nightingale Conant, 2003

Patrick Holford, *The New Optimum Nutrition Bible*, The Crossing Press, 2005

Malcolm Hollick, PhD, *The Science of Oneness*, O Books, 2006

Valerie Hunt, PhD, *Infinite Mind*, Malibu Publishing Co., 2000

Ervin Laszlo and Jude Currivan, *CosMos*, Hay House, 2008

Bruce Lipton, *The Biology of Belief*, Hay House, 2008

Dorothy Maclean, *To Hear the Angels Sing,* The Lorian Association, 2008

Joseph McMoneagle, *Memoirs of a Psychic Spy*, Hampton Roads, 2006

Lynne McTaggart, *The Field*, HarperCollins, 2001

—, *The Intention Experiment*, HarperElement, 2008

The Abbé Mermet, *Comment j'opère pour découvrir de près ou a distance. Sources, Métaux, Corps cachés, Maladies* (How I Proceed in the Discovery of Near or Distant Water, Metals, Hidden Objects and Illnesses), Maison de la Radiesthésie, 1952

Hamish Miller, *The Definitive Wee Book on Dowsing*, Penwith Press, 2002

Marlo Morgan, *Mutant Message Down Under*, Thorsons, 1995

Joseph Murphy, PhD, *The Power of Your Subconscious Mind*, Pocket Books, 2000

Sheila Ostrander and Lynn Schroeder, *Psychic Discoveries Behind the Iron Curtain*, Abacus, 1973

Dean Radin, PhD, *The Conscious Universe*, HarperCollins, 1998

— *Entangled Minds*, Simon and Schuster, 2006

Rupert Sheldrake, *The Sense of Being Stared At*, Crown Publishers, 2003

Ingo Swann, *Penetration*, Ingo Swann Books, 1998

P. M. Taubert, *Silent Killers*, CompSafe Consultancy, Australia, 2001

William Tiller, PhD, *Science and Human Transformation*, Pavior Publishing, 1997

Eckhart Tolle, *The Power of Now*, Mobius, 2001

— *A New Earth*, E. P. Dutton, 2005

Neale Donald Walsch, *Conversations with God: Book II*, Hodder Mobius, 1999

Richard Webster, *The Art of Dowsing*, Castle, 2002

Dr Robert Verkerk, *The Human Time Bomb*, Wellness Publishing, 2005

PERMISSIONS

Material from the following is reproduced with permission: Jude Currivan, Wayne Dyer, Lee Farrington, David Hamilton, Dr David R. Hawkins (courtesy of Veritas Publishing, www.veritaspub.com), Ervin Laszlo, Clare Lennard, Bruce Lipton and Candace Pert. Thanks to John Moss for granting permission to include quotes originally published in *Dowsing Today* (British Society of Dowsers, www.britishdowsers.org) from Prof. Alexander Dubrov (September 1993) and Dr Edith Jurka (December 1983). Special thanks to my clients who have allowed their case studies to be used. Grateful thanks to the estate of the late Hamish Miller for permission to quote from personal interviews and from *The Definitive Wee Book on Dowsing*. Many thanks to the following for allowing excerpts from our interviews to be published: George Applegate, David Ashworth, Maire Dennhofer, Professor Chris French, Dan Kahn, Dr Konstantin Korotkov, Annie Reed Henderson, Dr Keith Souter, Peter Taylor and Clive Thompson. And last but not least, thanks to Philip Argyle for designing the cover image and chapter motif, and to Eri Griffin for the internal artworks.

We hope you enjoyed this Hay House book.
If you would like to receive a free catalogue featuring additional
Hay House books and products, or if you would like information
about the Hay Foundation, please contact:

Hay House UK Ltd
292B Kensal Road • London W10 5BE
Tel: (44) 20 8962 1230; Fax: (44) 20 8962 1239
www.hayhouse.co.uk

***

Published and distributed in the United States of America by:
Hay House, Inc. • PO Box 5100 • Carlsbad, CA 92018-5100
Tel: (1) 760 431 7695 or (1) 800 654 5126;
Fax: (1) 760 431 6948 or (1) 800 650 5115
www.hayhouse.com

***

Published and distributed in Australia by:
Hay House Australia Ltd • 18/36 Ralph Street • Alexandria, NSW 2015
Tel: (61) 2 9669 4299, Fax: (61) 2 9669 4144
www.hayhouse.com.au

***

Published and distributed in the Republic of South Africa by:
Hay House SA (Pty) Ltd • PO Box 990 • Witkoppen 2068
Tel/Fax: (27) 11 467 8904
www.hayhouse.co.za

***

Published and distributed in India by:
Hay House Publishers India • Muskaan Complex • Plot No.3
B-2• Vasant Kunj • New Delhi - 110 070
Tel: (91) 11 41761620; Fax: (91) 11 41761630
www.hayhouse.co.in

***

Distributed in Canada by:
Raincoast • 9050 Shaughnessy St • Vancouver, BC V6P 6E5
Tel: (1) 604 323 7100
Fax: (1) 604 323 2600

***

Sign up via the Hay House UK website to receive the Hay House
online newsletter and stay informed about what's going on with your
favourite authors. You'll receive bimonthly announcements
about discounts and offers, special events, product highlights,
free excerpts, giveaways, and more!
www.hayhouse.co.uk